3595

Dr. W.C.M. Scott in his office (1980)

PSYCHOANALYSIS AND THE ZEST FOR LIVING

Reflections and Psychoanalytic Writings in Memory of W.C.M. Scott

Edited by Michel Grignon

With contributions by

C.E. Benierakis, J.B. Boulanger, C. Coulter, E.G. Debanne,
J.W. Freeman, M. Grignon, P. Lefebve, P.J. Mahony,
M. Meloche, H. Rey, G. Da Silva, W.C.M. Scott, R.H. Scott,
and O. Weininger

esf PUBLISHERS
BINGHAMTON, NEW YORK

Published by *Esf* Publishers
1 Marine Midland Plaza
Binghamton, New York 13901, USA
http://www.tier.net/esfpub/

First published 1998

*Thanks are due to the Scott family and to all contributors
mentioned in the Introduction for subsidizing, in part, the
printing of this book.*

Designed and produced by *Esf* Publishers,
Binghamton, New York.

Set in Cheltenham BT 11/10 pt. by *Esf* Publishers,
Binghamton, New York.

Printed on acid-free paper, smythe sewn and bound
in the United States of America.

The paper and materials used in this book meet the guidelines
for permanence and durability of the Committee on
Production Guidelines for Book Longevity of the Council on
Library Resources. ∞

ISBN 1-883881-27-7
Manufactured in the United States of America

The story of a loss, of grief, of mourning, of reparation and a new start with zest, may be short or may almost be lifelong. Our biggest problem is to help those grieving and mourning to become more efficient and become able to risk more in resolving mourning and making reparation and new starts and to risk even greater losses by loving to live more intensely (C. Scott, "Mourning, the Analyst and the Analysand," 1984, p. 6)

When we overcome our anger and disappointment at ignorance, we may learn to appreciate it. We have so much of it that we should make the best of it. When we are able to love our ignorance from which all new good will come, life may become easier (C. Scott, "On Positive Affects," 1981, p. 81).

Table of Contents

Acknowledgments

Michel Grignon

This book would not have been possible without financial help from Dr. Scott's family as well as from Dr. Costa E. Benierakis, Dr. Jean Baptiste Boulanger, Dr. Guy Da Silva, Dr. Elie Debbane, Dr. Michel Grignon, Dr. Paul Lefebvre, Professor Patrick Mahony, Mrs. Monique Meloche and Dr. Henri Rey.

Moreover, I wish to thank Dr. Florin V. Vladescu and Dr. Otto Weininger who kindly provided the typesetting, proofreading, and designing of this book through the generosity of *Esf* Publishers.

I would also like to express my deepest gratitude to Mrs. Doretta Batterton-Gatien who has been Dr. C. Scott's secretary for the last 25 years. Her precise memory, total dedication, and indefatigable energy contributed in the creation of this volume into a joyful work. All my thanks for her kindness, patience and humour.

I wish to say a very special thank you to my dedicated secretary, Ms. Odile Bourbigot whose meticulousness, willingness to work at odd hours, translation skills and constant kindness helped me put together this celebration of the work of Clifford Scott.

I also am very grateful to Karin Holland-Biggs, Ph.D., who kindly reviewed my writings and assisted me in a language that is not my mother tongue.

Many thanks to Jean Baptiste Boulanger who fostered and supported the project all along.

All my love goes to my wife, Luciana Barbuio, M.D., who accompanied me through the painful and exciting work of creation.

Lastly, all my gratitude to Eve Scott, who has generously given of herself at this difficult time. Despite her painful grief, she worked wholeheartedly with us to celebrate the life and zest of her beloved husband.

Introduction

Michel Grignon

A *Festschrift* was originally planned to celebrate Dr. Scott's ninetieth anniversary, but it did not materialize. After his death, I was determined to gather together some of his friends and his wife Eve Scott to publish a new *Festschrift*. Together with Jean Baptiste Boulanger, we were able to interest Otto Weininger and Florin Vladescu in the publication of this book. We all wish to thank Scott for having changed the history of psychoanalysis in Canada, and we would like this volume to represent the expression of the zest that he communicated to us and, hopefully, to mankind. He wrote, "Analysis leads to an increased ability to work and to love. This statement has almost become a cliché. The affect that best describes this increased ability is enthusiasm or zest. Zest only develops slowly" (1981, p. 572). In the spirit of Bion, I think that Scott was a visionary and that "he disturbed the universe" (Grotstein, 1981) of the Canadian Psychoanalytic Society. Like Bion (1970) I think that "there are not enough geniuses and those that there are must not be wasted" (p. 80). This book is meant as a celebration of the work and the spirit of W.C.M. Scott.

After the Memorial on May 25, 1997, it was decided that we would combine our personal contributions from the memorial with the more scientific papers. The composition of the papers should be read like a musical fugue consisting of personal and emotional points alternating with more intellectual and scientific counterpoints.

The first three chapters were written by Scott himself and members of his family. In his paper, which was written to be read on his ninetieth anniversary at Ste-Justine Hospital, Scott shares freely of some of his memories at the end of his life. Then Robert Scott, his oldest son, opens a vista onto the intimate life of his father with his family. Finally, John Freeman, the brother of Scott's second wife, Eve, describes Scott's wide interest in the vast expression of madness in opera. In addition, the book includes photographs of Scott at various ages, places, and periods of his career.

The next three contributors are long-term friends of Clifford Scott. Dr.

Henri Rey, a Mauritian psychoanalyst who trained in London and practiced most of his life at the Maudsley Hospital, describes the crucial psychoanalytic influence that Scott had at the Maudsley during Aubrey Lewis' time. Over the last two decades, while teaching alternatively in Canada and other countries, Henri Rey developed a very intimate relationship with Scott who used to send him most of his manuscripts asking for his opinions, corrections or reactions. Jean Baptiste Boulanger, a French Canadian psychoanalyst, relates the crucial historic event of Scott's resignation from the Department of Psychiatry at McGill University, which was determinant for the creation of the Canadian Psychoanalytic Institute as a truly independent body. In his scientific paper, Boulanger situates the work of Scott in continuity with Klein and Freud. Finally, Paul Lefebvre, who is probably Scott's most intimate friend, discusses the main themes of Scott's contributions to psychoanalysis.

The rest of the book was written by various contributors from the Quebec English branch of the Canadian Psychoanalytic Society and from the Société psychanalytique de Montréal as well as by psychoanalysts from all across Canada.

Professor Otto Weininger, Ph.D., Editor of the *Journal of Melanie Klein and Object Relations*, shares his experience with Scott as an editor. Scott had been Co-Editor of the *International Journal of Psycho-Analysis* and Patron and Honorary Editor of the *Journal of Melanie Klein and Object Relations*. In 1986, together with Dr. Paul Lefebvre, he formed a task force leading to the creation of the *Canadian Journal of Psychoanalysis* in 1991 which has since then become the official organ of the Canadian Psychoanalytic Society. The correspondence between Dr. Scott and Dr. Weininger is one example of the active and constant role that Scott had with many psychoanalysts in Canada and abroad.

Sharing with us the experience of his own supervision experience with Scott, the unpublished correspondence between Scott and Winnicott, and the private communication he had with James Grotstein, Professor Patrick Mahony sheds new lights on the complex relationship between Scott and the psychoanalysts Ernest Jones, Donald Winnicott, and Melanie Klein. Mahony's second paper in this volume, first published last year in the *Journal of Melanie Klein and Object Relations* (March 1997), is undoubtedly the first effort in the psychoanalytic literature to introduce readers to the work of Scott. The wide scope of subjects that he covers and the questions that he raises will hopefully stimulate more interest and curiosity in Scott's work.

My personal contribution to this book is an effort to articulate the intensity of my learning experience with Scott as well as the continual creativity of his art in which all rules are challenged, but where no compromise is accepted. My scientific paper shows that child analysis has been an underlying stimulation and a constant reorganizer of Scott's thoughts, providing him with a new understanding of neurotic and psychotic adults.

Costas Benierakis, an adult and child psychoanalyst teaching in both Montreal and Athens, discusses the vicissitudes of learning to talk and their complex relationship to child analysis, to preverbal experience, to envy and self-envy, to the progressive and regressive use of distancing in sessions, as well as to the various aspects of mourning.

Monique Meloche is a child and adult psychoanalyst of the Société psychanalytique de Montréal. She writes about her experience as Scott's analysand, supervisee, and later collaborator and friend. She is also the editor of a videotape, "Portraits of W.C.M. Scott," that was made from a selection of 19 taped interviews of Scott with Henri Rey, Paul Lefebvre, Pierre Drapeau and Monique Meloche herself.

Dr. Elie Debbane is a psychoanalyst living in Vancouver and teaching in Seattle. After reflecting on his experience with Scott, he demonstrates that the originality of Bion's thinking was highly rooted in his *Experiences in Groups.* In opposition to Freud where the core of the human psyche was formed by introjective identification, he discusses how for Klein, Scott and Bion "the totality of the individual then had to include both his introjective as well as his projective identification" (p. 176, infra). He elaborates on the concepts of transference and countertransference in connection to groups dynamics. Finally, Debbane evokes the group dynamics that are at play in psychoanalytic societies, theory and the analytic couple.

Dr. Guy Da Silva, who is a training analyst in the Société psychanalytique de Montréal, develops the links between Freud, Bion, and the neuropsychology of Edelman. Scott's interest in the psyche-soma problem originates in his relationship with Paul Schilder with whom he practiced for more than a year. Scott, with his Anglo-Saxon spirit, was always curious about the physical and neurophysiological expression of the vicissitudes of our emotional life and object relations. He would always refuse and critic any model of the mind where the body would have too little space.

I chose to end the book by including *Sessions,* a one-act play in nine scenes that was performed in Toronto in 1993 and in London, England, in 1997. This play represents an effort on Scott's part to share with the public the incommunicable experience of psychoanalysis, as he also did in a recent book (Raymond and Rosbrow-Reich, 1997).

Finally, with the aid of Doretta Batterton-Gatien, the complete bibliography of W.C.M. Scott has been compiled. It consists of 111 published articles and 429 unpublished papers. It should be read as an invitation as well as a challenge to explore and grapple with the genius of Scott in all its creative and destructive aspects.

References

Bion, W.R. (1961). *Experiences in Groups*. London: Tavistock Publications.
—— (1970). *Attention and Interpretation*. London: Tavistock Publications.
Grotstein, J. S. (Ed.) (1981, 1983, 1988). *Do I Dare Disturb the Universe? A Memorial to Wilfred R. Bion*, London: Karnac Books.
Scott, W.C.M. (1997). In: Laurie W. Raymond and Susan Rosbrow-Reich (Eds.), *The Inward Eye. Psychoanalysts Reflect on Their Lives and Work*. Hillsdale, NJ: The Analytic Press, pp. 279-309.

List of Contributors

COSTAS E. BENIERAKIS, M.D.
Member of the Canadian Psychoanalytic Society (Quebec English Branch).
Founding Member, Hellenic Association of Child and Adolescent Psychoanalytic Psychotherapy.
Child Psychoanalyst.

JEAN BAPTISTE BOULANGER, M.D.
Retired Professor of Psychiatry, Faculty of Medicine, Université de Montréal.
Past President of the Canadian Psychiatric Association.
Past President of the Canadian Psychoanalytic Society.
Founding Member, the Canadian Psychoanalytic Society.
Founding Director, the Canadian Institute of Psychoanalysis.
Child Psychoanalyst.

CLARE COULTER
Actress.

GUY DA SILVA, M.D.
Member of the Canadian Psychoanalytic Society (Société psychanalytique de Montréal).
Training and Supervising Analyst, Canadian Psychoanalytic Institute.

ELIE DEBBANE, M.D.
Member of the Canadian Psychoanalytic Society (Vancouver).

JOHN W. FREEMAN
Author and Associate Editor, "Opera News" (New York Metropolitan Opera).

MICHEL GRIGNON, M.D.
>Member of the Canadian Psychoanalytic Society (Quebec English Branch).
>Past President of the Canadian Group of Psychoanalysis for Children.
>Child Psychoanalyst.

PAUL LEFEBVRE, M.D.
>Member of the Canadian Psychoanalytic Society (Quebec English Branch).
>Training and Supervising Analyst, Canadian Psychoanalytic Institute.

PROF. PATRICK MAHONY, Ph.D.
>Professor Emeritus, Université de Montréal.
>Member of the Royal Society of Canada.
>Member of the Canadian Psychoanalytic Society (Quebec English Branch).
>Training and Supervising Analyst, Canadian Psychoanalytic Institute.

MONIQUE MELOCHE, Mss.
>Member of the Canadian Psychoanalytic Society (Société psychanalytique de Montréal).
>Child Psychoanalyst.

HENRI REY, M.D.
>Member of the British Psychoanalytic Society.
>Honorary Member of the Canadian Psychoanalytic Society.

ROBERT H. SCOTT
>Consultant.
>Son of Clifford Scott.

PROF. OTTO WEININGER, Ph.D.
>Founder and Editor of the *Journal of Melanie Klein and Object Relations*.
>Author of many psychoanalytic publications on child and adult psychoanalysis.

Memories and Reflections
on My 90th Anniversary (1993)[1]

W. Clifford M. Scott

Naturally, I was pleased when our Chairman came to discuss with me the Programme Committee's desire to "honor" me. She asked me whether there was someone in England, or the States, whom I would like them to ask to come to participate. I told her that I had many colleagues in England who might toast me, as well as roast me, and fewer in the States, but so many of my peers have died that I would much rather be honored by my Canadian colleagues. When she told me that had been her wish I was, of course, even more pleased.

The final credits on the video,[2] list those to whom I am more grateful than I can say—especially to Monique Meloche and sadly to our later colleague Bruno Cormier. To Ruby Cormier we are grateful for her work on transcription. You have been reminded of Henri Rey who would wish to be here. His first book is with the printers [Rey, 1994]. To Marie Emond, Chairperson of our Program Committee, to being in Ste-Justine Hospital, associated to the University of Montreal, and to being associated today with S.P.M. members, makes me very grateful and sad that there is no French on the tapes: *Je ne peux pas exprimer ma reconnaissance dans votre belle langue.*

Thinking of the relationship of the neurosciences to development led me to wonder how much infantile rage is an earlier form of Goldstein's (1948) description of the "catastrophic rage" of brain injured adults. I still think my earliest paper on this subject was important.

Sixty years ago this month, I became an associate member of the British Psychoanalytic Society. The first third of my life led in 1933 to my becoming an analyst. During the past sixty years, analysis has been my chief working interest. I feel very lucky to love my work. I continually look forward to new discoveries. Psychoanalysis is a young endeavor, and is trying to become "a science" and "a profession." I believe that many new truths will follow Freud's discovery of a new way of observing adults, and by Melanie Klein's and

Freud's daughter's discovery of new ways of observing children. Unfortunately too few have observed similarly the aged, the seriously disordered, and criminals. But the discoveries of analysis have been so very important that they will continue to be elaborated unless civilization is destroyed.

The thrill of making discoveries goes back a long time in my life. We often share with our patients their making discoveries of what had been discovered by many before. But some discoveries are new; I remember the thrill I had when, as a student, at the Atlantic Biological Station run by the Canadian Department of Fisheries in St. Andrews, New Brunswick, I discovered where flounders bred and later the thrill of discovering that the Barn-door skate occasionally developed a colloid goiter even though living in salt water with plenty of iodine!

When I came to medicine, psychiatry and analysis and their histories, my discoveries were mostly the sad discoveries of mistakes of my predecessors, but there were also new discoveries; and the thrills of being near important new discoveries, such as the discovery of insulin in Toronto, and discovering at Hopkins the very severe degree of inhibition of gastric-acid secretion which may occur in the severely depressed (published with Dr. Katzenelbogen, 1931). Discovering that the more I learned the more my vista of ignorance increased, and being thrilled to discover my knowledge is finite but my ignorance is infinite, it was interesting to share with others how they had discovered the same things.

Eventually reading Freud and having the good luck of having Melanie Klein as my analyst, and the many stimulating associates and teachers I had in the British Society from 1931 to 1954 led to reporting the projection that I found in a young schizophrenic girl I was treating successfully. At first she believed, not that she was Greta Garbo, but as she put it "Greta Garbo is me" (Scott, 1934) an idea which was confusing to her.

From my very early life I had been preoccupied by sadness. Gladness and madness seemed to be much more easy to understand. When I worked with Klein as she was developing her ideas of sadness emerging as a crucial stage of developmental achievement, with sadistic and masochistic tendencies having been more or less overcome, she described how tolerating sadness leads to the development of mourning with reparation. I shared her discoveries. It is another story why Adolf Meyer and Paul Schilder did not make the same discovery in their collaboration several years previously. It was a discovery to learn to repeat mourning often enough to make the best of sad jobs to create hope to carry on to find zest and enthusiasm in life again.

I had luck being a student intern, for 18 months, under Farrar, in the 120-bed Toronto Psychiatric Hospital before graduating.

I was lucky by my 14 months in the active 8,000-bed Manhattan State

Hospital in New York City. I was lucky indeed to learn and share the intensive work at Phipps (Johns Hopkins) and learning so much from Adolf Meyer and Paul Schilder. Meyer sent me to Boston and again I was lucky that Macfie Campbell after a year there gave me a three year Commonwealth Fellowship which allowed me to learn more neurology and train as an adult and child analyst in London. There I was lucky in my analyst, my supervisors, and colleagues.

The world was depressed sixty years ago—doctors were on welfare in Canada, but passing my exams to allow me to practice in the United Kingdom gave me new hope and allowed me to work in the London Society and Institute until the war began—this period was exciting. Again luckily I was able to remain a clinician throughout the war and learn much about applied and short-term psychoanalysis rather than being sidetracked into administration.

From war's end until I was invited to visit McGill in 1953, life was busy and productive. Much as I loved London I was excited about Canadian academic possibilities, and was glad indeed to return to my home ground.

From the beginning of my discovery as an infant of feeling wakey and waking up and being sleepy and later inferring that I had gone to sleep and had "dreamt," I have been interested in waking and sleeping and not just in sleep-dreams and day-dreams. Only in recent decades have I thought more seriously of the conflicts of waking and sleeping as the conflicts between two instincts realizing that in his last paper Freud had advised us to pay more attention to sleeping as an instinct than had been done previously. This article of Freud (1940) has been criticized by one of the best American teachers as an article by an old man which should not have been written. I feel we should respect all ages and although young adults are supposed to be more creative than at any other time we should respect the possibilities of the creative activity at any age. I am glad you wanted to listen to some of the things I happen to have said even though I am a little bit older than Freud was when he wrote his *Outline*.

It is not easy to talk about splits, doubles, multiples, or the beginning of subject and object, and inner and outer object relations. The change from reflexes to reflections; the change from swallowing when your mouth is full; to saying a mouthful which becomes an earful for someone to understand; are difficult. Freud (1919) tried but gave up after he wrote his paper on "The Uncanny." He came back to it in his last paper in writing that we should think more of sleep as an instinct. Klein became interested in what she called inner and outer objects and the transformations which led to projective identifications, as well as introjective identifications which Freud had paid much attention to earlier.

Jones' last paper discussed giving up the word "mind" and finding something better. Soon after I gave my (1948) first paper on the body scheme to the British Society and soon Winnicott (1954) took these two ideas up in his next paper to the Society in which he talked about his idea of "psyche-soma." His paper was published only several years later but his idea of "psyche-soma" has stuck. He told me that my ideas would never be written about until long after I was dead. He might have said the same about Jones' ideas. These ideas had been with me since my mother gave me my first *Alice in Wonderland* and wrote on the fly leaf "For into my heart you have stolen, like sunbeams in shadows creep"—a jumble of anatomical, criminal and psychological words going beyond subjects and objects, to Winnicott's cleaning lady who complained: "Oh, doctor, it's when my insides gets on top of me, that's what gets me down" (personal communication). Tolerate that confusion if you can, and you will get somewhere, which reminds me of the test invented by my Boston associate, Coon, who became involved in the treatment of Harvard students, as Taylor Statten became involved in the treatment of Toronto university students. Coon said that there is hope for the schizophrenic when he learns to tell his ass from a hole in the ground. Forgive me this slip to the simple—it's all too easy to rise to the complex in talk. Jones invented a new useful meaning for the word "complex"; just as someone invented "engram" for the bits of memory in the brain. Freud said that when people stop trying to understand him, or deny that what he was saying is useful, or call what he says nonsense, or even something criminal, at least they would dream of it. Perhaps you will dream of some of the things I have said and understand them better—I have often done that myself.

When asked to say these few words more or less in the middle of this meeting my ambivalence came up, and I hoped I could say something suitable. I wonder what you felt about thinking of and listening to bits of what I have said and seeing something of the different ways I have looked at different times during the last more than ninety years. Every time I remember those years I remember something new and hope for something new during the rest of my life. Just as now I wonder will I say something newer and better today than I have ever said before and will it be worth saying or will it only be a repetition without a difference. There is more than one way of saying the same thing but some ways are better than others.

I think of questions and I think of first words. In the video there were my answers to many questions. Most were my way of saying something that others have said in their words so often before. Perhaps something was new, something I had said to myself that I had never said before out loud. When others heard it they may have made some good use of it or they said to themselves I heard all that before.

When I think of a lifetime I think more of the future of life. Awaking each morning to this world and to some of its beauties, may be a bit like, for the first time, watching one's baby wake up, usually we think of such an experience as being after birth but the more we know about lifetimes, the more we become curious and find out more things about awakenings before birth which are repeated, not countless times, but a finite number of times. We each woke the way we woke this morning and the fact that my being awake now, or at least more or less awake, and believe there will be a last time I will wake up is perhaps the simplest way of talking about death. Others may watch and wonder will I wake but eventually they will believe I entered my last sleep. The stories of lives are each unique and some of them are written at length. My teacher Jones spent his last years writing his three volume story of the life of Freud which became not only the story of a life but the first good textbook of psycho-analysis. Jones was very pleased when it was recognized by some as a textbook.

The big books of my life have been firstly the Bible, the first words of it being the first verse of Genesis: "In the beginning God created the heaven and the earth" (Genesis, 1:1). The first verse of the Gospel according to John is: "When all things began the Word already was, the Word dwelt with God and what God was, the Word was" (John, 1:1-2).

This is of course a new translation. The introduction to the *New English Bible* (1961), namely the translator's notes, are an excellent description of the problem of telling a story in new words appropriate to our times. I was reared of course on the King James version (1995) which still sounds better and more mysterious to me. "In the beginning was the Word, and the Word was with God, and the Word was God. The same was in the beginning with God" (John, 1:1-2).

When you think of me and wonder how did he begin so do I often wonder the same thing. And I only hope my first words were the equivalent of what I have mentioned to you so often since you have known me: "Oh what a beautiful morning! Oh what a beautiful day!" Of course it was different! But at least when I first woke up I am sure I wondered and questioned without words: "What is going on?," "Who is it?," "Where is it?," "When is it?," "What is it?," "How did it come to be?," and "Why is it?" and then more complicated questions: "What will happen if?" ("woof" as a child condensed it) or "What is going to happen next?," "What will happen if they do something?" or "What will happen if I do something?" and soon as the vista increases the question in condensed form becomes woof-woof: "What would have happened if?" Part of waking up is "what have I been doing?" What was my dream? Will I remember or forget it? This takes us to the history of dreams and to the fact that they are often told and become shared. I think of the dream I have read most often, a dream told by a bachelor to young girls, but chiefly to Alice. A lonely bachelor who loved to take pictures of naked little girls of his married friends. He told a story of a dream that began with a vision. A little girl had been complaining to herself that her older sister was reading a book that did not have pictures. She saw a rabbit take a watch out of his pocket, look at it and say "I must hurry." She followed in a dream and eventually woke to remember a dream in her. A Russian writer, a woman, who spent most of her life in France, now married to an artist, was interviewed when about my age. When asked about her artist husband she told of her wonder that so much can be told by a picture in contrast to what can be told by a story. She said "our language changes and it may be a hundred and fifty years before it will catch up with what a picture can show now." Many artists have tried their hand at illustrating Alice in the wonderland (Carroll, 1865/1986).

Dreams are important like the words "I had a dream" and the dreamer was murdered but his dream of respect for man lives on and is relived far away near wars and near places where the searches for peace are being negotiated. These places are linked to us as we listen to the voice of the newscaster, and read the papers daily before we sleep.

Alice's dream has been read by more people in the world than any other dream. It has been translated into many languages. How often do we, like the little rabbit, think of time and of what we wish we had done and think we should hurry! Was he wondering as we wonder what would life have been like could we do it all again. But of course we go back and sleep, and dream of doing things differently and perhaps wake and do not want to remember the dream. But perhaps we do something a little bit better and we wake to remember, and act out our dream of being better today than we were yesterday.

The first love story I was read was Hiawatha's wooing of Minehaha:

As unto the bow the cord is,
So unto the man is woman,
Though she bends him, she obeys him.
Though she draws him, yet she follows,
Useless each without the other! (Longfellow, 1960, 1975, 1984, p. 91).

Work woos us and sixty years ago this month, when I became a member of the British Psychoanalytic Society, psychoanalytic work has wooed me ever since as it has wooed most of you here. The stories of love of life, love of people and love of work have dominated the professions and their histories and these stories are the marvels of the history of civilization. The attempts of Freud and his colleagues to found a new profession are repeated in each of us. What do we profess when a child asks: "What do you do? What do people come to you for? How do you earn your living?" The simplest, of course, is to tell the child who asks that people come complaining and we listen to their story and talk to them and try to understand more about their complaints than they do and with sympathy we try to help them by telling them how life might be different and better. The complaints may be confusing or they may be simple to begin with or become simpler as we listen as they repeat the story over and over again. I think of my first patient. His complaint was that before he married he could love his wife and now that they were married he could not but she told him that he could in his sleep but if she woke him he stopped being able to. He wanted to be able to wake up and love her as he had in the past. My last patient had even a simpler complaint: I wanted to feel more intensely. We all want to live and in some way a more intense life of more intense feelings but we look back on our answers to some of the questions I often ask: when did I feel most intensely happy? most intensely angry? most intensely sad? most intensely frightened? most intensely guilty? and you may ask yourself the same questions over and over during your life. But life is not always intense: sometimes there is fatigue, we are tired of it all and we want to go to sleep, or we are exhausted without wanting to go to sleep. But we learn that we can recover and be at peace.

Analysis is not much older than 100 years. The Greek dramatists almost discovered analysis as Zavitzianos has shown us. Elizabethan Benedictines also almost did and perhaps there were many others who almost did. But it was Freud and his pupils who discovered and elaborated the analysis of adults. Their pupils did the same for analysis of children and a few others approached the analysis of the aged in health and illness. These recurrent observations of parts of lifetimes will lead to, we know not where, but will not stop and will lead, as they have in the past, to new discoveries and the recognition of new conflicts. Freud tackled a dangerous field of work in which the greatest dangers and all their lesser forms are: murder, suicide, seduction, rape, and masturbation. For a few years, the world has faced *glasnost* (facing new truths about old ignorance and lies) and *perestroika* (what are we going to do about new truths?). One life is short and any one life only contains a limited number of acts, acts of the shapes, that are recognized or created. Freud and his pupils, and their pupils, survive to observe bits of lifetimes and try to help some individuals live happier lives, and more productively. Some of these will become analysts and our heritage we leave with them. As Einstein said: "The hope for mankind lies in the study of lifetimes." A lifetime is not long enough, the single individual is powerless to study many lifetimes, let alone adequately even one lifetime but co-operatively beginnings are being made and the complexities of lifetimes are being increasingly recognized but at the same time are subject to denial and, as it were, and many say, "what is the use." We can all look at a newly born baby and watch it opening its eyes and feel the awe of a life beginning, and if we are too depressed about what is before the infant we may feel "what is the use" but if the infant lives we will certainly not live to see what use it will make of its lifetime. We can only hope that the uses of lifetimes will be more and more interesting to more and more lifetimes without end.

Some may say: Oh! he is too old. Why does he not keep quiet and let us talk? I still do like to listen to others. I am reminded of a toast I learned years ago:

Here's to you,
Good as you are,
And bad as I am.
I'm as good as you are,
Bad as I am.

Notes

1. Having been asked to comment on the video I had prepared the following, but as time was not available I only made a few spontaneous remarks.
   Prepared for the 90th birthday celebration of W. Clifford M. Scott, Ste-Justine Hospital, Saturday, September 18, 1993.
2. See Monique Meloche, *A portrait of W.C.M. Scott*. Videotape presented to Dr. Scott on the celebration of his 90th birthday.

References

Carroll, Lewis (1865, 1986). *Alice's Adventures in Wonderland*. Illustrated by Peter Weevers. London: Hutchinson.

Freud, S. (1919). The uncanny. *SE*, 17: 217-256. In: J. Strachey (Ed.), *Standard Edition of the Complete Psychological Works of Sigmund Freud*, 24 volumes. London: Hogarth Press and the Institute of Psycho-Analysis, 1953-1974.

—— (1940). *An Outline of Psychoanalysis. SE*, 23: 141-207.

Goldstein, K. (1948). *Language and Language Disturbances*. NY: Gennestaton.

Longfellow, H.W. (1960, 1975, 1984). Chapter 10. Hiawatha's wooing. In: *The Songs of Hiawatha*. London and Melbourne: J.M. Dent & Sons Ltd.

Rey, H. (1994). *Universals of Psychoanalysis in the Treatment of Psychotic and Borderline States*. Edited by J. Magagna. London: Free Association Books.

Scott, W.C.M. and Katzenelbogen, S. (1931). Functional achlorhydria and the histamine test. *Amer. J. Psychia.*, 10: 829-837.

Scott, W.C.M. (1934). *A delusion of identity*. Unpublished paper read to the British Psychoanalytical Society, November 21.

Scott, W.C.M. (1948). Some embryological, neurological, psychiatric and psychoana
lytic implications of the "Body Scheme." *Int. J. Psycho-Anal.*, 29: 141-155.

The New English Bible (1961). Oxford University Press, Cambridge University
Press.

The Holy Bible (1995). King James Version. Grand Rapids, MI: Zondervan
Publishing House.

Winnicott, D.W. (1954). Mind and its relation to the psyche-soma. (Paper read before
the Medical Section of the British Psychological Society, 14 December 1949
and revised in October 1953 for publication in 1954.) *Brit. J. Med. Psychol.*,
27: 201-209.

Fig. 2. Reverend Robert Smyth Scott and his wife, Katherine Munro Hopper, in 1902.
They were married in 1901 and Clifford Scott was born in 1903.
Credit: The Estate of W.C.M. Scott.

Fig. 3. Katherine Munro Hopper and her son, Clifford Scott, at his christening (1903)
Credit: The Estate of W.C.M. Scott

Fig. 4. "The Manse" in Metz, birthplace of Clifford Scott.
Credit: The Estate of W.C.M. Scott.

Hillsburg.

Fig. 5. View of Hillsburg, the village where Clifford Scott spent most of his childhood.
Credit: The Estate of W.C.M. Scott.

Fig. 6. The Main Street in Hillsburg.
Credit: The Estate of W.C.M. Scott.

Remarks to Be Read at the Memorial Celebration for Father (May 25, 1997)

Robert H. Scott

Father was born on March 11, 1903 in a small town in Ontario, the son of a Presbyterian minister. He died in Montreal on January 19, 1997. He entered life three years after the end of the nineteenth century and in the year that the first airplane flew; he left it three years before the beginning of the twenty-first century and almost thirty years after men first walked on the moon.

Father grew up in rural Canada and that life a century ago—in an environment fundamentally different from ours today—filled his memories and shaped many of his attitudes. He spoke often of his childhood and of days spent with parents, sisters, and neighbors in a small, closely-knit rural community. He recalled both the specific tasks of daily life and the seasonal events which were central to the life in a very different time. While his childhood was evidently a happy one, it was complicated by his father's vocation, by his own intelligence, and by his parents' high expectations for him.

As a teenager, Father moved to Toronto to attend high school and then went on to receive his B.Sc. and MD degrees from the University of Toronto in 1927. He began his post-graduate medical education in Baltimore, New York and Boston and, in 1930, traveled to Europe to undertake psychoanalytic training. While studying in Germany, Father met Richard's and my Mother. They married in 1933 and made their home together in England. Father's career developed quickly during the subsequent two decades as he became very active in the psychoanalytic profession not only as an analyst but also as a teacher, scholar, and leader.

In 1954, our family moved to Canada. Father often talked about his roots in Canada and the opportunity to return to his native land was one which he felt almost compelled to accept. The move was exciting to me as a child but must have been difficult for both of my parents. Father ended an active career in England in mid-stream and needed to establish a new base and make new professional connections. Mother had to move the family, establish a new home, and make her own network of relationships in a new country—for the second time in her life. While Mother was quite happy in Montreal, her and Father's relationship did not blossom in Canada and their marriage ended in the early 1960's. Father had the good fortune to find a wonderful second partner to share his life. He and Eve were married in 1970 and shared almost thirty years together.

Since I left Montreal in 1960 to attend university in the United States and did not return, all of my interactions with Father after age seventeen were through letters, telephone calls and all too infrequent visits. Five years later, Richard also left to study in the United States and then in the Middle East not to return until the late 1970's.

Father was a very great presence in the lives of all of his family. My memories of him and of things done with him are many, vivid, and almost exclusively wonderful. I know that I could not have had a more interesting Father and I doubt very much that I could have had a better one.

As Father's life was drawing to a close in January, I said to my wife, Diane, that, while I wished he would go on for ever [this was a family joke about Scotty who, until recently, seemed never to age and rarely to tire!], I found myself thinking not about sadness and the inevitable loss but, rather, about all of the achievements he had made during his long and fruitful life. This, I think, is the mark of a good life well lived—that others can and do count your successes and accomplishments and see the good you have done and the mark you have made on the world. I hope that my family and friends will feel as positively about me when, in the fullness of time, it comes to them to remember me.

Let me remember Father here with you today by talking briefly about three aspects of his family relationships: a child's view of him, his interactions with adult family members, and his view of a child.

A Child's View of Father

Father was forty when I was born and was, consequently, already very well established in his career. He was, of course, delighted by my early memories recounted later in life: being stung by a nettle, leaning over a railroad bridge while a puffing locomotive passed beneath, marveling at the size of a tractor, being awakened at night by a bird which had flown down my bedroom chimney, and asking "what animals are those?" on passing a field full of tanks in post-war England. These memories—all before age three—delighted Father but never seemed particularly significant to me.

In London, when I was between five and ten, Father would see patients on

Saturday until noon. Then, he would often take me out to lunch—just the two of us. We always went to a different place [this meant that we did not return to restaurants we liked and that the statistics were against us given the state of post-war English cooking!] and we talked about what we saw, what we ate, what we had done recently, and what we thought. We went to Indian, Chinese, Italian and British restaurants. My favorites were the hotels where a string orchestra played while we ate.

I remember enjoying these outings very much. They were special and they made me feel special. In addition to the family warmth I felt, I also remember how much I learned. I came to think that Father knew everything—well, almost everything—and, more important, that what he did not know could be discovered. Often, we would return home from one of these outings to look up some fact or information in the encyclopedia or to undertake some project to prove or disprove a point. I came to see Father as a very wise man, a great teacher, and as one with a tremendous interest in other people.

Adults with the Family

Whenever we visited Father or he visited us, it became the tradition for he who rose first to prepare breakfast. Until the last decade of Father's life, it could be either of us; recently, it was usually me. We would eat together around his or our kitchen table, read the paper, and listen to the news. Then we would start to talk about something—anything; a political event, some business news, an issue facing a family member, or a recent artistic exhibit or performance. The conversation would then range from that starting point in all sorts of directions to cover problems of our society, how the world could be improved, and how the future might unfold.

In these conversations, we all saw Father's psychoanalytic approach encircling his everyday life. But we also saw his boundless enthusiasm, his energy, his interest in connections—real and hoped for—between events and feelings, and his belief that life was an endless, wonderful journey of discovery. With Father, we enhanced our joy in conversation, exercised our logical and debating skills, and always emerged with some new viewpoint or insight. However, these conversations were sometimes very frustrating to him, particularly when I was younger and even brasher than I am today. Father did not want conversations to end or conclusions to be reached; I was—and most of the others in the family were—looking for clear answers whenever they could be found. But we always learned a lot from these conversations both about the substance being discussed and about Father's and our own thought processes.

These conversations were great events and often lasted for hours. Eventually, a cease fire would be declared, breakfast would be cleared away and lunch prepared. Then we would continue!

Father's View of the Child

Father's life was built around the study and use of the mind. Conversation and writing were the methods of study. But there was one type of event about which he had very little to say and that was the profoundly happy event. I remember well calling Father to tell him that one of his grandchildren was getting married or was expecting a child. I remember them calling him to tell him that he had become a great grandfather. He had *nothing* to say except how happy he was. He knew that these events needed no study or comment or embellishment—they spoke for themselves very loudly and he knew how wonderful they were. In his relative silence, he spoke volumes about his feelings of joy at birth and at the continuation of the generations.

Diane and I are very active gardeners. Father enthused about our garden and explored it carefully each time he visited. We loved to see him enjoy it. He often spoke about how much it reminded him of his parents and of gardens he had seen as a small child. In 1983, when he celebrated his 80th birthday, we invited him to stay with us for a while in Boston. For his visit, we decorated our guest room with primroses, his favorite flowers. After he left, we planted those primroses in the garden. They have grown to become quite a large patch and bear one of Diane's botanical tags which reads "80th, Birthday Primroses."

Whenever he visited us in the summer, he would sit and read for hours in a chair under one particular tree. Our favorite picture of him—with a rose in his lapel—was taken under that tree. Father's life has now ended and his chair in our garden and at our table is empty. There can be no new experiences with him. There are, however, thousands of memories which we cherish, which serve as examples about how to live a life, and which tells every day that he was a wonderful teacher, a thoughtful friend, and a tender parent. Like the primroses, those memories grow and evolve over the years. But also like the primroses, they are very beautiful, unique, and special.

All of his family love Father very much. While we will miss him greatly, we will live forever with our recollections of his far ranging intellect, lively wit, endless curiosity, sincere tenderness, and boundless love.

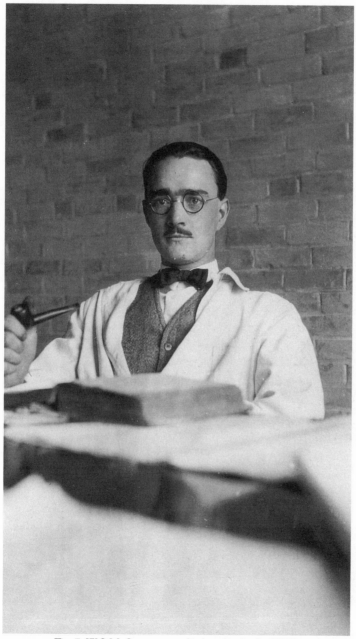

Fig. 7. W.C.M. Scott as a medical student in the 1920's.
Credit: The Estate of W.C.M. Scott.

Fig. 8. The medical students, members of the Seventeen Club.
"A number of us spontaneously formed a group called the Seventeen Club
where we presented and discussed various ideas with each other" (*Autobiography*, in press, p. 60).
Credit: The Estate of W.C.M. Scott.

Fig. 9. W.C.M. Scott at the end of Medical School in the 1920's.
Credit: The Estate of W.C.M. Scott.

Fig. 10. Picture of Clifford Scott with his first wife
and their two children, Robert and Richard.
Credit: The Estate of W.C.M. Scott.

Notes for Scotty's Memorial Service (May 25, 1997)

John W. Freeman

Though I was not a patient or student of Scotty's, I sensed about him the qualities of a good teacher. One such quality is that you continue learning from him when he is no longer there. I do not mean only because of his example or principles or ideas, but because of the process and direction of thought he has initiated in you—or, may I say, inspired.

What I recall most about conversations with Scotty is not what we discussed but how he led the talk always in some unexpected direction. In that respect, these were thought-provoking conversations, even if they started with the most mundane topic.

Very often, Scotty's side of a conversation would be to pose a series of questions. At first, this felt to me like a chess game in which my moves were perpetually being checked. It took time to realize that his questions were speculative and exploratory—that I was not expected to propose answers, and that it was not failure or stupidity if I could not.

President Eisenhower, on entering the new United Nations Building in New York, is supposed to have looked at a mural and said, "You don't have to be crazy to be a modern artist, but it helps." This echoes the popular perception of the artist as a law unto himself—inspired, intuitive or simply avoiding through fantasy the realities that most people face most of the time.

Scotty did not have a primary concern with art or a connoisseur's intimacy with it, but he was curious about everything, and he understood the artist as someone who tries to interpret experience, to give it form and communicate something about it. Technical skill and control come into play to convey the most disordered emotional expression.

When we discussed mad scenes in opera, he was not interested so much in the music per se as in the way the composer tried to recapture and restructure the nature of an emotional outburst—how the spontaneity of the moment can be recreated through a considered art form.

In his published interview with Virginia Hunter (1995), Scotty told of a patient who took her clothes off during her session and tried to sing and dance —apparently Irving Berlin's song "You don't need analyzing. . . you're not sick, you're just in love" (p. 202), from *Call Me Madam*. Scotty said, "She couldn't even dance as well as she wanted to" (p. 203). To convey her sense of personal liberation to a theater audience, she would have had to be a good dancer and be able to sing well.

In a letter of June 1996, again about mad scenes in opera, Scotty suggests the need for "a more detailed discussion of the point of the relationship between the mad singing or speech and the creativeness somewhere." To put it in Freudian terms, how and where does the process of sublimation come into play?

Concerning the script of an interview between myself and a New York doctor[1] (which was to have been published, along with some recorded examples) concerning madness in opera scenes, Scotty writes further, "I think the problem would be: would you or the psychiatrist be saying something about whether the production conveyed the madness, or any understanding of it, to the listener?"

At the end of his interview with Virginia Hunter, Scotty talked about people he had known who realized they were dying and called to say goodbye. Last January 17, shortly before his own death, I received this fax message via his secretary:

> Dr. Scott has been in the hospital for over a week with pneumonia. He has some good days and bad days. He read the article you sent him about [Bellini's opera] *I Puritani*,[2] and dictated the following: "Thanks for bringing my attention to what I enjoy so much but can't understand with my imagination or memory as I would like. Bits remind me of what I am going through, expecting to die very shortly. I hope you will be able to write a long book about madness in music for psychiatrists who can read music."

I had never thought of writing such a book, but as usual, Scotty had gone and put another idea in my head.

Notes

1. During the 1970's there was a short lived project sponsored by Lederle Laboratories called *Madness in Opera*. The first part (an LP album with accompanying text) was published, but the second, for which I was taped in conversation with a psychiatrist, was not; it remained only a manuscript.
2. Albert Innaurato, *Crazy for You*, Staged for the Metropolitan Opera, January 1997, pp. 8-11.

References

Batterton-Gatien, D. (January 17, 1997). Letter to J.W.F.

Hunter, Virginia (1995). An interview with Clifford Scott. *Psychoanal. Rev.*, 82(2): 188-206.

Fig. 11. Dr. Clifford Scott, Dr. Henri Rey and Dr. Bruno Cormier (1987)
at the 75th anniversary of Dr. Henri Rey.
Credit: The Estate of W.C.M. Scott.

Dr. W.C.M. Scott in England

Henri Rey

In March 1996 I received a letter from Dr. Scott and a: "manuscript on loan, hoping that you will be interested in reading it and letting me know what you consider is missing and what is redundant, as well as a note of your general impression of my efforts."

This manuscript entitled *Becoming a Psychoanalyst* is an amazing document starting with Scott's birth and until age 31, that is: "when I had finished my education, and became a Doctor, a Psychiatrist, a Psychoanalyst and a member of the British Psychoanalytic Society."

It is not possible to do better than Clifford Scott himself on these events since birth and his interpretation of his life itself afterwards.

I myself joined the Maudsley in 1945. During my time as a registrar I came to know Dr. Scott, attended his teaching in psychotherapy and later became a great friend to him, a wonderful friendship. . . .

In 1954 Dr. Scott returned to Canada. The teaching of Psychoanalysis in his country started more or less with him and all psychoanalysts there and up to his death in 1997, owe a debt to him for years to come.

I remade contact with him on one or two occasions when I went to Quebec and naturally by exchange of letters as well.

However, since 1978 I return every second year to Montreal as a visiting professor for periods of six months each time. During these six month periods Scott and myself spent hours visiting each other, talking to each other about life and about psychoanalysis.

We had meals at each other's place. Our wives became friends. Dr. Scott was not only a psychoanalyst but he was a man of incredible culture in all subjects I can think of and at the same time he was a great family man. He loved his family.

In 1989 I met some serious troubles with my health and I could not travel anymore, but we kept on writing to each other until the end came for him.

I will only write now about the time at the Maudsley Hospital that he left in 1954 and only about one particular work subject as we proceed. At the Maudsley Scott became a Consultant Psychotherapist and taught registrars. He became a great friend at work with Professor Aubrey Lewis. Scott during his time in the States had been a great admirer of Professor Adolf Meyer. Aubrey Lewis shared also the same admiration for Meyer. The way he organised the teaching at the Maudsley was greatly inspired by Meyerian techniques. When I knew Aubrey Lewis well I used to tell him with a big smile: "Professor Lewis you are the only one and last Meyerian on earth," and Lewis would laugh with evident pleasure. At this point I must add something most important about Professor Lewis.

Psychoanalysts outside the Maudsley had built up a sort of active attitude to Aubrey Lewis as a deadly enemy to psychoanalysis and that he rejected completely analysis in the teaching at the Maudsley. Nothing could be more untrue. It was Aubrey Lewis who introduced psychoanalysis at the Maudsley, psychoanalysts as teachers and created a department of psychoanalytical psychotherapy. I have no doubt that his friendship with Clifford Scott contributed to all this. If only one had seen Aubrey and Clifford having lunch together at the doctors' canteen you would know how they got on. . . .

I want now as my next aim to say something about an experience I felt when I first attended a psychotherapy seminar with Dr. Scott, together with a number of registrars. After a while people started finding this very difficult and gradually stopped coming. However I started feeling that although I had the same difficulty to understand and to apply this understanding, that after a while sometime after a seminar, it all became clear about what he said. I talked to my registrar friends and soon they began sharing that experience. Let me just add that when I went to Montreal much later, I related my story to colleagues who told me then that they had also noticed something of that sort. Shall we call this impression we had, or some of us had, a fantasy we experienced about this tremendous knowledge appearing clear a little while later, but not immediately.

Dr. Scott when we knew him had an enormous practice in treating very serious mental patients including schizophrenics, manic-depressives and personality disorders. He treated some for a few minutes and others for hours a week. In his (1995) own words: "Between 1933 and 1936, the experience I had at the Maudsley, treating patients for a wide range of times—from an hour a day for several months, to five minutes a day, week or month—was extremely enlightening." He had learned the language of psychotics and some of their fantasies. Very few psychoanalysts in those days had a similar experience. I would like now to explain how I think he used this knowledge in his teaching, at least in my fantasies later on when there was more knowledge perhaps on my part.

In 1975 a long paper appeared in the *International Review of Psychoanalysis*, entitled "Remembering Sleep and Dreams." In this paper Scott mentions sleep as an instinct and recalled that Freud had also had this idea. But the main and repeated belief for Scott is that what matters is what happens at the particular phase of going to sleep and precisely then, and then precisely at the point of waking up.

This precise moment he went on working on it and in 1986 Scott presented to the Canadian Psychoanalytical Society a paper entitled: "The broken links between sleep and the unconscious and waking and the conscious." Some modification of this paper appeared in 1988 as: "Repairing broken links between the unconscious, sleep and instinct, and conscious, waking and instinct."

What goes on in the "mind" and "body" at that precise moment had been occupying Scott's thoughts for years. What happens when words begin to fade away, perhaps dreaming starts in some sort of way and the body or body-image begins to count in a more effective way. Then appears the reverse as waking up starts. For him this means understanding partly awake and partly asleep as modern theories imply nowadays.

Scott recalls that Freud (1900) in one instant had a bright thought, it became *The Interpretation of Dreams* and its development occupied a lifetime and not only for him but for so many other thinkers.

Dr. Scott points out that such words as conscious and unconscious are sophisticated terms derived from some advanced language and not the language of going to sleep or starting waking up.

Before we go further about Scott's views regarding waking and going to sleep, we have to consider that Clifford Scott was analysed by Melanie Klein.

Melanie Klein was the first to seriously demonstrate that children could be analysed by using certain methods such as play, drawing, painting and so on as well as not being afraid to use interpretation.

Dr. Scott had acquired a great deal of experience with analysing and treating some very difficult children. So we can understand that he thought that going to sleep or waking up and dreaming had a great deal to do with how children, young children, have in mind at those moments. Further it is amazing that he had as one of his supervisors Melanie Klein herself and he says that did not cause difficulties as Melanie Klein was quite capable of not mixing the two activities. That leaves us with a lot of thoughts!

We must also add his great friendship with Winnicott who nearly had analysis with him but they decided not to do so because of their friendship. However Winnicott was fully involved with children analysis and treatment.

So I guess we can see how there was some connections in Scott's mind when going to sleep and dreaming and waking up and certain activities connected with infant representations and images and wishes. We must add to that all the new work on observing infants and even foetuses inside mothers.

That state of partly awake and partly asleep perhaps also reminds us of Winnicott's transitional objects and transitional phenomena. So he could start using his knowledge of the body-image that he had learned with Schilder and the various activities of the body. He also became very interested with one syllable sounds and words like bad, mad, piss and so on before the use of more sophisticated words like conscious and unconscious.

In a letter dated December 1992, addressed to Dr. Guy da Silva of which he sent a copy to me, there is a paragraph about certain complexities for the infant regarding the loss and reparation of the object. I quote: "Being glad that sad, glad that mad, mad that sad, begin and their reversals appear; sad that glad, mad that glad and sad that mad. The memory of the coincident memories has much to do with the confusion of the patient and the analyst who has to remember to interpret the actual sequence over and over again before the complexity becomes tolerated and beginnings of attempts at reparation are seen and heard."

Now we begin to see what Scott had in mind when he supervised both registrars beginning to treat difficult patients and even with experienced analysts. We are beginning to understand Clifford Scott!

In repairing the broken links between sleep and the unconscious and waking and the conscious Scott also considered not only dreaming but the part played by the body and its behaviour.

He became aware that the analyst sitting behind the patient lying on the couch ahead of him, the analyst was loosing a great deal of information and specially for the patient and sometimes the analyst, when falling asleep during a session occurred. I will not discuss all that but just mention that Scott tried to sit in his chair placed at the feet of the patient and observe his mimics and his postures and the movements of his body.

This was also part, I think, of his idea that sleep is part of an instinctual activity, of going to sleep and waking up and dreaming.

So we come to dreaming. With being awake and going to sleep we have to consider the role of diurnal residues in the making of dreams and vice versa the role of sleep residues in being awake. I will leave out of the discussion the immense part played by the brain but concentrate on the psychological part. It is necessary to once more remember that Scott was analysed by Melanie Klein. Therefore the whole concept of the inner object is vital. The inner object and therefore that part of memory, includes in my view not only the present life of a person during ontogenesis but also has been contributed to by phylogenesis.

It contains the present being modified by the future. The inner object has become a fundamental concept in psychoanalysis. Therefore we can say that falling asleep involves all sorts of transformations for the inner object and obviously the reverse when becoming awake. Remember Melanie Klein also for the maturation and passage from the schizoid-paranoid to the depressive position and for Clifford Scott its importance.

I hope that I have somewhat clarified how the delay between Scott's interpretations of what we experienced, as registrars, beginners and sometimes more knowledgeable persons, and a little later being able then to understand, had arisen. He was moving from the conscious to the unconscious making us becoming, so to speak, partly asleep and then partly awake and finally awake and understanding.

At those particular moments he was able to convey to others in a way that they would themselves experience, the state of the patients' mind, and become aware in their own mind of that state.

Will my old friend forgive me in case I have not been successful in the exposé of his thoughts. I have tried with the help of our unforgettable friendship to do so.

There only remains the sleep from which no one wakes up and in Clifford Scott (1988) words: "This sequence [sleep–dream–waking, etc.] is constantly repeated, until—we hope—we reach a second childhood when, ideally, sleeping and dying become more nearly the same thing, just as we used to feel they were before we discovered that sleep and death could be so different."

References

Freud, S. (1900). *The Interpretation of Dreams. SE*, 4, 5. In: J. Strachey (Ed.), *Standard Edition of the Complete Psychological Works of Sigmund Freud*, 24 volumes. London: Hogarth Press and the Institute of Psycho-Analysis, 1953-1974.

Scott, W.C.M. (1975). Remembering sleep and dreams. *Int. Rev. Psycho-Anal.*, 2(3): 252-354.

—— (1986). The broken links between sleep and the unconscious and waking and the conscious. (Paper presented to the Canadian Psychoanalytical Society, Edmonton, June 29.)

—— (1988). Repairing broken links between the unconscious, sleep and instinct; and the conscious, waking and instinct. *Free Assns.* 12: 84-91.

—— (December 1992). Letter to Guy Da Silva.

—— (1995). *Becoming a Psychoanalyst*. Autobiography, in press.

Fig. 12. First National Training Committee of the Canadian Institute of Psychoanalysis (1961-1962 and 1962-1963).
Standing: André Lussier, Alan Parkin, Alistair W. MacLeod, Nathan B. Epstein
Sitting: Johann Aufreiter, Jean Baptiste Boulanger and W. Clifford M. Scott
Credit: Canadian Psychoanalytic Society

A Last Tribute to Dr. W.C.M. Scott

Jean Baptiste Boulanger

William Clifford Munro Scott was born in Metz, Ontario, on 11 March 1903. When he was eight years old a friend murdered both his parents and later shot himself. This oedipal tragedy became, according to Dr. Scott's reminiscence, "the incident that spawned [his] career" (Hunter, 1995, p. 194). As Dr. Scott later recalled, "When I asked why he had killed his mother and father, I was told he was crazy. When I asked why he was crazy, I was told because he killed his mother and father. When I asked, 'What is crazy?' I was told, 'Nobody knows.' All these answers disappointed me, but knowing and liking the boy kept me questioning and asking myself why people become crazy" (ibid., pp. 194-195). While he was a student at Parkdale, he first read about Freud's ideas in a small book, found in the High Park Public Library, The Psychology of Insanity by Bernard Hart (1912).

In 1919, he enrolled in medicine at the University of Toronto and graduated in biology (B.Sc., 1924) and in medicine (M.B. 1927), having served two years of internship at the Toronto Psychiatric Hospital (1925-1927). His curiosity in the mysteries of the mind led him to pursue, from 1927 to 1931, his psychiatric training in prestigious centers of New York, Baltimore and Boston. He numbered among Adolph Meyer's eminent students who became the outstanding teachers of psychiatry in North America. This unusual and precocious interest in the working of the mind and these formative years of higher education were undoubtedly decisive in his choice, since 1931, of psychoanalysis as a dedicated life-work.

In 1982, Dr. Scott (1982a) publicly referred to his "analysis (1931-1933) with Melanie Klein" as his "own greatest stimulus" (p. 182). The statement needs some qualification: the receptor should not be underestimated. Eighteen months after her epoch-making "Contribution to the psychogenesis of manic-depressive states" (Klein, 1935), Dr. Scott began "analysing in an institution several patients with. . . severe manic-depressive disorders" (1938a) and, in 1938, reported at the Fifteenth International Psycho-Analytical Congress the first analysis of a psychotic patient "under treatment for two years" (1938b).

His most recent clinical contribution was delivered in 1980 at the First World Congress on Infant Psychiatry; it recounts a five-month "Psychoanalysis of a boy of 26 months with a 20-year follow-up" (1980). Dr. Scott stands among the greatest of Melanie Klein's progeny, and we are proud to honor in him a founding member of the Canadian Psychoanalytic Society.

More than half of my life and all of my psychoanalytic years have been shared with Dr. Scott within the Canadian Psychoanalytic Society. He became my mentor in my terms of office as President of the Society and has remained a constant source of inspiration.

We met for the first time in 1953, prior to his taking charge of psychoanalytic training in the Department of Psychiatry of McGill University. My initial reaction to his courteous and friendly visit was somewhat guarded. Five years later, a spokesman for a majority of psychoanalysts affiliated with the McGill Department of Psychiatry pledged their loyalty primarily to the University in the event of conflicts of competence between the Society and the Department of Psychiatry regarding psychoanalytic training and graduation. I felt it was my duty as the Society's President to lead a coalition of unfettered members against the intrusion of a foreign power in the development of "the psychoanalytic movement" in Canada. The University's training program was given a death blow by Scott's resignation from his appointment in 1959, becoming the tenth long awaited recruit to form the two-third majority required for the foundation of a distinct body, the Canadian Institute of Psychoanalysis—Institute canadienne de psychanalyse, designed "to promote theoretical and practical training in psychoanalysis for competent students; to promote and conduct research in psychoanalysis" (Boulanger, 1988, p. 4). At the crucial sixth AGM of the Society, on 1st October, 1960, the appropriate motions were presented, carried and confirmed by mail ballot.

Dr. Scott had accepted the appointment in good faith and, feeling that he had been deceived by the Professor of Psychiatry whom the invited speaker for the first Dr. Ewen Cameron Lecture, referred as "not a Freudian" (Himwich, 1969, p. 3) by any means but only needing to have "confirmed psychoanalysts on his staff" (ibid.). He displayed the rare courage of not renewing his contract and, at the age of 56, of submitting to examinations for medical licensure and starting a new career in private practice. His commitment to the development of the psychoanalytic movement was crucial in the creation by our psychoanalytic society of an autonomous training Institute.

My initial suspicion toward Scott was gradually superseded by a more complex attitude, brought about mainly by my close professional association with him. I knew that I had overcome my ambivalence when I heard my daughter of five remark, while we were passing by Dr. Scott's home: "This is the house of my friend who and daddy's friend." I may here quote from a letter of January 20, signed by Dr. Scott's widow and his two sons, announcing: ". . . the death of Dr. W. Clifford M. Scott on January 19, 1997. . . . As a husband and father he was thoughtful, considerate, supportive and unusually tender."

In 1959, after his resignation from McGill University, he accepted an appointment as consultant at the Montreal Children's Hospital, where he began singlehandedly training child psychiatrists in child analysis. Indeed, Dr. Scott practiced the Freudian and Kleinian tenet that the adult originates in the child; consequently, to his mind, a complete psychoanalyst should be trained in the analysis of both children and adults. Twenty years later, his efforts resulted in the inauguration of a training program in child analysis under the auspices of the Canadian Institute of Psychoanalysis.

In 1955, Dr. Scott was the first and only child psychoanalyst in Canada. In 1996, the number of practicing child analysts had increased to twenty-five. A "Canadian Group of Psychoanalysts for Children" was founded on May 30, 1991, and, the following year, Dr. Scott delivered at our AGM the inaugural lecture of the Group's official integration in the scientific activities of our Society. Dr. Scott had fulfilled most of his dream for psychoanalysis since his return to Canada.

It would be fastidious to review his published and unpublished works; one is literally amazed by the scope of his scientific interests, from embryology to speech, and by the creativity of his psychoanalytic process. I had the fortunate opportunity of editing a French version of an unpublished paper, read in 1980 to the Advanced Institute for Analytic Psychotherapy in New York (Scott, 1985) and presented, in 1982, to the French Branch of the CPS, Société psychanalytique de Montréal (Scott, 1982b). The title combines some of the main themes of his theoretical research: "Narcissism, the Body, Phantasy, Fantasy, Internal and External Objects and the Body Scheme" (Scott, 1985); the content integrates fifty years of working through with these fundamental concepts and, together with the impressive monograph issued in 1975 by *The International Review of Psycho-Analysis*, "Remembering, Sleep and Dreams" (Scott, 1975), constitute, I believe, the essence of his legacy in the development of psychoanalytic thought.

He was a teacher in psychiatric Centers of London and Montreal, Honorary Member of both the British Psycho-Analytical Society and the Société psychanalytique de Montréal, a Training and Supervising Analyst in both the British and Canadian Institutes of Psychoanalysis, Co-Editor of *The International Journal of Psycho-Analysis*, Patron to and Honorary Editor of the *Journal of Melanie Klein and Object Relations*, Director of the London Clinic of Psycho-Analysis and President of the British Psycho-Analytical Society and, later, of the Canadian Psychoanalytic Society. By virtue of all these activities, Dr. Scott influenced the history of the psychoanalytic movement in one of its oldest and in one of its youngest ramifications. His leadership on the Canadian scene has been much akin to that of Ernest Jones in Great Britain—to quote Scott writing about his respected teacher, "advocating greater tolerance towards diversities or even divergencies."

Dr. Clifford Scott exemplifies the quality considered by my last analyst, Maurice Bouvet, sole French object relations theorist and clinician (1956), as the mark of a true analyst, *l'impavidité* (Bouvet, 1955-1956), in the exploration of unconscious processes, a fearless and dauntless stance, which led him, in the footsteps of Freud and Klein, to the origins of waking, sleeping and dreaming, the emergence of feelings, "bad, mad, sad, glad," and the beginnings of thought and language.

I am pleased to quote from a personal letter of Dr. Scott, dated a few days after his seventy-fifth birthday: "It is difficult indeed to express my gratitude for having been able to work and live in Montreal for so long and for having your friendship during all these years" ("your" is a collective term).

"Zest," as Scottie teaches and lives it, has a contagious property and I have not been exposed for all these years to the infection without some consequence. My admiration and gratitude, the offsprings of love's triumph, I wish to share, in this tribute, with his friends gathered to celebrate his life and work.

References

Boulanger, J.B. (1988). The critical years. In: P.A. Dewald (Ed.), *The History of the Canadian Psychoanalytic Society: The First Two Decades.* (Oral History Workshop #28, unpublished and read at the 77th Annual Meeting of the American Psychoanalytic Association, Montreal, May 5, 1988.)

Bouvet, M. (1955-1956). Séminaire de technique. Institut de psychanalyse, Paris.

——— (1956). La clinique psychanalytique: la relation d'objet. In: S. Nacht (Ed.), *La Psychanalyse d'aujourd'hui.* Paris: PUF, pp. 41-121.

Hart, B. (1912). *The Psychology of Insanity.* Cambridge, England: Cambridge University Press, 176 pp. (The Cambridge Manual of Science and Literature.) Quoted in the *Globe and Mail*, Toronto, 11-04-1997.

Himwich, H.E. (1969). First D. Ewen Cameron Memorial Lecture. In: G.F.D. Heseltine (Ed.), *Psychiatric Research in our Changing World* (International Symposium, Department of Psychiatry, McGill University, Montreal, 3-5 October 1968.) Amsterdam: Excerpta, 1969: 93.

Hunter, V. (1995). An interview with Clifford Scott. *Psychoanal. Rev.*, 82(2):188-206.

Klein, M. (1935). A contribution to the psychogenesis of manic-depressive states. In R. Money-Kyrle et al. (Eds.), *The Writings of Melanie Klein*, 1: 262-289.

Scott, W. Clifford M. (1938a). On intense affects encountered in treating a severe manic-depressive disorder. (Unpublished and read at the 15th International Psycho-Analytical Congress, Paris, August 2.)

—— (1938b). Psychoanalysis of a manic-depressive patient in an institution. (Read at the 15th International Psychoanalytical Congress, Paris.)

—— (1947). On the intense affects encountered in treating a severe manic-depressive disorder. *Int. J. Psycho-Anal.*, 23:139-145.

—— (1975). Remembering sleep and dreams. *Int. Rev. Psycho-Anal.*, 2(3): 252-354.

—— (1980). Psychoanalysis of a boy of 26 months with a 20-year follow-up. (Unpublished paper presented at the 1st World Congress on Infant Psychiatry, Cascais, Portugal, April 3.)

—— (1982a). Melanie Klein: 1882-1960. *Psychia. J. Univ. Ottawa*, 7:149-157.

—— (1982b). Le narcissisme, le corps, le phantasme, le fantasme, les objets intérieurs et extérieurs, le "schéma corporel." (Unpublished paper translated by J. B. Boulanger and presented to the Société Psychanalytique de Montréal, December 16.)

—— (1984). Psychoanalysis of a boy of 26 months with a 20-year follow-up. (Unpublished and read at the Canadian Psychoanalytical Society (Q.E.), October 18.)

—— (1985). Narcissism, the body, phantasy, fantasy, internal and external objects and the "Body Scheme." (Read at the Advanced Institute for Analytic Psychotherapy, N.Y., May 16, 1980.) *J. Melanie Klein Soc.*, 3: 23-49.

—— (1997). *Mourning and Zest – Mourning and Melancholia*. (Unpublished mss., 295 pp.)

Fig. 13. View of Wildbad where Clifford Scott had his analysis during the Summer of 1932, "two hours of analysis a day for four weeks" (Interview conducted by Phyllis Grosskurth with Dr. Clifford Scott. *J. Melanie Klein Society*, 1(2): 3-26).
Credit: The Estate of Dr. W.C.M. Scott

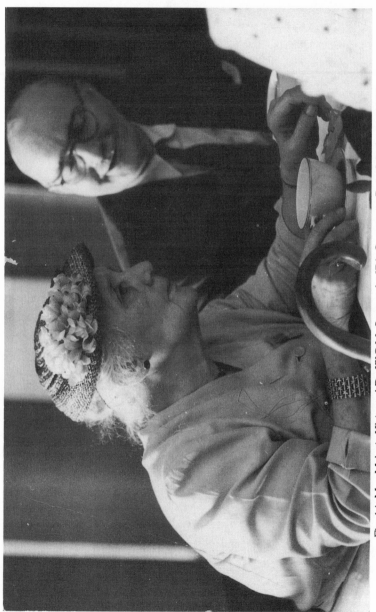

Fig. 14. Mrs. Melanie Klein and Dr. W.C.M. Scott at the IPA Congress in Paris, July-August 1957. Credit: Dr. Hans Thorner.

Fig. 15. Diner to celebrate Melanie Klein's 70th birthday in 1952. From left to right (seated): Marion Milner, Sylvia Payne, Clifford Scott, Roger Money-Kyrle, Eric Clyne. Standing: Melanie Klein, Ernest Jones, Herbert Rosenfeld, Joan Rivière, Donald Winnicott. Seated: Paula Heimann, James Strachey, Gwen Evans, Cyril Wilson, Michael Balint and Judy Clyne.

Credit: Canadian Psychoanalytic Society.

From Freud to Klein[1]

Jean Baptiste Boulanger

I t would be folly, or in more appropriate Anglo-Saxon parlance, madness on my part to emulate this ten-minute "tour de force," this delicacy of a choice Scottian vintage. The impact of Scott's comments, written or uttered, on the psychoanalytic knowledge of mourning, depression and mania is better appreciated when they are historically connected.

It is not surprising that we should be led by the Freudian paradigm of the analytic situation to the "royal road" of mourning, thus establishing a "genetic continuity" between Freud's "third phase" and the "Kleinian development" (Meltzer, 1978). I should like to continue in the same vein, with a special emphasis on the contributions of three other "early analysts" to the architecture of the monumental *Mourning and Melancholia* (Freud, 1917): a turning point in Freudian ideology and the starting point of the Kleinian tradition.

In 1910, Freud (1910; Nunberg and Federn, 1967) compared suicide, mourning and melancholia. Independently, the following year, Abraham (1911) related depression to grief, depressive psychosis to obsessional neurosis, and both to a conflict between libido and hatred. At the Vienna Society, on the penultimate day of the year 1914, Tausk (Nunberg and Federn, 1975) described a narcissistic personality in depressive patients. In February 1915, Freud had written a draft of a paper, and sent a copy to Ferenczi and Abraham. In his comment, Abraham distinguished melancholia from obsessional neurosis, attributing an "oral factor" to the former and "anal-erotism" to the latter (Jones, 1955, p. 368). The paper was finished on May 4, 1915 and published two years later (Freud, 1917). The final product could scarcely have been construed from Freud's original concoction, in 1895, of "*melancholia. . . (as) mourning over loss of libido*" (Bonaparte, 1950, p. 103).

In the meantime Freud (1915) had "used Ferenczi's (1909) term" of introjection and his own "mechanism of projection" to establish "the object-stage," where "pleasure and unpleasure signify relations of the ego to the object" (Freud, *ibid.*, p. 136). Ferenczi (1909) had previously introduced the concept of introjection as the key to the understanding of transferences, symptom formation and psychological structure. In Freud's (1917) formulation, it became the link between mourning, melancholia, identification and "the critical agency commonly called conscience."

"The great discovery," attributed by Klein (1959) to "Freud and Abraham" (with the strange omission of Ferenczi), of introjection and projection enabled her to posit "the double process of introjection and projection" at the core of inner life and of unconscious phantasies.

Reviewing *Civilization and its Discontents* (1930) at the Vienna Society on March 20, 1930, Freud disclosed that it had been written with the purpose of generating greater insight in feelings of guilt. Sterba (1982) quotes him as "concerned to promote the concept of the feeling of guilt to its very end. The feeling of guilt is created by the renunciation of aggression. Now it is up to you to play with this idea. But I consider this the most important progress in analysis" (p. 116).

In his essay "a view taken in particular by Jones, Isaacs and Klein" is presented by Freud (1930) as enjoying "a predilection in the most recent analytic literature" and differing from "a view which I have earlier recommended. . . . The idea (is) that. . . any thwarted instinctual satisfaction results. . . in a heightening of the sense of guilt. A great theoretical simplification will, I think, be achieved if we regard this as applying only to the *aggressive* instincts . . . . Only the aggressiveness is transformed into a sense of guilt by being suppressed and made over to the super-ego" (p. 138). This is a radical change in psychoanalytic theorizing, since the onslaught of Adler's (1908) *Aggressionstrieb* and Freud's (1909) spurning of "the existence of a special aggressive instinct" which would threaten his darling libido.

Such an innovation could only follow the recognition, "in welcome fashion," of a "newer view. . . rightly emphasized by Melanie Klein" on the severity of the superego, previously connected by Freud (1930) to the severity of one's upbringing. "Experience shows, however, that the severity of the super-ego which a child develops in no way corresponds to the severity of treatment which he has himself met" (p. 130). Freud's admission marks the return of the repressed "psychic reality." "Now," he writes, "we can at last grasp two things perfectly clearly: the part played by love in the origin of conscience and the fatal inevitability of the sense of guilt. Whether one has killed one's father or has abstained from doing so is not really the decisive thing. One is bound to feel guilty in either case, for the sense of guilt is an expression of the conflict due to ambivalence" (*ibid.*).

The year following Freud's (1926) partial revision of his toxic theory of anxiety, Klein (1927) began relating "criminal tendencies in normal children" to the fear and guilt induced by an unmodified early super-ego, thus explicating Freud's (1916, p. 333) previous description, "known to Nietzsche too," of "criminals from a sense of guilt." In *Die Psychoanalyse des Kindes* (Klein, 1932), anxiety and guilt will be attributed respectively to an earlier and to a later organization of the superego. Eventually (Klein, 1935), the persecutory and depressive forms of anxiety will be clearly differentiated, the latter being identical with the sense of guilt and their common derivation from aggressiveness being denoted by the same substantive.

Again, Freud (1912) had paved the way. He has clearly adumbrated the Kleinian "positions" in *Totem and Taboo*, "on a basis of emotional ambivalence, the simultaneous existence of love and hate towards the same object" with their specific differences: "the law of talion, which is so deeply rooted in human feelings" (*ibid.*, p. 154) and "the creative sense of guilt" (*ibid.*, p. 159) whose "reparative tendency" was later adduced by Klein (1948).

How strikingly "Freudian" is Freud's enunciation of the depressive position: "the feeling of guilt is created by the renunciation of aggression" (Sterba, 1982, p. 116). How typically "Kleinian," or, as Mrs. Klein would certainly prefer, how "Freudian" are Freud's last pronouncements on "hate" and "aggressiveness," from which, according to Jones' (1940) obituary, "he seemed to pass over rapidly, to extremely abstract. . . conceptions" (p. 13).

In the definitive statement of his "position" on "anxiety and instinctual life," Freud (1933) "put(s) it to (us) like this. . . scarcely a novelty. It looks like an attempt at a theoretical transfiguration of the commonplace opposition between loving and hating" (p. 103). Replying to "Princess Marie's question about aggression," in 1937, he begins his "lecture" by disowning "what I had to say about it in earlier writings (as) so premature and casual as hardly to deserve consideration" (Jones, 1957, pp. 493-494); he then touches on various related aspects, including "the impulse to investigate"—Klein's *Wisstrieb* (1932, p. 158) or Bion's "K" (1962, p. 43)—and terminates on "the theme of ambivalency, which is still very puzzling" (Jones, 1957, p. 494).

Note

1. Discussion of Dr. W.C.M. Scott's paper, "Mourning, the analyst, and the analysand." (Presented to the Canadian Psychoanalytic Society [Quebec English Branch], Montreal, October 18, 1984, and published in *Free Associations*, 1986(7): 7-9; first appeared in the Spring issue of *Free Associations*, 1987(8): 132-136, and in the *J. Melanie Klein Soc.*, 1987, 5: 18-24. Modified reprint with kind permission of the *J. Melanie Klein Soc.*

References

Abraham, K. (1911). Notes on the psycho-analytical investigation and treatment of manic-depressive insanity and allied conditions. In: *Selected Papers on Psycho-Analysis* (transl. D. Bryan and A. Strachey). London: Hogarth Press, 1927.

Adler, A. (1908). Des Aggressionstrieb im Leben und in der Neurose, *Fortschritte der Medizin*, 19.

Bion, W.R. (1962). *Learning from Experience*. London: Maresfield Reprints.

Bonaparte, M. et al. (Eds.) (1950). *The Origins of Psychoanalysis: Letters to Wilhelm Fliess, Drafts and Notes: 1887-1902 by Sigmund Freud* (transl. E. Moshbacher and J. Strachey). New York: Basic Books.

Ferenczi, S. (1909). Introjection and transference. In: *First Contributions to Psycho-Analysis* (transl. E. Jones). Boston: Badger, 1916.

Freud, S. (1895). Letter to W. Fliess, 7.1.1895 - Draft "G" "Melancholia". In: M. Bonaparte et al. (Eds.) (1950), *The Origins of Psycho-Analysis* (Transl. E. Mosbacher and J. Strachey). New York: Basic Books.

—— (1909). *Analysis of a Phobia in a Five Year Old Boy. SE*, 10:5-149. In: J. Strachey (Ed.), *Standard Edition of the Complete Psychological Works of Sigmund Freud*, 24 volumes. London: Hogarth Press and the Institute of Psycho-Analysis, 1953-1974.

—— (1910). Contributions to a discussion on suicide. *SE*, 11: 231-232.

—— (1912). *Totem and Taboo*. SE, *13*:1-161.

—— (1915). *Instincts and Their Vicissitudes. SE*, 14: 117-140.

—— (1916). Criminals from a sense of guilt. *SE*, 14: 332-333.

—— (1917). Mourning and melancholia. *SE*, 14: 243-258.

—— (1926). *Inhibitions, Symptoms and Anxiety. SE*, 20: 87-174.

—— (1930). *Civilization and its Discontents. SE*, 21: 64-145.

—— (1933). *New Introductory Lectures* – Lecture XXXII. Anxiety and instinctual life. *SE*, 22: 81-111.

Jones, E. (1940). Sigmund Freud (Obituary). *Int. J. Psychoanal.*, 21: 1-26.

—— (1953). *Sigmund Freud: Life and Work*, vol. 1. London: Hogarth Press.

—— (1955). *Sigmund Freud: Life and Work*, vol. 2. London: Hogarth Press.

—— (1957). *Sigmund Freud: Life and Work*, vol. 3. London: Hogarth Press.

Klein, M. (1927). Criminal tendencies in normal children. In: R. Money-Kyrle et al (Eds.), *The Writings of Melanie Klein*. vol. 1. London: Hogarth Press, 1975, pp. 170-185.

—— (1932). *Die Psychoanalyse des Kindes*. Wien: Internationaler Psychoanalytischer Verlag.

—— (1935). A contribution to the psychogenesis of manic-depressive states. In: *The Writings of Melanie Klein*, 1: 262-289.

—— (1948). On the theory of anxiety and guilt. *Ibid.*, 3: 15-42.

Klein, M. (1959). Our adult world and its roots in infancy. *Ibid.*, 3: 247-263.

Meltzer, D. (1978). *The Kleinian Development*, 3 volumes. Strath Tay: Clunie Press.

Nunberg, H. and Federn, E. (Eds.) (1967). *Minutes of the Vienna Psychoanalytic Society.* New York: Int. Univ. Press. Vol. 2 (1908-1910).

—— (1975). *Minutes of the Vienna Psychoanalytic Society.* Vol. 4 (1912-1918).

Scott, W.C.M. (1947). On the intense affects encountered in treating a severe manic-depressive disorder. *Int. J. Psycho-Anal.*, 28: 139-145.

Sterba, R.R. (1982). *Reminiscences of a Viennese Psychoanalyst.* Detroit: Wayne Univ. Press.

Tausk, V. (1914). Contribution to a psychoanalytic exposition of melancholia. In Nunberg H. and Federn, E. (Eds.), *op. cit.*, vol. 4, pp. 272-274.

Fig. 16. From left to right: Dr. Philippe Moreau, Mrs. Helen Lefebvre, Dr. Paul Lefebvre, Mrs. Evelyn Scott, and Dr. Clifford Scott (Kingston, 1971).
Credit: The Estate of Dr. W.C.M. Scott.

Some Predominant Themes
in Clifford Scott's Work

Paul Lefebvre

I t can easily be said that Clifford Scott possesses a lot of what his Irish
forebears called the gift of speaking and writing. The key word here is
prolific, if we consider that since 1924 till now there have been 111 published papers and 429 unpublished works in various forms such as articles,
discussions, essays, lectures, book chapters, interviews and broadcasts.

In the limited time I have I will only try to underline what seemed to me the
salient themes that recur in his writings and of course these will be familiar to
you.

Clifford Scott's basic vision of psychoanalysis was always an essentially
developmental one, from birth (or even before) to death, and covering all the
phases in between. As if he felt, as George Santayana once said: "There is no
cure for birth or death except the capacity to enjoy the interval!" In his work
Scott continuously addressed the many obstacles to such enjoyment. He therefore wrote about the broken links between consciousness and unconsciousness
as derivatives of the broken links between the sleeping and the waking state.
Remembering sleep and dreams in life and in the analytic situation is a frequent
focus of his writing. Inevitably this tied in with body experience and he wrote
extensively about the "body scheme" and its links with psychosomatic vulnera-
bility. His indebtedness here to his early teacher, Paul Schilder, was evident.

Beyond his own analysis with Klein, it was his experience of analytic
treatment of children and of psychotics that he considered so fundamentally
formative in his professional development and we know he wrote extensively on
these subjects. In his papers on the treatment of schizophrenia and manic-
depressive illness he showed a very individualistic developmental stance, not
bound by linear "positions" as others wrote about, but focussed on continually
oscillating affective states—between madness and sadness and post-mourning
gladness, which would endlessly evolve throughout the life-span of the individual. Thus he wrote a great deal about mourning and reparation, as opposed to

the subject's need for restitution, i.e. the need to be paid back for past losses and deprivations instead of mourning them creatively. In this design, affect theory and instinct theory remained paramount in his writing.

Scott's work with children and psychotics also led him to write a great deal about the distinction between ego fragmentation or splitting, as opposed to ego doubling and multiplication, as illustrated in his caution to differentiate psychoses, neurotic dissociation and the so-called multiple personality disorder.

I cannot avoid another of Scott's most original contributions and that concerns his theorizing about envy and what he described as self-envy, like the envy of the waking self having forgotten a dream and envying the sleeping self that created the dream and lived it. Recently an analyst (López-Corvo, 1995) has written a book about dissociative states with fantasies of self-envy and he has quoted the insights of Scott in the preface (p. IX) and the acknowledgments (p. XIII) as an inspiration for his own work.

I cannot omit to underline the range and scope of Scott's interests as a psychoanalyst. His papers covered the status of care in mental hospitals, observations on schizophrenic drawings, on delinquency and criminology, the psychodynamic aspects of drug therapy, the psychology of religious experience and near-death experience, the effect of motion pictures on the public, the history of science and civilization, the impact of Einstein's theory of relativity, the problem of psychedelic drugs, the relevance of psychoanalysis to education, the problem of child abuse and the question of remembered fantasy or fact—a problem so topical these days—and, of course, the problem of the Nuclear Age. In this latter respect I have to say that I was glad to join with him and then others in the early 80's, stirred by a shared concern for the children of this and later generations, to establish the "Group of Canadian Psychoanalysts against Nuclear Weapons," which united over time with similar groups in the USA and Europe. Essentially, it is clear that the range of Clifford Scott's interests and preoccupations covered virtually every area of human experience.

Throughout his work, it is in the very fabric of Scott's writing and speaking that he continually encourages his readers and listeners to reach for a level of tolerance for ambiguity and even ignorance in order to attain not less but more understanding.

And this leads me to say a few words now not about the writings of Scott per se but about the writer, i.e. not about the content but the style of his work.

And here we come up against a glaring paradox. Although Clifford Scott always practiced what he preached by always writing with simple words, he has had a reputation here and there of being difficult to understand. There is no doubt that his vision of development is complex and there is also no doubt that some of the things he says are *blindingly* simple. I have a clear memory of sharing a conviction among our small group in training that there were "gems" in what Scott told us but that we struggled a lot to grasp their full significance. I later got to see that this was largely *our* problem. Why does the style appear at times challenging and ambiguous? Largely, I think, because Scott carried the theory of emotional development back to earliest infancy and therefore part of the work was devoted to the verbal exploration of what is preverbal, and the use of purely technical vocabulary here would be useless and devoid of meaning. Scott therefore needed a style removed from the jargon of psychology and he wrote one paper about the perils of what he called "gobbledygook." There is another reason for the challenge that his language presents. He writes, I think, about the intermediate space of experience between "fact and fancy," where ambiguity has to be tolerated and even valued in order to gain better understanding. You will of course recognize a hint of someone else in this last comment and rightly so.

Many of us know that Clifford Scott over many years enjoyed a deep personal and professional relationship with Donald Winnicott. It was not an experience of filiation but rather one of shared differences and affinities. It is said that Winnicott used to tell his students in his characteristically impish way: "All you are going to get out of me is chaos!" He was borrowing without acknowledgement, as usual, the terminology of ancient Greek philosophy which contrasted cosmos, i.e. the universe, as an orderly harmonious system, with chaos, as the confused state of primordial matter. Winnicott recreated this distinction by telling his students that the chaos they would get out of him was the description of experience in a transitional space between reality and fantasy, the space where creativity begins, if ambiguity, contradictions, paradoxes, and coexisting opposites are not only tolerated but valued. Whatever their differences in other respects it seems to me that this vision of development was a shared affinity between Scott and Winnicott. It is relevant, I think, to recall that this capacity for the simultaneous perception of opposites has become recognized as the hallmark of creative individuals in science as well as in art. It has been called Janusian thinking. Scott in this respect recalled Freud telling Jones, and Jones telling Scott, and Scott telling me and everyone: "When you get stuck, think of the opposite". . . meaning "You might learn something new."

I was fortunate in this respect in that quite by accident Clifford Scott and I discovered in the early 70's that we belonged to the same athletic Club. After games of squash, which he also taught me, we for many years would share dinner at the Club and talk about everything including, of course, psychoanalysis. It is throughout these years that I could let his "style" as a not-me object come into me to be processed until it eventually came out my way as if, which was partly true, I had created the new understanding myself. This is what leads me to the conviction that all of Clifford Scott's students and colleagues will be able to go back to his writings year after year, after year, finding in them each time some new approach to a truth and some new stimulus to reflection.

We all know that Clifford Scott is the oldest—but many of us feel that he is still in many ways the youngest member of our Society.

My own personal experience of the Scott connection will never be a "broken link" but rather an enduring and cherished source of inspiration from a person who, as they used to say about Thomas More, four hundred years ago, was always "his own man" and "a man for all seasons."

Since this was first written we have learned that Clifford Scott died in January 1997.

My wife and I could say to Scotty that we thank him for all the years of wisdom, support and love, and that we cherish the memories and dearly miss the friendship.

Scotty would, I think, appreciate as our wish the old adage of his Irish forebears, "be blessed with soft winds and gentle light."

Reference

López-Corvo, R. (1995). *Self-Envy. Therapy and the Divided Inner World.* Northvale, NJ: Jason Aronson.

Letters from Dr. Clifford Scott

Otto Weininger

In 1983 I started a journal. The journal is devoted to the understanding and exploration of the works of Melanie Klein and object relations. An interview with Dr. Clifford Scott, by Professor Phyllis Grosskurth was published in the first volume of this journal. Their conversation added much to our understanding of Melanie Klein's thoughts and work. To this day, I feel their contribution helps clarify and unify the serious differences seen in present psychoanalytic approaches.

Phyllis Grosskurth's conversation with Dr. Scott has helped all of us to understand the problems inherent in psychoanalytic frameworks, as well as to realize the origins of the problems that have developed amongst the adherents to these special schools of psychoanalysis.

> You see in contrast to being able to predict what is going to happen before it happened, you must be certain that you are truly seeing what is happening. If you see a ball going up you know that eventually it will come down. Like the screaming baby, you know it's not going to scream forever. It's either going to be fatigued, or go to sleep. There are certain alternatives, and you don't know which one is going to happen. Is it going to be fatigued before it goes to sleep, or go to sleep before it gets fatigued. . . (p. 25).
>
> She [Melanie Klein] had an extremely analytical mind. She always looked very carefully for evidence, for facts and sequences of facts. She had quite a memory for them. If anyone wanted to generalize, she would always force them back to the material (Grosskurth, 1983, pp. 19-20).

The interview went to press after several people, myself included, read and reread the article, hoping to find any errors or omissions. We thought that we had been able to identify and correct the mistakes, but were we mistaken.

I wrote to Dr. Scott in January 1984 to let him know how pleased we were to publish his interview and to invite him to publish his work in the journal.

This was my first of many, many letters to him, and a correspondence which continued for close to twelve years, ending with the last letter I can find to me

The Ontario Institute for Studies in Education
252 Bloor Street West, Toronto, Ontario M5S 1V6   Tel. 923-6641

Department of Applied Psychology

December 20, 1988

Dr. W. C. Scott
488 Mount Pleasant Avenue
Westmount, Quebec
H3Y 3H3

Dear Dr. Scott:

I am enclosing some further notes on "Sleep"--and a bit of a use of
some of your words. I've tried to extend these notes from the past note.
Hope it makes sense.

I think we are going to change the Journal's name to <u>Melanie Klein and
Object Relations.</u>   What do you think of this name for the Journal. I am
getting a lot of comments about the title, and I think this might be a
good compromise--I hope so. I've put it to Pat Grosskurth, John Wisdom,
James Grotstein, and others, and they agree. Do you?

Jan. 2/89

I look forward to hearing from you.

Best regards and Happy New Year.

*I do! — and
include an editorial
explaining the change —*

Sincerely,

Otto Weininger, Ph.D.
Professor

*I'm reading the new
Anna Freud Biography —
fascinating. What an*

P.S. also — *Thanks for the notes.*

OW/jt   *I'll answer later.*

*advantage it would have been had
she and Melanie communicated rather
than contested too sadly Freud couldn't
contain 2 daughters! Perhaps he would
have wanted to analyse Melanie to know more about
her but also about Anna. Greetings etc*
Clifford Scott

Affiliated with the University of Toronto

Fig. 17. Letter from O. Weinger to Clifford Scott, and Scott's hand written reply.
Credit: Dr. Otto Weininger.

in February 15, 1996.

In his answer to my first letter, he began to help me understand what it means to "correct the proof"—Dr. Scott wrote in February 1984,

> I am sorry that I did not have a chance to correct the proof—recently I have often been amiss in not insisting that I see the proof before something I have written has been published. The last time it was because the editor made too many corrections —many of which changed the meaning! In this case it was because neither Dr. Grosskurth nor yourself, picked-up mistakes or nonsense (February 1, 1984).

As you might imagine this sent me reeling. I became determined to proof-read more accurately, have others reread the proof, and also to send the galley to the author.

This was Dr. Scott's first letter to me. Through his letters he began to teach me how to be an editor, how to read the proofs and how to communicate with authors.

> May I suggest that somewhere in the journal you should have a note about the Melanie Klein Society, the price of the publication to subscribers and the cost of reprints if the article submitted is accepted for publication, etc. (February 1, 1984).

Thus began my apprenticeship as Editor of a psychoanalytic journal. Dr. Scott has taught me many aspects about being an editor. He has taught me with a kindness and honesty I hope I have been able to pass on to both my students and those who work with me clinically.

Dr. Scott began his twelve year correspondence with me as a teacher, a mentor and a guide—always teaching with sympathy and compassion.

When I asked him what he would like me to do about the mistakes in his interview with Professor Grosskurth, he was clear and direct.

> I think you should publish the errata I sent in the next issue of the Journal you edit (March 20, 1984).

And that is just what I did. The errata appeared in the next issue of the journal (*J. Melanie Klein Soc.*, 1984, 2[1]:151-152).

Dr. Scott's article "Narcissism, the body, phantasy, fantasy, internal and external object and the 'Body Scheme'" was published in June 1985.

Throughout our contacts whether by letter, telephone, or infrequent meetings in person, he was to remain my teacher and a staunch supporter of the journal. When I was in "trouble," and I seem often to have been in "trouble," I could and did call to ask for his opinion and advice. He always—"came through for me." It is a debt I do not know how to repay—but it is an experience and education that I can now pass along by being "there" for those who depend upon me and need me in times of "trouble."

My relationship with Dr. Scott gradually altered—he began to help me cope with certain differences as he saw them between psychotherapy and psychoanalytic psychotherapy.

> Already I have found that you are up against the difficulty many others are up against in making a clear distinction between psychotherapy, psychoanalytically oriented psychotherapy and psychoanalysis of children. . . I have always found that in work and supervision how amazing it is that a young child can begin to value and make good use of an analytic setting which is created of course by the analyst (May 9, 1984).

As my conversations with Donald Winnicott gave me a sense of permission to talk and write about my work with young delinquents, so now Dr. Scott gave me a sense of freedom to criticize what was "passing" for "play therapy." I felt freed to talk, write and supervise students in Kleinian psychoanalysis of children. Before this, I felt forced to restrict my work with students to what was being described as child treatment—play therapy. Finally I could be open about the work I was doing.

Dr. Scott and I began to correspond about "ideas," concepts, theory and practice. I was able to explore the set up of the appropriate psychoanalytic playroom, materials used in the playroom and interpretations in the transference relationship, not only with children but also with adults.

> Your question about the need for "integrative resolution" of the phantasies of the internal and external Mother if development is to proceed effectively is interesting. My answer is: Recurrently conflicts have to be resolved to allow development to proceed. Sequences of conflict will need to be integrated—or sequential resolutions, each better and better, of one conflict will need to be integrated. Fantasies (not phantasies—as I reserve this spelling for the presentation or recollections of the time before fantasies and facts can be separated) of the internal mother (IM)— good, bad, or sad, frightened or frightening, guilty or guilt provoking and all degrees between, etc. need to be integrated as well as linked in integration to a similar sequence of outer mother (OM). This may seem complicated but the developing toleration of greater complexity is part of development (June 11, 1985).

Dr. Scott never stopped helping me to cope with the difficult job of being an editor. He was always clear and direct with his criticism and his compliments.

In 1986 Dr. Scott began his letter to me, "Dear Weininger"—no longer "Dear Dr. Weininger," however it took me until 1993 to address him as "Dear

Clifford." Our letters were always about our work, mine as a teacher of psycho-analysis, a psychoanalytic psychologist, a researcher, writer and editor. His letters helped me to understand the different roles I had with my students and patients. I found his comments were always very considerate and especially helpful to me as Editor of the *Journal*. I wrote to him about my understandings of his concepts, I tried to help him find publishers for his work and offered the *Journal* as another vehicle for his writings. Through our correspondence he found out about my interest in art therapy and he wrote,

> Perhaps some day when I split the book (*Grief and Zest; Melancholia and Mania*) into two we can discuss the part which has to do with art therapy and you might be able to suggest where I might seek publication (March 7, 1986).

We wrote about setting up psychoanalytic branches in various Canadian provinces, about reviews of books. We wrote and talked about how to privately publish a bilingual Canadian psychoanalytic journal.

> My hope is to publish many short articles, clinical material without much theory, letters, etc., as well as longer articles. I think there is a place for such a journal, especially to bridge the gap between psychoanalytic journals and those dealing with psychoanalytically oriented psychotherapy (October 15, 1986).

In 1986 we began to write to each other about being asleep and being awake, about "sleep and the unconscious and waking and the conscious."

In 1987 I asked Dr. Scott if he would consider being a patron to the *Journal*. He closed his return letter of June 25, 1987 with these kind words:

> Thank you very much for considering me as a patron. I would be very pleased indeed to be honored in this way. I refused to become a patron of the psycho-analytic/psychotherapy training in Toronto but valuing your Journal as I do does not say anything about the training of the people whose articles you publish. They are a very heterogeneous lot. All the power to them! Truth in humor—no doubt!

Our correspondence about sleeping and waking continued and Dr. Scott added,

> I hope we might collaborate a little bit more by correspondence. I thought that I would get some criticisms from you but all you say is that my paper was "thought provoking." It is a paper that Manfred Bleuler complimented me on greatly and I am sure there is something in it but I do not know how to put it in the best way (November 15, 1988).

I was, of course, concerned to say something directly about this paper—I enjoyed it, and knew that wasn't enough to say. So I wrote the following:

If you write about sleep and the sleeper, then you are putting the sleeper into a different state than he already is—and once that happens he is no longer asleep!, at least for those of us who are reading about his sleep. Also if I talk about sleep, then I have to put feelings and body sensations into my awake language and that not only misses things I sense, but may be distant because I have not language to talk in the "unconscious." I think it is similar to my problem when I say to some of my students to learn how to talk to the unconscious directly! I get blank stares at first but I try to explain and perhaps I am somewhat successful at doing this. Dreams are the same, in a sense I think that the language of the asleep dream is the language of the dream unconscious and the awake dream is a distortion of this (Weininger, November 8, 1988).

Dr. Scott answered:

You put it clearly but if you take a few moments you will see how difficult it is to become clearer and clearer and clearer about what you said: "Talk to the unconscious directly and you get blank stares." When you talk to a sleeping person, or to a person who is going to sleep, or a person who is waking up, what language do you use? Or if you hypnotize a person and tell them to go to sleep but still keep on listening to you and do what you tell them to do, you put them in this paradoxical state in contrast to the state in relationship to human development, or the hygiene of sleep, by talking in more and more detail about their problems of waking and their problems of going to sleep which are all concerned with the problems of what they are going to do about the dreams they did have; will they remember them? Will they forget them? Can they talk about them or are they dreams which they have no words to express, or if they are going to sleep are you going to talk about the dreams they plan to have, until you run out of words to talk about them, but we do know that memories go back to that time and of course when one is very wide awake to times before one had any language, any words at all, to put that into language of words is very difficult. One sees this over and over again in treatment by asking a patient when they make a noise to try to put the noise into words, if it could be put into words what would the words be? If it is a memory from the time before they had words, now that they have words what words would they use? The same with an action of a body part, often the body part is "saying something" and so one can ask the patient if the body part could speak what would it say? I am often amazed at what fantasy comes out and what words are used.

Then you come to "the language of the sleep dream is the language of the dream unconscious" and "the wake dream is a distortion of this"—those statements if you make them clearer are worth a paper and would bring you in touch with what Lacan talks about and the problem of the "rebus." How do you describe a picture? Or how are pictures used to tell something? In talking about picture books for children, I do not know whether you know the Penguin publication "The Ultimate Alphabet" by Mike Wilks, but if you don't you should get a copy as soon as you can. We saw his twenty six paintings exhibited in the foyer of the National Theater on the Southbank in London last year. Pictures of hundreds of objects beginning with "A" for example, many realistic and many fantastic, abstract, etc. (November 15, 1988).

We continued our correspondence on sleep, and who knows, but perhaps someday, when I've found a few more of Dr. Scott's letters (I thought I had put his letters in a safe place—maybe so safe, that I've lost the safe place and now I know they are safe—even from me!), I will try to put together his and my writings so that we may be able to have a wider discussion with the many people who are interested in sleeping and waking. But for now—I just wanted to give some indication of our writings about sleep and waking.

On December 20, 1988 I wrote to Dr. Scott,

> I think we are going to change the Journal's name to *Melanie Klein and Object Relations*. What do you think of this name for the Journal. I am getting a lot of comments about the title and I think they might be a good correspondence—I hope so. I've put it to Pat Grosskurth, John Wisdom, James Grotstein, and others and they agree. Do you? (Weininger, December 20, 1988).

Dr. Scott replied,

> I do—and include an Editorial explanation of the change—I'm reading the new Anna Freud Biography—fascinating. What an advantage it would have been had she and Melanie cooperated rather than contested so badly. Freud couldn't contain 2 daughters!! Perhaps he would have wanted to analyze Melanie to know more about her but also about Ferenczi (January 2, 1989).

And so the name of the *Journal* was changed. His words about the name change were to me an understanding of unspoken thought—he clearly brought home to me, at least, that part of the history of psychoanalysis which has truly not been dealt with—but which has created so many controversies, distortions, omissions and political back stabbings. Dr. Scott was the "honest-broker"—he spoke the truth and had the courage to say the "Emperor wears no clothes."

As our correspondence continued, I began to write to Dr. Scott about my patients. Sometimes we would continue this correspondence through telephone conversations, during which I was able to thank him for the many years he helped me to become the Editor he could approve of, to thank him for teaching me about "sleep and awake," and to thank him for his patience in reading the notes about my patients and later, my remarks on his work. Dr. Scott was always clear about what his thoughts were on these notes, and I was able to tell him how much I learned from him. I am grateful that I could tell him all this and more, and I was especially grateful that he wrote a preface for my book, *View from the Cradle: Children's Emotions in Everyday Life*, published by Karnac in 1993.

My psychoanalytic history would not be nearly as rich were it not for Clifford Scott. I cherish the letter I received from him in 1996, where I was able to experience his joy.

> Greeting! At last my manuscript of an autobiography from birth to completing analytic training, getting married and ceasing to be a student and taking positions I could earn a living and teach, is off to the publisher. During the writing of it, and considering the many papers that were given the year before last at the time of the 75th anniversary of the *International Journal of Psychoanalysis*, I had a dream which added a couple of lines to the children's prayer.

> > Now I lay me down to sleep
> > I pray the Lord my soul to keep
> > If I should die before I wake
> > I pray the lord my soul to take
> > If I should wake before I die
> > I pray the Lord my day to make (February 15, 1996).

And within months Clifford died—and left us a legacy of his humanness, his thoughts, his patience, his considerateness, his continual curiosity about children and people and the beautiful way he worked to understand why we do what we do, why we think what we think and why we feel what we feel.

He made many of my days. I miss him.

References

Errata (1984). *J. Melanie Klein Soc.*, 2(1): 151-152.

Grosskurth, P. (1983). Interview conducted by Phyllis Grosskurth with Doctor Clifford Scott, October 8, 1981. *J. Melanie Klein Soc.*, 1(2): 3-26.

Scott, W.C.M. Letter to O.W. February 1, 1984.

—— (March 20, 1984). Letter to O.W.

—— (May 9, 1984). Letter to O.W.

—— (June 11, 1985). Letter to O.W.

—— (1985). Narcissism, the body, phantasy, fantasy, internal and external object and the "Body Scheme". *J. Melanie Klein Soc.*, 3(1): 23-49.

Scott, W.C.M. (March 7, 1986). Letter to O.W.

Scott, W.C.M. (October 15, 1986). Letter to O.W.

—— (June 25, 1987). Letter to O.W.

—— (November 15, 1988). Letter to O.W.

—— (January 2, 1989). Letter to O.W.

—— (February 15, 1996). Letter to O.W.

Weininger, O. (November 8, 1988). Letter to W.C.M.S.

—— (December 20, 1988). Letter to W.C.M.S.

—— (1993). *View from the Cradle: Children's Emotions in Everyday Life*. London: Karnac Books.

South Close
Walberswick
Suffolk
8ᵗʰ Aug. 1939

Dear Scott,

I hope you have had a good journey back, – the holiday traffic must have been terrific later on in the evening. – and you were wise to leave in time.

Your suggestions for the Don Juan paper have been very stimulating and helpful.

When you asked me about the meals you had at SouthClose I was rather absent minded – still thinking about what we had been talking before – and not quick enough to return to you straight away the money you left behind for this purpose. But as soon as you

Fig. 18a. Letter from Melanie Klein to Clifford Scott, August 8, 1939 (top section).

had gone I so much disliked the thought of it that I prefer — though the in itself it is not important either way — to return to you the money and to think that you have been, as I intended you to be, my guests, at South Close.

We have had to-day a perfect day, spending most of it with Michael at the beach. The sun was shining and the water was so attractive that we had a bathe. Michael took to it very nicely, — the fun prevailing over the anxiety, and he enjoyed himself thoroughly with making "cakes" in the sand, throwing "stones" and paddling.

I hope you are going to have a pleasant and beneficial holiday. Give my love to Mrs Scott senior and junior. With best wishes

Yours sincerely
Melanie Klein

Fig. 18b. Letter from Melanie Klein to Clifford Scott, August 8, 1939 (bottom section). Credit (figs. 18a and 18b): The Estate of W.C.M. Scott.

42, CLIFTON HILL,

St. JOHN'S WOOD, N.W.

19th February, 1943.

Dear Scott,

Thanks very much for your letter. I thought the
notes about Darvin were fascinating and I handed them
round to friends; I have not yet got them back, but I
shall not forget to return them to you.

It was nice that you could come to the Meeting, and
I liked your contribution very much. Last Meeting was
much better in some ways; you will read the contributions
and I hope you will particularly enjoy Susan Isaacs reply.
The effect was that the pace of the discussions, and I
think also the temper of it is altering to the good; it
has been suggested and unanimously agreed to by the
Meeting that further questions to Susan Isaac's paper
should be put forward at the next Meeting, which will be
on the third Wednesday in March, and that speakers
should have a longer time limit and replies to these
questions and contributions by Susan Isaacs should be
forthcoming at a further Meeting.

I was so glad to hear that Mady is well and I can
imagine how you are both looking forward to the event;
I hope you will let me know soon.

You mention that you will come to the Meeting on
March 3rd, I take it that you are speaking of the
psycho-analytic Meeting? That is not the Meeting on
which the discussion will be continued, but Dr.
Rosenberg is going to read a paper for membership. If
you have time and let me know beforehand I shall be
very pleased to see you.

With best wishes to Mady
and yourself
Yours sincerely
Melanie Klein

Fig. 18c. Typed letter from Melanie Klein to Clifford Scott, February 19, 1943.
Credit: The Estate of W.C.M. Scott

W.E.H.,
Whitchurch,Cardiff
23/2/43

Dear Mrs.Klein;
        Thanks for your letter. Mady is fine and
sends you greetings. We are both looking forward
to March 12th when her doctor says she should go
to hospital if nothing happens before.
        I am glad to hear that the discussion
of Mrs.Isaacs paper continues. I was writng Matthew a
few days ago and said that I thought that discussion
of each paper would take some time and that much
would be worn off in the going over and over the
various aspects of the topics discussed.
        The next paper -Introjection and intro
Projection - is,I think,the crucial one as it is
in connection with ones belief in the intricacies
of these mechanisms at all stages that technique and
interpretation depends.
        I may be coming down to a committee
meeting of the Royal Medico-Psychological Assc. on
Wed. afternoon March 3rd and when I wrote you I did
not know that there would be a Psa. meeting that night.
I hope to be able to get to the meeting but am sorry
that I will not likely have time to see you between
the end of my afternnon meeting and the beginning of
the Society meeting even if you were free. I will
be coming up later in March to an EMS meeting and
will likely have more time then.
        Sincerely,

Fig. 18d. Typed letter from Clifford Scott to Melanie Klein, February 23, 1943.
Credit: The Estate of W.C.M. Scott

WELBECK 5050.

47, QUEEN ANNE STREET,

W. 1.

15th December 1949.

Dr. W. Clifford M. Scott,
49 Queens Gate Gardens,
S.W.7.

Dear Scott,

I hope you did not feel that my paper
let down the Section last night. Somehow
or other the discussion was spoiled, I think,
not by Dr. Heimann's criticisms but by the
length of her speech. I thought Wisdom was
much too long too although in a way more
sensible.

I did feel that I had really put down
something that belonged to the bit of clinical
work with this case, which has been a very
severe tax on the whole of me for two years
and which is coming through to a successful
conclusion. After the end of the evening,
however, I felt that I had not been able to
convey what is in my mind. I see what you
mean that the Body Scheme is not the patient's
diagram of himself but is an objective statement of the individual by someone else. Some
time or other I want to hear you talking about
the difference in the Body Scheme concept
following the arrival of the individual at the
stage at which he could use a circle as a
diagram of himself.

Fig. 18e. Letter from D.W. Winnicott to W.C.M. Scott (December 15, 1949), p. 1.
Credit: The Estate of W.C.M. Scott.

(Continued on p. 82)

W.C.M. Scott and Otherness

Patrick J. Mahony

I shall focus on three topics of great significance which Scott kept private. The first topic concerns Scott's earliest memory in his whole life. He revealed to me that during his analysis with Melanie Klein he recovered the memory of himself, at the age of eight months, looking at his mother's glove and wondering whether it was right side out or wrong side in. Afterwards I often thought that this early event constituted a creatively organizing as well as creatively disorganizing experience in Scott's life. It stirred up his enduring preoccupation with the complexities of point of view, space, and the question of origins. In an extraordinary meeting of circumstances, Scott's infantile memory was fired up some three decades later when he went into supervision with Ernest Jones. During the supervisory interviews Jones repeatedly mentioned Freud's self-help device for thinking: Freud said that when he was baffled by the unconscious, he would think of the opposite. Freud further stated that if he were to post a single maxim at the head of his bed that he could look at everyday, it would be none other than: Think of the opposite. Scott never forgot Freud's wishful maxim, but true to himself Scott gave it his own particular twist, namely: Think not just of the opposite. Rather, how many opposites can you think of? And which of them are both the most and the least opposites? And then ask yourself for strange opposites, such as: What is the opposite of intuition? And what is the opposite of experience? Such questioning, we all fondly remember, are vintage Scott.

The second topic I wish to share with you relates to Scott's relationship with Winnicott. While ranking Winnicott at the forefront of psychoanalysis today, the standard accounts of his life and work minimize Scott's influence. In them we read simply that Scott analyzed Winnicott's two wives and also his brother-in-law, period. The unpublished letters between Scott and Winnicott, however, yield a very different and hitherto unknown story. That correspondence shows the exceptional personal and clinical influence which Scott wielded over Winnicott for a number of years.

In order to describe their story further, I shall turn to Winnicott as witness.

-2-

As I am writing this I see more clearly
that the Body Scheme as an observer's concept
does include the whole individual from the
beginning, developing into an individual who
can feel to have an inside and an outside and
a boundary.

I am sorry I did not take the trouble
really to bring in Freud's paper because it
gave Dr. Heimann a justified criticism. I am
not so sorry about leaving out Klein because
one cannot drag in everyone and in any case
I cannot see why Mrs. Riviere was so very
angry. Even Melanie herself seemed rather
annoyed because afterwards she rather
sarcastically apologised to me for being such
a nuisance and causing me such a lot of
trouble! I think that one can fully
acknowledge Klein's work and yet feel that
there is something else, and I am not
absolutely certain that this particular
patient would have thrived under analysis
with Melanie.

Naturally analysts always get worried
when one talks about contact with patients
and I realise that this is dangerous
territory. Nevertheless I feel that when
there is an absolutely genuine regression
to a very early stage of development there
must be something wrong with an analyst who
cannot provide contact if it is needed.
Such contact, when it has to be provided,
puts a very big extra strain on the analyst,
and I would never give it if I could avoid
it.   Curiously enough there is a greater
strain on the analyst when the patient is
psychotic, as one of my patients is, and whose
psyche, in so far as it exists, is in the mind
and unrelated to the body so that in my

Fig. 18f. Letter from D.W. Winnicott to W.C.M. Scott (December 15, 1949), p. 2.

(Continued on next page)

-3-

relation to her I have to have no body and
simply communicate with her mind through my
mind. The effect of this in the countertransference is that I dream that I have no
body on the side I am next to her. In that
case it would be a relief to me if she were
able to want physical contact, but only a
relief from a very severe tax that is put on
me through her having no body. It would
still be a strain relative to the ordinary
analytic situation in which there is no
physical contact.

I am awfully sorry to have had to miss
nearly all the meetings over which you
presided. I thought last night you looked
very much at home in the Chair and I am sorry
that you are leaving it.

With good wishes,

Yours,

D.W. Winnicott

D.W. Winnicott.

Fig. 18g. Letter from D.W. Winnicott to W.C.M. Scott (December 15, 1949), p. 3.

Bear in mind that when Winnicott looked for someone to analyze his wife, he asked neither Strachey nor Joan Rivière with whom he had been in analysis for fifteen years. Rather, he asked Scott, saying, "I do not feel like trusting this type of case to anyone but yourself" (letter of Sept. 12, 1938). A year later, Winnicott wrote to Scott, "My gratitude to you is unbounded" (letter of Oct. 16, 1939). Meanwhile and for years to come, Winnicott would send his scientific manuscripts to Scott for commentary and correction. In 1945 Winnicott summed up his professional gratitude this way, "I cannot thank you enough for the new light you shed on things for me" (letter of Jan. 8, 1945). In a subsequent letter the increasingly grateful Winnicott declared to Scott: "Your paper is extremely valuable and you will have to gradually educate the [British Psychoanalytic] Society to see how valuable your approach is: in fact [it is] invaluable" (letter of Mar. 26, 1947).

I will restrict myself to refer to one more letter. In it, Winnicott thanked

Scott for analyzing his second wife, Clare, who decided to become an analyst. Apart from that, the letter reveals as no other the astounding extent of Winnicott's far-reaching indebitude—during the treatment of Clare, Scott served Winnicott as his third and proxy analyst. I quote at length:

> Clare has developed enormously under your analysis and I really do believe that when she now says she wanted to be a psychoanalyst, this is indicative of an essential independence. . . . I take this moment to thank you for what you have done for me via the treatment of Clare. I needed help ever so badly which she could give. . . . If you had not been available I would have not been able to let my relationship with her develop. . . . I can never thank you enough for this that you have done for me, apart from all you have taught me in psychological understanding.

The letter ends: "With my deepest gratitude. Yours" (letter of June 19, 1949).

In sum, it is totally unknown in psychoanalytic literature what a pervasive role Scott played in Winnicott's life as scientific guide, as friend, and as a kind of third analyst over the years. That multi-sided influence becomes all the more remarkable when we reflect that Scott was six years younger than Winnicott.

My final topic involves a twist in the story about gratitude. In her greatest work, *Envy and Gratitude*, Melanie Klein approvingly mentions Scott twice— once, about an unpublished case history of his,[1] and then about his novel idea that splitting may affect the continuity of experience not only in space but also in time, as in the activity of sleeping and waking.[2] Unfortunately, though, she did not express gratitude for Scott's major contribution to her volume. The unknown story about it is this. Klein asked Scott to criticize her original manuscript which bore the simple title *Envy*. In his reflexive way of thinking about a singular opposite, Scott went on to tell Klein, "you write about envy but say nothing about gratitude" (James Grotstein, private communication). Then Klein promptly expanded her work and reentitled it, *Envy and Gratitude*. In my opinion, the added passages which dynamically relate envy and gratitude rank among the finest in all psychoanalytic literature. It would be consistent with Scott's sense of wondrous curiosity that I quote a sample from those passages for which he is ultimately responsible:

> Enjoyment and the gratitude to which it gives rise. . . mitigate. . . envy (Klein, 1975, p. 310). . . .
>
> Gratitude is essential in building up the relation to the good object and underlies also the appreciation of goodness in others and in oneself (*ibid*, p. 187). . . .
>
> If envy is strong, goodness cannot. . . become part of one's inner life, and so give rise to gratitude (*ibid*, p. 254). . . .

There are very pertinent psychological reasons why envy ranks among the seven "deadly" sins. I would even suggest that it [envy, and not pride] is unconsciously felt to be the greatest sin of all, because it spoils and harms the good object which is the source of life. This view is consistent with the view described by Chaucer in *The Parson's Tale*: "It is certain that envy [and not pride] is the worst sin that is; for all other sins are sins only against one virtue, whereas envy is against all virtue and against all goodness" (*ibid*, p. 189).

In the guise of a conclusion, we could imagine Scott here today listening to my memorial and then saying: "Well, it is one thing to talk about wonder, it's another thing to wonder about wonder, and it's another thing again to have zest in your wonder." Scotty himself, we know, did not merely advocate a zestful wonder. He lived it—dreamfully, wakefully, until the end. For that and much more, we are grateful.

Notes

1. "In the discussion following the reading of this paper" ["Notes on Some Schizoid Mechanisms"], "Dr. W.C.M. Scott referred to another aspect of splitting. He stressed the importance of the breaks in continuity of experiences, which imply a splitting in time rather than in space. He referred as an instance to the alternation between states of being asleep and states of being awake. I fully agree with this point of view " (Klein, 1975, p. 6fn).
2. "W.C.M. Scott in an unpublished paper, read to the British Psychoanalytic Society a few years ago, described three interconnected features which he came upon in a schizophrenic patient: a strong disturbance of her sense of reality, her feeling that the world round her was a cemetery, and the mechanism of putting all good parts of herself into another person—Greta Garbo—who came to stand for the patient" (p. 9fn).

References

Grotstein, J. Private communication.
Klein, M. (1975). *Envy and Gratitude*. London: Delacorte Press.
Winnicott, D.W. September 12, 1938). Letter to W.C.M. Scott.
—— (October 16, 1939). Letter to W.C.M. Scott.
—— (January 8, 1945). Letter to W.C.M. Scott.
—— (March 26, 1947). Letter to W.C.M. Scott.
—— (June 19, 1949). Letter to W.C.M. Scott.

Fig. 19. Clifford Scott sitting in his psychoanalyst's chair.
Credit: The Estate of W.C.M. Scott.

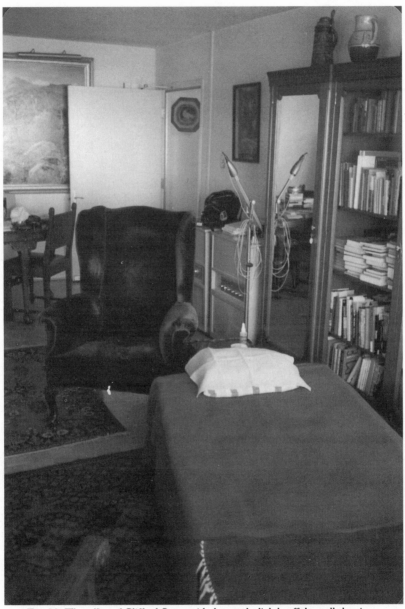

Fig. 20. The office of Clifford Scott, with the couch slightly off the wall showing
a long mirror which enabled patients to see him (1980's).
Credit: The Estate of W.C.M. Scott

Fig. 21. Clifford Scott and Doretta Batterton-Gatien, his devoted secretary
for the past 25 years (1987).
Credit: The Estate of W.C.M. Scott

An Introduction to Clifford Scott:
His Theory, Technique, Manner of Thinking and Self-Expression

Patrick J. Mahony

B y virtue of more than 60 years of clinical experience and his close professional relationships with many of the leading psychiatrists and analysts of this century, Scott is a piece of psychiatric and psychoanalytic history. He studied under Paul Schilder and Adolf Meyer, the most influential North American psychiatrist in our time. He became Melanie Klein's first analytic candidate in analysis, and was one of the pioneering few who began to analyze schizophrenic and manic-depressive patients on a regular basis. He had supervision with Klein herself, with Ernest Jones, and with Ella Sharpe. Scott analyzed Winnicott for one session and both of Winnicott's wives for a number of years. And he himself supervised a host of notable analysts, including Masud Khan. Finally, he was *a* if not *the* principal figure who established psychoanalysis in Canada.

Scott has further historical distinctiveness. I know of no one, from Freud to Winnicott and up to the present day, who has left such a unique record of having treated so many different kinds of fascinating and sometimes strange patients. And within that overall unique record some of the individual cases themselves are unique within the annals of psychoanalytic treatment. That record stands as a testimony of Scott's "long sitting" wakeful concern about strange clinical phenomena. He observed them, analyzed them, and had enough wonder left over to write them up for us. Perusing that record, as we shall do, is like a visit to "Scotsland."

Even a cursory examination of Scott's writings and conferences will reveal his omnivorous reading as well as his abounding interests in many fields, from the pure and social sciences to all the arts. Bearing in mind Scott's proposal that we take all that Freud told us as one big dream (Scott, 1986c),[1] the educated lay reader may further enjoy the minuteness of Scott's perceptual observations and his constant attention given to initial appearances of clinical phenomena. And the analytic reader in particular will experience the evidence of a relatively new kind of clinical management which is worthy of the eponymous adjective Scottsian.

In Scott's clinical theory we recurrently come upon five basic thematic subjects: instincts, primary narcissism and states, the body image, the ego's development in the pain-pleasure interaction, and the sleeping and dreaming dynamic. For Scott, instinct and drive are without difference in the beginning (Scott, 1987b). Contrary to Klein, he believes that aggression is reactive, not primary, and that the death instinct is a disorganization of what is inherited (Hunter, 1995, pp. 196-197). Considering the other end of the life cycle, Scott agrees with Flugel (1953) about the need to look for evidence of new instinctive behavior in the senescent dying person; but whereas Flugel stresses the difficulty of clinically showing that the earliest kind of aggression is self-aggression, Scott suggests that it would be more profitable to look for early oscillating behavior producing inactivity (Scott, 1953a).

Scott's other major difference with Klein concerns primary narcissism: whereas she felt that object relation is there from the beginning, he feels that initially there is a primary narcissism before object relations (Hunter, 1995, pp. 196-197). Primary narcissism is either oceanic bliss or what Scott has called catastrophic chaos; in those states are found much consciousness and movement; a confusion between phantasy, perception, memory, action, and anticipation; but no stable boundaries, no insides and outsides, no me, and not me (Scott, 1978b; 1982, p. 152). Both states of primary narcissism can be returned to in partial or total regression (Scott, 1985).

Scott also situates the later primary states of patients in terms of the two archaic polar states: an oceanic bliss, such as in orgastic and creative moments, in which all time and space are one and all affects flow into one good feeling; and catastrophic chaos, such as in depressive nihilism, panic attacks and paranoid crises, in which the universe, our body and its contents are fragmented, and the overall affect is that of hate, distress, despair, and fear (Scott, 1975c, p. 341). In contrast to much contemporary emphasis on the pleasure and pain in the polar cosmic and chaotic states, Scott has found the factor of boundlessness more important (Scott, 1975c, pp. 340-341).

Klein described at length how the disillusionment of primary narcissism is followed by the paranoid-schizoid position. Scott (1985) faulted Klein, however, for the neglect of time within her spatially biased conception of object relations and splittings—thus, for example, he urges the integration of Klein's notion of part and whole objects with the relationship of present newness, the memory of the past and the anticipation of the future. Likewise, Scott disputes Freud's hypothesis that the first split into good-inside and bad-outside takes place concurrently rather than sequentially. Also, relevant here is Scott's (1978a) theory that ego development occurs in tandem with the capacity of making discriminations: the discrimination of hallucination being first, followed by that of sensation, phantastic image, and memory image.

Scott's (1985) theory centrally involves the corporeal schema succeeding primary narcissism. The child's body schema includes a temporal complexity about his past, present, and future; it also refers to that conscious or unconscious integrate of sensations, perceptions, conceptions, affects, memories and images of the body from its surface to its depths, and from its surface to the limits of space (Scott, 1948b, pp. 142-143; cf. 1985). If the ego arises from corporeal sensations coming principally from the surface of the body, it rather early becomes an introjection from this surface. A new splitting between the boundary of the body and what is "projected into the interior" gives rise to the psychic apparatus (Scott, 1985, p. 29). Boundaries, it follows, also include depth. Still, we must recognize that Freud's designation of the ego as a mental projection from the surface of the body is a metapsychological formulation of the earliest splitting, for the mind does not exist as an entity (Scott, 1948b, p. 152).

Alongside zonal development, the ego unfolds through an overall pleasure-pain dynamic occurring in five stages and marked by various regressive, progressive, and oscillating tendencies. To simplify radically: early on, the child lives in a preambivalent (Scott, 1964a, p. 374) cosmic bliss and catastrophic chaos, attended by splitting and confusion that affect megalomania and persecutory feelings. From this organized or disorganized narcissistic oneness occurs a progression to many kinds of ambivalence, involving two affects, and multivalence involving more than two affects. The progression continues on to sadomasochism; then a capacity to bear or inflict pain without being sadomasochistic; next, a working through a manic state of denial, envy and admiration; and finally, a zest for reparation of past damage and an anticipatory openness to new objects and opportunities (Scott, 1981b, pp. 1-4; 1986a, p. 8; 1988, pp. 130-131) so that one may "risk even greater losses by loving to live more intensely" (Scott, 1986a, p. 9). Indeed, whereas normal mourning resembles minimal mania, optimal mourning betokens a zest which is realistic and firm, not idealized and triumphant (Scott, 1964a, pp. 375, 377). It should be emphasized that the repetitive regressions interrupting ego development should be called vicious spirals and not vicious circles, for the repetitions are never the same (Scott, 1985, p. 35).

Of capital theoretical and technical importance is that within the above five overall stages there are three kinds of micro-sequences: impulse-desire-satisfaction; impulse-desire-increasing tension-pain-some disorganization-satisfaction;

and impulse-desire-increasing tension-disorganization and hate-regression to sleep. These micro-sequences may be fused, separate, or oscillating in memory, as manifested in dreams and clinical associations. A case in point is depression. In the earliest form of depression, the child becomes aware that he can love and hate the same object that can be both gratifying and frustrating (Scott, 1948a, p. 4). Although appearing together, later manifestations of love and hate might not be fused, but rather oscillate rapidly; if the rapid manifestations can be slowed down to a fraction of a second, the oscillating nature of the ambivalence can be grasped (*Mourning and Zest*, pp. 116-122).

The most distinctive characteristic of Scott's theoretical orientation is his investigation of what I might label the dormancy triangle (going to sleep-sleeping-waking). Broadening his investigation, he has traced the vicissitudes of insomnia, sleepiness, going to sleep, (over)sleep, dreaming (and its relation to hypnosis), waking, and wanting to be awakened, all of which may be remembered, forgotten, or anticipated. As a parallel to what we might call the "ultimate scenes" of conception, birth, and death in our lifespan are the recurrent scenes of the dormancy triangle. We can now understand them as organizing and/or disorganizing scenes in the psychology and psychopathology of everyday life.

Just as Winnicott (1953) speaks of the perpetual task of keeping outer and inner reality of transitional experience separated and yet interrelated, so Scott (1975c, p. 318) wants us to focus on the transitions from being awake to being asleep to being awake. Condensed in these transitions are problems of relationship with the two instincts to the conflict between love and hate. To date, Scott (*ibid.*, p. 263) insists, there has been little in child research about the waking ego's discovery of sleep, its discovery of going to sleep, or its discovery of waking up as well as the integration of going to sleep, sleeping, and awakening. All these discoveries have a continuous history with the widespread difficulties which adults have in sleeping and waking.

Much as Lewin (1954a, p. 494) insisted that all psychopathology must be related to sleep and dream psychology, Scott (1975c) has stressed the clinical neglect of dreaming situation or dormancy triangle in which the dream is set—the activities of waking and sleeping seem all too often relegated to an out-of-bounds reserve or sanctuary, in part because listening to dreams induces sleepiness (*ibid.*, p. 282). Said somewhat differently: there has been an imbalance between the clinical attention accorded to both the analytic process and analytic situation on one hand, and to the dreaming process and the dreaming situation on the other. Scott cautions that the exclusion of the dormancy triangle from analysis is as much a universal amnesia as the infantile amnesia we expect to undo during analysis (*ibid.*, p. 324). Indeed, in his numerous articles and conferences over the years, Scott has not tired of claiming that adequate psychological mindedness must include an awakenness to the dormancy triangle. If Freud disturbed sleep of the world, it has somewhat dozed off, and both Lewin and Scott have tried to wake it up again to the richness of dreams and their staging.

The preceding discussion may serve as a contextual setting for the rest of this essay. Since Scott has not written any sustained account of his experience as a child analyst, I have dispersed many of his insights into child psychology throughout my essay's first four parts. The subjects of those four parts are respectively: the dormancy triangle, dreaming, Scott's clinical technique, and his manner of thinking and self-expression. Let it be said that the subjects of the dormancy triangle and dreaming far from exhaust Scott's technique, so that much of what remains to say about it constitutes the fourth part of my essay. I have elected to end with a kind of appendix, a selective collection of Scott's unforgettable clinical vignettes, fittingly entitled "Scotsland."

I. The Dormancy Triangle

a. Going to Sleep

A quick survey of Scott's comments on sleepiness prepares us for his insights into going to sleep itself. The awakened state prior to going to sleep may be analyzed for its defensiveness. When the clinical focus shifts to the defensive history of a patient's sleepiness, working through produces a not only greater perceptiveness and honesty about it but often sleep as well (Scott, 1975c, pp. 276, 342). In this regard, patients report two kinds of blankness, one accompanying sleepiness and the other not, although the latter might be a defense against sleepiness and sleep—oscillations occurring between the two blanknesses may come from there being too much content in the inner or the outer world to decide what to talk about (*ibid.*, pp. 295, 297). The blank state described as "I have nothing to talk about" often defends against sleepiness or falling into sleep (Scott, 1952, p. 1); that sleep, let us mind, might itself be a defense rather than a primary state (Scott, 1975c, p. 342). When in fact sleep is defended against by states described as "blankness" and "I have nothing to talk about," Scott's technique is to ask for associations to the question, "If you slept, how would you like to awake or be awakened?" (*ibid.*, p. 314).

The first phase of the dormancy triangle proper is going to sleep. Although Freud spoke of the instinct of sleeping, he neglected to recognize the instincts of going to sleep or waking.[2] If we investigate the instinctual wishes to sleep and the wish to wake in their interrelated totality with all other wishes (*ibid.*, p. 271), we would illuminate the manifestations of narcissism (*ibid.*, p. 342).

Heinz Hartmann (1964) for his part stressed that we learn about the regressive relationship between the ego and the id by studying falling sleep, a state when the ego abandons itself to the id just as it does in coitus (*ibid.*, p. 323). Rey has suggested that the superego has a different sleep-wake cycle from the ego as regards to the epistemophilic function; perhaps the later conscious superego goes to sleep and the primitive superego with its good and bad objects awakens (Rey, 1992, p. 446).

Regardless of the fact that we all have sleep rituals or ceremonials (Freud, 1915-1917, p. 264), the ability of greater awareness to waking up than to falling sleep (Scott, 1975c, p. 324) has resulted in the relatively few introspective reports on that subject. Going to sleep and waking up may consciously be parts of one and the same short, sudden process and may not be initially separated, as they are later by the consciousness of having slept (*ibid.*, p. 314). A thought of sleep may be a memory or an anticipation of a disguised wish to sleep (*ibid.*, p. 273), but consciousness of breathing is often the last conscious content that we remember (*ibid.*, p. 348).

Going to sleep has its own peculiar history in childhood. It takes time before the child realizes that he cannot say as much about going to sleep as about waking up (*ibid.*, p. 339). The later child's conception of unconscious and conscious is related to his early watching sleepers and remembering himself waking and becoming sleepy and wondering about going to sleep and waking up later (Scott, 1978b). The child changes from initially wanting to sleep with his mother; later, when he goes to sleep, he wants companions in bed partly as a substitute to comfort and to be comforted by—he may put his companions to sleep before he falls asleep, or he may expect them to sleep only after he does and to be there as the first recognizable reality when he wakes (Scott, 1975c, p. 286).

b. Sleep

In that of all the animals, only birds and mammals sleep, human sleep is but a few seconds on the evolutionary scale. Phylogenetically, that is, our sleep has a rather recent history. In somewhat parallel theoretical fashion, Freud began by thinking of sleep as an instinct only in the *Outline*, written at the very end of his life. Sleep is a partial instinctive activity in that it recurrently rather than constantly satisfies (Scott, 1975c, pp. 309-310). The object and source of the sleep instinct is the body, and its aim the bodily function leading to satisfaction (Scott, 1986b). That satisfaction is best described by one's state upon waking and the full feeling of having regressed "to the narcissism of oneness, to the world of dreams, with no inner or outer world distinguished" (Scott, 1975c, p.

339).

In the course of our development, sleeping and its normal or abnormal libidinal and aggressive activity in sleeping and waking states, are not well understood (*ibid.*, p. 258). In the absence of the maximal satisfaction in the sequence impulse-satisfaction, a reduced satisfaction in the sequence impulse-desire-tension-pain may result, ending in disorganization, then hate, with a consequent possibility of fatigue and then narcissistic sleep (Scott, 1986b, pp. 7-9). We must recognize two kinds of narcissistic sleep: sleep may be a prime example of the pleasure principle and maximal narcissistic libidinal activity— oceanic bliss; or maximal aggressive narcissistic activity—catastrophic chaos (Scott, 1975a; 1975c, p. 280).

Beliefs, attitudes, and fantasies toward sleep show much variety. In Freud's view, we are aware that we are asleep (Freud, 1900, p. 571); he himself felt a "somnambulistic certainty" that he placed a long lost and forgotten object in a desk drawer which he then opened (Freud, 1901, p. 140). Other evidence of the activity which goes on even in sleep is the exceptional time sense that only some people have in sleep (Scott, 1975c, p. 331). Duration of sleep-need perhaps varies more from person to person than any other primary need except perhaps orgasmic need (*ibid.*, p. 348). The two-year-old child not only shows increased difficulty in going to sleep, but he has difficulty in getting out of sleep; he temporarily loses the knack of waking up, but at adolescence he may show a similar clinging to sleep (Scott, 1948b, p. 145). A child can also get annoyed at not being able to stay awake to find out what it is like to be asleep (Scott, 1976b).[3] Generally speaking, fantasies about sleep can range from hallucination about being asleep (Scott, 1975c, p. 278), to the commoner introjections or projections, namely, "Do I go into something or does something go into me?", "Do I go into sleep or am I overcome by sleep?", "Does it go into me?" (*ibid.*, p. 311). Finally, in times of danger, such as war, those who sleep best were often those who had come to terms with the possibilities of being killed while awake or asleep (*ibid.*, p. 259), and they awoke with a short-lived cathexis of an omnipotent creative wish and its fulfillment, i.e., "a world and an ego are created" (*ibid.*, p. 279).

Scott's technical reflections about sleep are worthy of note. First of all, sleeping with a person or being with a person who sleeps is rarely mentioned in analysis, perhaps on account of both transference and countertransference problems (*ibid.*, p. 347). Analytic treatment, we should acknowledge, may progress "when equal importance is given to the interpretation of repression of concern about sleep, and the frustration of having to wake up to tell dreams" (*ibid.*, p. 327). What is more, we must analyze the patient's early childhood stages of real anger and pleasure, frustration and satisfaction in relation to the issue of sleep during sessions (*ibid.*, p. 318).

If more attention is paid to defenses against sleeping and looking as well as to their substitute and primary instinctive aspects, an increased amount of sleeping and looking may enter the analytic situation (Scott, 1952, p. 5). Scott found that with patients resisting sleep, the easiest way to bring the nature of the aim of the sleep wish into consciousness was to ask for associations to the question, "If you slept, how would you like to wake or be wakened?" (*ibid.*, p. 1). But if they seem to sleep, his technique was to ask them whether or not they were sleeping at least five minutes before the end of the interview (Scott, 1975c, p. 295). The analyst should bear in mind that talking with patients about consciousness and unconsciousness and partial instincts related to sleep often leads to defensive silence or verbal confusion, a confusion comparable to the trouble a child has in talking about sleep and in going to sleep (*ibid.*, p. 338).

c. Waking

Although we ignore what waking before birth is like, we do know that the source of the waking instinct is the body; its aim, the bodily function leading to satisfaction; and its object, the body from its surface to its depths (Scott, 1986b). The origin of the waking instinct dates back to the uterine conflict between sleeping and waking (*ibid.*). Our life began by waking, not sleeping; thus, the core psychic unit in our lives is waking-sleeping and not the contrary (Scott, 1975c, p. 278). The instinct of sleeping fuses with waking from the dream state and fuses again with the later waking state when the dream is remembered (Scott, 1987b). But it is an open question as to when sleepiness and wakefulness are first connected with sleep (Scott, 1975a, p. 350).

Being instinctually motivated, the wishes to sleep and to wake are rooted in the unconscious (*ibid.*, p. 268). Consciousness is an instinct, whose first object is the dawn of ego-object relations in its minimal or narcissistic form (*ibid.*, p. 338). At the point of waking, the conflicts between the wish to sleep, the wish to wake, the wish to dream, the wish to remember the dream and the wish to forget the dream may be condensed (Scott, 1975a). Those conflicts, ranging from transitory to persistent, affect the breadth and intensity of our awakenness (Scott, 1990a). Perhaps the first defense on waking is against unconscious processes which would lead to a wake-dream or hallucinosis (Scott, 1975c, p. 277).

Mothers teach children to go to sleep, but they wake up in their own way (Scott, 1986b). Although we slowly learn that we did not create the world to which we wake (Scott, 1990b), the change from the state before sleep to waking may at times be felt as sudden or even magically omnipotent (Scott,

1975c, p. 339). A world and an ego are born (Scott, 1952, p. 1)! Not only can waking up be slowed down, but it can also be speeded to become as fast as anything we can do, thus it might act as a defense against being conscious of the transition from sleep to waking, or from dream to memory of dream, or to perception (Scott, 1975c, p. 280). Adult experiences of greatest speeds and sudden change can often by reconstructed by going back to the infantile discovery of the slowness or speed of going to sleep and waking up. The child is apt to have the illusion of his sleeping and waking as simultaneous, and only later, by realizing that it has slept for some time, understand the "sudden change" and the difference of the two activities (*ibid.*, p. 343).

A big problem is a lack of concern about that which happens in dreams, if anything, before we wake up, and which can become a dream residue upon our waking. This waking up to something we were never awake to before is very related to creativeness which may loosen primary repression as distinguished from secondary repression (Scott, 1986b).[4] In his last paper of 1979, Bion wrote of wake work on the remembered dream while we are awake (Scott, 1986b). It was the early Freud, however, who coined and thrice used the term "wakework."[5] Just as we carry out dream work on the dream in sleep, we do wake work on the remembered dream while we are awake (Scott, 1990a).[6]

We know much about the later derivatives of looking and sleeping (e.g. the visual sleep dream) but little about the origins of the connection between looking and waking (Scott, 1952, p. 3; 1975c, p. 260). Since optical fixation is a physical voluntary innervation possible in the awakened stage only, a person in a dream eagerly trying to read something will wake imminently (Scott, 1975c, p. 260).[7] Prominent examples of infantile wancies are the following: Will the baby find mother inside on waking? Will baby wake to being inside mother, and for a time believe all he sees and hears, is mother's insides? Will the world into which baby wakes be a world without mother, without a meal, and only cries and perhaps a sad repeated journey of troubles, until all ends well again as part of repeating but changing cycles? (Scott, 1990b). More complex wancies include Lewin's (1946) well-known triad of oral wishes (to eat, be eaten, and sleep). That triad may also appear in passive-active terms (to feed, sleep, to eat into, versus to be fed, to be put to sleep, to be eaten). Projective-introjective dynamics underlie other wishful variants (to be fed, to be eaten, to be encompassed by sleep versus to feed, to eat into, to encompass sleep) (Scott, 1975c, p. 341).

There are many stages of sleepiness discovered during the development of different ways of waking. We can wake up to forgetting, or forgetting that we have forgotten, or remembering to remember (Scott, 1986b).[8] Sooner or later one wakes to remember that he awoke; one wakes to being awake to being awake and begins to anticipate sleeping (Scott, 1987b). Proclaiming his advanced thinking in those papers delivered in 1986 and 1987, Scott tried to heal the broken links between the polar instincts of sleep, unawareness and the unconscious on the one hand, and waking, awareness, and consciousness on the other. He questioned whether we add anything to the term "waking" by saying that we are "aware" or "conscious"—whether, that is, we are merely giving a new name to the meaning of reflection. Although it would be quite a linguistic exercise to describe to a child what "aware of being awake" means (Scott, 1986b), we can talk to our colleagues about awareness and consciousness as well as unawareness and unconsciousness. Would it not be clearer, Scott proposes, to say "awake to being awake," thus being explicit about the type of reflection? (Scott, 1990a).[9]

The transitional states of going to sleep and waking up are rarely talked about after infancy, even in treatment (Scott, 1987b). The need to understand the types of conflict and the speed and manner with which they are solved may be a long time coming into any analysis. In the treatment of these issues, so many repetitions of early types of waking, alone or with someone who was awake or asleep, have to be worked through (Scott, 1975a).

Ever pursuing insight into the dynamics of sleeping, waking and sleep-wake conflicts, Scott interpreted defenses against the indifference to memories of sleep and awaking (Scott, 1990a). Yet he readily admitted the difficulty in deciding how awake or asleep patients are, or how fused, confused, or quickly oscillating are their states of sleeping and waking (Scott, 1987a). During interviews, moreover, some examples of fast waking and some examples of fast falling asleep were used as defenses against memories of a sleep dream or a day dream. Scott urged the reconstruction of the defenses against waking up for the 3-4 a.m. feeding and the reactions to the first regularly missed feeding and other experiences of waking up and not being fed, which led to memories of waiting (Scott, 1952, p. 2; 1975c, p. 342).

Patients may also keep themselves awake for fear that they would sleep too long (Scott, 1975c, p. 346). When someone remains unconscious of having awakened, he or she may come to the interview and, instead of telling a dream, will talk as if the analytic situation is continuing a dream. To change that situation, we must interpret the patient's denial of having awakened, or interpret their delusion of still being asleep and being able to wake up in the place where they went to sleep (ibid., p. 325).

It is also instructive to follow Scott's technique with patients having serious waking problems. Two of his clinical examples merit citation:

Twice I have interpreted that a certain female patient was waking in her sleep, that she believed me to be part of a dream in which, if she woke, she would be in bed at home, but I believed that she woke. In both instances, the patient suddenly changed; she was confused in finding herself awake in session and remembered dreaming of being in analysis with me, then went to sleep again and came to the interview the next day walking in her sleep (Scott, 1987a, p. 13).

A manic depressive who would not lie down during the first months of treatment took sedation for sleeplessness. She would fall into stupors from which, as she said, she suddenly woke up. My interpretations of anxieties about going to sleep were ineffective until I addressed her anxieties about waking up. Then it became apparent that sleep was death for her and that she felt that my interpretations were fostering her suicide. Later she spoke of perplexity as to whether she was awake or not, and on one occasion after this she asked me not to awaken her lest the awful things come to be. I interpreted this as a delusion of sleep—that she was treating me as her dream, as an entirely internal object (Scott, 1975c, p. 296).

II. Dreaming

Scott devoted major attention to dreaming, the activity that is literally embedded within the dormancy triangle. The instincts of sleeping and waking are fused and can be conflicted in dreaming (Scott, 1990a).[10] Our sleep restores primitive narcissism and effects the withdrawal of cathexes of consciousness until broken through by the consciousness of the dream; with sleep as its preconscious part, the dream itself recapitulates the history of disillusionment of primary narcissism, which, to an important extent, occurs upon one's waking from earlier dreams (Scott, 1975c, pp. 256, 284, 308).[11] Some children and adults can tolerate and exploit fantasy which is near to hallucinosis in vividness; in others, the ego's contribution to the sleep-dream may also be the wish to dream rather than to hallucinate (*ibid.*, p. 277)—a dynamic supporting Garma's (1967) insistence that the fulfillment of a wish is a dream's defense against the primary revival of the trauma in hallucinated form (*ibid.*, p. 282). Scott also investigated sleep and dreams that are themselves hallucinated instead of being remembered (*ibid.*, p. 259). In the case of many unremembered dreams, the waking ego is envious of the dream function and spoils the link between the dream and waking life (Scott, 1974).

Scott's insatiable interest in dreams has extended to every type: those of the feeble-minded (Scott, 1975a); the dream with laughter in it (*ibid*); the vaguest or minimal dream—Lewin's (1953b) dream screen or blank dream (Scott, 1975c, p. 313); the hateful oneiric kind ending in the satisfaction of hate, and the convulsive and traumatic, hateful kind leading to pain (Scott, 1953a); and the most difficult dreams in which a person sleeps and wakes up in the dream (Hunter, 1995, p. 203). Scott has noted dreams themselves rarely contain sleeping people or timepieces and rarely about the dream state (Scott, 1975c, p. 324). And he has found that the dualistic-laden images of the mirror and horizon frequently symbolize sleeping and waking (*ibid.*, pp. 342-343). According to his further findings, premenstrual dreams are apt to be erotic, and postmenstrual ones maternal (*ibid.*, p. 254). And he has identified the type "vista dreams," which, arriving at a critical change in the analysis, span much of the patient's life and require an interpretive attention lasting over many sessions (Scott, 1974; 1975c, p. 263).[12] Scott (1990a) regrets that he had neither a patient who dreamt of being hypnotized nor one who, if he slept, associated to hypnosis.

Reports of children's dreams have a special place in Scott's writing. It happens in a child's dream that he goes into mother, or that his very dream remains outside or even disappears deep inside. In one instance, "the dream vanished into a cupboard in the room, the door of which was too heavy and the catch too complicated for the child to manipulate, and he did not wish to tell the secret to any adult whom he might have asked to help him—the place represented the interior of his mother's body" (Scott, 1975c, pp. 316, 344). Scott has observed that the child may dream about his attempts to understand the beginning of speech and so dream of spoken speech and understood and then upon waking, hear mother's voice and is only able to baby-talk (*ibid.*, p. 344). He has suggestively asked whether the infant who wakes and babbles to itself and returns to sleep is babbling about babbling or about waking, dreaming, and sleeping (*ibid.*, p. 282). He has urged analysts to learn a notation to register the sound a patient heard in a dream, which itself was a memory of an earlier sound, e.g., a memory of an attempt to imitate mother's sound or a memory of an attempt to get mother to imitate its sound (private communication, 1976).

According to Scott's observations, the child's development of boundaries prepares him both to understand and tolerate the phenomenon of the double in his dreaming and nondreaming life. But for the double to have meaning, the child must first solve some of his problems with internalization and externalization, as well as with the stabilization of the inside-out and outside-in. The child, that is to say, must first be able to incorporate the world on going to sleep and externalize it upon waking, and he must develop stable boundaries that lead to feelings of outsideness, insideness, and besideness (Scott, 1975c, p. 342). If, however, the child's dreams are exciting, or frightening, he may still be confused about the person waking him up and about what he remembers (or hallucinates) of the not yet forgotten or not yet disappeared dream. This situation is especially confusing when the dream contains the persons who have come to wake the young sleeper—or then again, the child may be desirously dreaming of his mother, only to be woken by his father (Scott, 1986c). An enlightening contrast is found in the example of the psychotic who, upon waking, had a hallucinatory regression to the time before he could discriminate and tolerate his dream as a double of the external world (Scott, 1975c, p. 340).

The I-thou experience has its roots in the discovery of the double: "I the hallucinator-rememberer-anticipator/thou the hallucination-memory-anticipation" versus "I the perceiver/thou the perception." Repetitions of this discovery sometimes occur when a patient in session, instead of first bringing up his awakening perceptions and their relation to the dream, talks immediately about the dream from which he has just awakened (Scott, 1976b). A complication arises when the analyst figures in such a dream; if the patient sleeps in order to deny the analyst's doubleness and thus to make him only into an internal figure, he must eventually wake and overcome this frustration by talking (Scott, 1975c, p. 349). We come upon a further complication when a dreamy patient suddenly realizes that he has not recognized that he was talking to himself rather than to the analyst; one reason for this is that the patient may remember playing the peek-a-boo game with his mother—the game of talking and looking away and looking back, the game of magical appearance and disappearance, magical destruction and recreation, and maintaining a memory and then discovering the double of the memory in the external world (*ibid.*, pp. 341-342).

Scott's technique with dreams also shows his originality. In an overall sense, he has extended Ferenczi's comparison of the analytic session to a dream: its beginning can be symbolic of going to sleep, its ending symbolic of waking,[13] with the analyst figuring in that pervasive dream (*ibid.*, p. 349). Scott went on to consider that repression is the most important aspect of patients' dreams in the analytic situation (*ibid.*, p. 327), an idea foreshadowed in Freud's (1925, p. 128) tenet that dreams best fill their function if they are forgotten (in the words of Lewin [1953a], "to remember the dream is a quasi prolongation of sleep. . . while forgetting the dream repeats and stands for waking up" [Scott, *ibid.*, p. 323]).[14] To that effect, Scott (1986b) is ever alert to interpret the part played by both the ego and superego in forgetting. Believing that certain things could be discovered only if they sleep and dream in session, some patients fend off sleep and even repress the wish to sleep in the presence of the analyst (*ibid.*, p. 346); they may even engage in talk as a defense of dreaming about being in/away from analysis or as a defense to wish for a dreamless or a more talkful sleep (*ibid.*, p. 277).

Throughout Scott's clinical work the relationship of minor disorders of both sleeping and waking to the forgetting and remembering of dreams[15] is at the forefront (*ibid.*, p. 256). He also keeps in view the optimal relationship among specific acts of dreams, sleep, and waking (*ibid.*, p. 284). Equally important are the connections between the manifest dream and the patient's first thought on waking, his manner of waking, and his emergent attitudes to the dream (*ibid.*, p. 332). Scott has found that in the fear that their dreams will bore the analysts, some patients identify with aggressive parents who once rejected or forgot their child's dreams. The child who called out on waking up might have been told, "Go back to sleep," or "You've only been dreaming"; and the next morning he might not have been asked to remember the dream and talk about it (*ibid.*, pp. 36, 327-328).[16]

Scott has specified a number of ways in which he has extended the concept of day residue. For example, there is both dream residue and wake residue in the next day's dream. A depressive dream may continue as a residue fended off by a manic, wakeful state (Scott, 1964a, p. 374). When a patient dreams on the couch, the day residues can include a sessional immediacy.[17] In the remembered dream, in the background there is always the dreamer's wish that in the next sleep he will continue the dream in the next sleep. Such a continued dream will involve as day residue, the dreamer's memory of being awake the day before and of what he did with the dream (Scott, 1975c, p. 288).

If for Freud dreams are the royal road to the unconscious, for Scott dreams during the analytic session are the shortest royal road to the unconscious and to infantile amnesia.[18] To those patients who cannot remember their dream, Scott interprets their possible regret upon waking that he was not present there when the dream might have been remembered and told immediately (*ibid.*, p. 324). When he thought the sleeping patient was dreaming, he would wake him and ask to be told the dream right away, the point being that the account might differ from one given by the dreamer who would wake up of his own accord (Scott, 1964b).[19] But in Scott's general understanding, the reported dream may be taken as the first association to the dream itself (Scott, 1975c, p. 332).[20]

Mindful of Freud's observation that our thought activity changes to images as sleep takes over, Scott was interested in the issues of visuality and light in dreams. Two of his vignettes about technical management may suffice. In one patient, the feeling that everything was brighter when she closed her eyes was related to her idealized wake-dreams that ever since childhood contained light brighter than day. While working through the link between wake-dreams and sleep-dreams, their light began to show variations similar to the variations of the light. Another patient once slept and woke up without opening his eyes and wondered whether the light he saw was a memory of the light of the dream or the light of a lamp in the room coming through his eyelids. Scott discovered that the light represented the external analyst, whereas the internal light represented his dream, himself, and what he had already obtained from others. The patient opened his eyes to discover the room darker than expected, a circumstance reflecting his belief that he had obtained more from Scott in the past than he expected to obtain in the shorter time left in the analysis (*ibid.*, pp. 342-343).[21]

III. Scott's Clinical Technique

A few introductory words should be said about Scott's organization of the analytic setting and framework. He places a rather wide couch away from the wall, thus putting the patient in a freer space that facilitates his free association. Reflecting his stress on the patient's body schema and regression to early stages, Scott had a cloth at hand since he felt Kleenex was inadequate for "a bout of really active crying"; he also had a blanket available, as well as a bowl ready for vomiting (Scott, 1970). Drawing on his own experience of having two analytic sessions a day for a certain period, Scott (1984b) holds that every analytical candidate should have longer sessions for a period in his personal analysis and should also offer them to his own patients (*ibid.*, p. 150).

A key Heisenberg principle guiding Scott's technique concerns the necessity that we be aware of our procedural limitations from the very onset of any analysis. The more we are supposedly "objective" and refrain from altering the observational scene, the less we interpret and the less we learn about a patient's ability to change; but the more we interpret, the more we disturb our perceptions about the patient's mental status at rest (Scott, 1964b, p. 4; 1962, p. 346.). In a private communication (1976), Scott showed further how Heisenberg's principle of indeterminacy undercuts clinical observation:

> The mouth may speak what the body part spoken of cannot speak, and in fact, a child may say that he is saying what the part would say if it could speak. The difficulty of speaking about speech and speaking about the mouth is also relevant insofar as the very act of speaking changes the sensation in the mouth from the sensation which was intended to be spoken about. A memory rather than an ongoing sensation has to be spoken about.

Such phenomena are necessarily altered as one tries to explain them to different audiences, such as to the child patient, to his mother, and to one's colleagues with different training and competence (*Becoming an Analyst*, pp. 108-112; Rey, 1992, p. 3).

Driven by his own curiosity and sympathetic understanding (1981b, p. 4), Scott incited his patient to be ever more truthfully curious (*Becoming an Analyst*, p. 11). To this end, Scott (1986c) interpreted in order that the patient became free to associate in questions, much like the child saying:

"What's that? What's that? What's that?" (*ibid.*, p. 9). To stimulate his own curiosity, Scott (1982b) kept in mind Henry Rey's (1992) interrogatory formula: "What part of the subject, when and where, in what state and for what intention, does what, to what part of the object, when and where, and with what consequences for both the subject and the object?" (p. 56). Concomitant with those self-reminders is Scott's (1985) particular focus on the corporeal schema as perceived consciously or symbolically by the patient. A turning point in Scott's technique occurred when he began to ask patients to try to tell everything that they *could* say, rather than everything that came to their mind (Scott, 1985)—but the problem remains of their proneness to indulge in recounting the past instead of the present, and to narrate what happened instead of what is happening (Scott, 1975b).

Lastingly impressed by Adolf Meyer's tenet that "whatever makes a difference is significant" (*Mourning and Zest*, p. 189), Scott (1984a) strove to have his patients join him in being "wakefully discriminatory" (*ibid.*, p. 462). Included in that observational goal are the speed, length, sequencing and repetitions of events—the repetitions themselves are important for containing inevitable significant differences and for possibly indicating a defensiveness toward new behavior (*Mourning and Zest*, p. 197). Scott (1984b) also noted how patients made their maximal discriminations and greatest integrations of what they were part of and what their words were for "everything that exists" (*ibid.*, p. 152). Affective and temporal factors, however, interfere with the capacity to discriminate. Thus, when aggression and anxiety are maximal, there is hardly a chance of making discriminating perceptions and accepting symbolizing activity (*ibid.*, p. 153). Temporally, an accelerated oscillation may lead to confusion and even elude perceptual discrimination (Scott, 1986c). Since the period of oscillation must be reduced to the region of 1/10 to 1/100 second before the elements are consciously discriminated and seen as discontinuous, the patient's awareness of ambivalence and its components will be accordingly affected (1953b). From the analyst's point of view, first the patient's inactivity will be detectable, then confusion, and finally the oscillation between recognizable love and hate (*ibid.*).

It is quite revelatory of Scott's (1962) corporeal orientation in assessing pathology that to Anna Freud's list of factors (such as frustration tolerance, anxiety tolerance and capacity for substitution) he added the rate of growth and sleep patterns, and variations of orgasm, fertility, parturition, and lactation as well as speed of reaction (*ibid.*, p. 239). Given the variations in sensorial sensitivity, Scott urged that we observe the greatest and least importance that patients individually lend to touching and being touched, tasting and being tasted, smelling and being smelled, hearing and being heard, and seeing and being seen (private communication). It was only gradually, however, that Scott thought of certain similarities between child and adult analysis that extended to both ego development and emergence of new discriminations and visual fields between analyst and analysand, all being related to the child's early nondiscrimination between a mouthful and an eyeful (Scott, 1970).[22]

Scott (1984a) has recurrently insisted on the analyst's discrimination that is crucial to decide whether transference is a regressive or a progressive defense rather than more related to insightfully working through (*ibid.*, p. 463). Hopelessness or minimal hopefulness may give rise to pathological regressions and pathological progressions (*Mourning and Zest*, p. 168). The always present possibility of regression to magical restitution and progression to reparation are often confused both in patients and in clinical descriptions, the clarification of that confusion being indispensable for analytic progress (private communication). To that effect Scott (1986a) helped patients work through sado-masochistic developments, manic denial, and idealization so that they would become zestful in reparative resolution. Especially in transitional depressive-manic periods (Scott, 1960, p. 500), Scott closely watched sequences of behavior, the slow or sudden changes of emotions, and their pinpoint balances, with the aim of assisting patients to go from a confusional state of tolerating oscillating affects to the satisfied state of tolerating their complexity (*ibid.*, p. 502).

A principle element in Scott's (1986b) technical armamentarium was his particular way to foster the remembering of broken links and forging of new ones in every session. Scott attempted to link: (1) preparing to sleep, dream, and wake; (2) the subsequent sleeping and dreaming; and (3) the waking to remember some dreaming and going on to daydream about the dream and eventually beginning to plan to act. "Why," Scott advanced, "can't we talk about the links between everything, something, and nothing? Why can't we talk more easily about all times, sometimes, and never?" (Scott, 1990a). Scott (1986c) also wanted to be the person "who speaks to the young child, or to the child in the adult, using words to make a link with the early experience of the nothing prior to its anger-motivated transformation into something" (p. 16). In that fashion, Scott underlined the child's angry, transitional intolerance of nothing and held out as exemplary Bion's attention to less and less, enabling him to discover how a symbol of nothing could become the beginning of thinking.

Tapping on his own infantile anxiety about becoming too spontaneously loving and happy (*Becoming a Psychoanalyst*, p. 162), Scott often interpreted that patients fear "becoming too spontaneously loving and happy like a baby and remembering the early years when they were too spontaneous, too loving— so that somebody stopped them" (Hunter, 1995, p. 196). In a further development of interpretive technique, Scott (1981a) asked patients about their memories and anticipatory fantasies of maximal experiences,[23] e.g., when they were happiest, angriest, saddest, most frightened, most guilty, most fatigued, and in the greatest pain, as well as under what circumstances could they imagine becoming so in the future.

Visual activity plays a cardinal role in Scott's (1970) analytic treatment. A basic premise grounding his practice is that despite fixated impressions, our looking is actually a continuous scanning, since the two to ten saccadic eye movements per second escape our conscious awareness. In his observation of infants, he concluded that sometimes they gape or have an open mouth or eyes, as if they are discovering a nothing, an absence, or the disappearance of hallucination (private communication). Looking can become more remarkably complicated in actual child analysis: the child frequently talks about wanting the therapist to watch; or wanting the therapist to watch him watch the therapist do something; or even wanting to watch the therapist do something without being able to watch him watch the therapist.

Scott has made an additional number of fascinating interpretations about the impact of fantasy on visual perception in adult analysis. The patient who feels that he is being stared at rarely mentions that it is with one eye or the other —actually, one has to be some distance away from anyone to become conscious of the fact that one can look at both eyes, rather than at one or the other. Although it is not possible to judge correctly whether one is being looked at mostly on the chin, right eye or left eye, people mostly have the illusion that they can tell. Some patients may persevere by looking at the analyst and hoped that his expression will change, thus a defense against looking away or closing the eyes to see more clearly what the wish is. Looking at a minor detail of facial expression will often stimulate the wish or act to fend off the wish to analyze the analyst. Mutually concurrent talking by the analyst and patient is less compatible than a mutually concurrent looking, which is often related to kissing, fighting and other mutual acts.

Scott (1970) also has found that patients repeat habits they formed in childhood when they were trying to discover many aspects of their body, especially when they were curious about how much they gave out and took in with their eyes and mouth. Such patients may show inhibited partial stretching, yawning, and other significant body movements. Other patients may be looking through or into the analyst, putting him into the distance, bringing him close, or bringing inside only as an image (Scott, 1976a).

Scott does not hesitate to alter the visuality of the analytic setting. For the purpose of fostering development after the transference has been understood, he might have the patient speak to him before a mirror and relate his attendant inhibitions in so doing. In those difficult periods where another analyst might invite the patient to sit up, Scott (1985) preferred to see whether his sitting at the foot of the couch would put the patient at ease. Also, when patients brought in memories of the way they looked and talked or wanted to do so, he often moved a chair toward the foot of the couch near the patient's feet. Scott (1970) explained, "If a patient is facing me but can very easily look away, I can observe his expression when he looks at me or elsewhere, and I then detect the relationship between speech, memory, anticipation and looking" (p. 11).

Two relevant vignettes further demonstrate Scott's clinical flexibility and inventiveness:

1. "Once while treating a depressed patient who at times became stuporous and stared straight ahead, I interpreted how the content of the visual field became a substitute easing her to wait for what was wanted in the mouth. During my interpretation, I began to walk around the couch into the patient's visual field so that my speech and her sight of me were part of the same experience. My previous interpretations in an unaltered setting had not been so effective" (Scott, 1970, p. 18).

2. On another occasion, Scott (1985) relied on a different visual parameter. "I asked a patient to try self-analyzing before a mirror for three minutes in my consultation room because she wanted to work alone. Upon my return to the room, she said that she had been incapable of speaking and looking at the mirror. When I placed my chair between the mirror and her, she discovered that I did not change as much as she had expected and then became capable of perceiving for an instant the excitement on her own face" (p. 44).

Scott's technical handling of the analytic setting also attended to its many acoustic aspects, including the inhibition, repression, and transformation of noise. Sometimes he explained the counsel of free association to patients this way: Try to talk, and if you can't talk, try to make some kind of noise, and if you don't know what kind of noise to make, just guess. By inviting the patient to lie down, Scott affirmed, it is as if we are asking him to regress to the period when the baby cannot sit but can roll around and make plenty of noise (Scott, 1975b)—the period of the child's native tongue preceding the acquisition of his mother tongue (Scott, 1989). Scott's (1958) working hypothesis was that when speech is used as a defense against noise, analysis may be slowed; however, when patients understand that noise just as well as speech may speed and foster analysis, they will make more noise (p. 1).[24] On such occasions Scott (1952) may have also imitated the nonverbal sound the patient made (p. 4).

Scott's understanding of the repertoire of noises is instructive. Screams of sobs and joy lead to fatigue; screams of rage can last much longer (private communication). Significant clapping in body movement may extend to inhibited hand-clapping and knee-clapping, etc. (Scott, 1958, p. 4). The ambiguous sound "ah," meaning no, yes, or a question, may be reversed into "ha" or combined into "aha," "ugh,"which is often taken as a sound of disgust, may be a sound of welcome bringing the internal and the external object together, or it may represent "a return of the swallow," as one patient put it (ibid, p. 2).

Elaborating on noises, Scott (1958) wondered why analysts had not become more clinically interested in the problems of those who had to learn to speak in belch after having lost by operation part or all of their larynx (p. 2). Persistent snores may obtain gratification combined with denial of the noise of the sleep-disrupting snore.[25] Sniffing may show disdain but also unconscious or conscious agreement. A short snort is usually related to the rejection or ejection of something unpleasant or to inhibited laughter (attempts to put the snort into words usually produce laughter). Between the upper noises of the larynx (such as belches) and the lower noises of bowel and bladder lie borborygmi; these are liable to occur at significant moments as derivatives of swallowing-belching, or anal output. A defensive interrelation may exist among alternate coughing, burping, and bopping. Finally, an inhibition of speech may sometimes be due to the oscillation of noises inside: a certain patient felt that no matter what kind of noise she might make, a nice noise would have to be followed by a nasty one, and vice versa (ibid., p. 3).

Scott brought to the fore other locutory variations in the analytic scene. He stated that sometimes a patient, while keeping his mouth wide open but not listening, may watch the movements of the analyst's lips and tongue. Such cathexis equally shared by open eyes and mouth gives the opportunity of interpreting regression to the time of lack of discrimination between the eyes and noise made by the mother and the rest of the world (Scott, 1952, p. 4). Analysts also confront the problem of who is listening: Is the patient listening to what he says? Does he make his audience his only listener? (Scott, 1975b). Is there an inner analyst being spoken to when a patient's voice drops or when a patient remarks that he has forgotten where is or was (Scott, 1976a)?

Scott reflected on still other possibilities:

> Sometimes I would be able to say something simple and noticed that the patient did not stop talking though his or her face registered a reaction to what I said. Sometimes I noticed that when I said something, a patient might begin to speak, but when I was silent, he or she fell silent as well (Becoming a Psychoanalyst, pp. 195-196).

In the final account, analysts will agree with Scott (1976a) that, except some singers and actors, few patients in analysis overcome their inhibitions to put anger, joy, or sadness into anything like the energetic speech approximating the energy of their primary noise. Taking one more step, Scott (1981b) proposed that self-analysis be carried out not by closing one's self up in inner speech but rather by talking to one's self out loud—such an analysand's zest for self-analysis relates to his belief about the good role he played in the self-analysis of his own analyst.

IV. Scott's Manner of Thinking and Self-Expression

Scott had a remarkable ability to empathize with and convey the infant's mental world. Closely bound up with mode of infantile perception and expression but not identical with it are the condensing and displacing characteristics of primary process, all of which Scott could subject to acute analysis. When at its best, his mentational and scriptive manner illuminated and mimetically dramatized its message—and in such moments one can detect a definite change in the tone of Scott's prose with its quickened rhythms. At other times, the balance was tipped, so that a removed, analytic perspective was lost, and the pace of rational elaboration gives way to expository confusion marked by impulsive thrusts of fantasy-like associativeness—or to mix metaphors, at other times in his discourse Scott seemlessly sewed his own comments into a child's phantasmagoria and interior monologue. The upshot is that the reader was offered streams of marvelous insights swirling into each other.

To further delineate Scott's communicative style, I find Einstein's timely yet troubling counsel to scientific writers most serviceable: "we write either correctly or understandably." Seen within the context of Einstein's maxim, Scott, although striving for accuracy, tried to say so much or even too much at once. Expository control was not his forte. Although he had made several attempts to organize the grander design of psychoanalytic thought, he struggled to maintain a controlled logical progression over sustained pieces of writing. It is often easy to shuffle his paragraphs and longer expository units like a deck of cards, without any resultant difference in thematic development. Even within Scott's paragraphs and individual sentences, one tends to miss a tight logical coherence—his efforts at linking are undercut by awkward punctuation and syntax (incidentally, the latter word from an etymological point of view means placing together or linking).

A related problem inhabits Scott's aim of communicative simplicity. On one hand, he wanted "to lead a simpler life by using simpler words and playing the game of small words in long sentences and long stories" (Scott, 1986b, p. 1).

On the other hand, that aimwas subverted by his endorsement of Whorf's postulate that the more a word is used the shorter it becomes and the more meanings it has (Scott, 1986c), a phenomenon that also affected the language of science (*Mourning and Zest*, pp. 28-29). In effect, Scott (1986c) resembled both Freud and Bion, who, he said, were more multiguous than ambiguous. Yet within that multiguity or in spite of it, Scott (1970) bemoaned the fact that our current technical terms, although adequately describing later stages of development, did not suffice for the earlier elemental stage. "We need to do so much work," Scott (1987a) reminded us, "to put into words what happened before words were understood or used" (*ibid.*, p. 8).

In reading and listening to Scott over a number of years, I have been ever impressed by the paradoxical freshness and lawful patterning of his creative discourse. While analyzing it, I have drawn up a series of ad hoc categories (they also may be used, however, as an analytical grid in the mapping out of infantile mentation and adult phantasy life). Within each of the thirteen categories I have furnished clarifying examples drawn from Scott's texts:

1. *Klang association*:
   a. "Analysis works to undo the ignorance summed up in the maxim 'I wit, I wot but I forgot' or 'I understand that I understood but I've forgotten'" (private communication).
   b. "I wit, I wot, but I forgot. Mind is such an odd predicament for matter to get into. What is matter? Never mind. What is mind? Never matter" (Scott, 1975c, p. 1).

2. *Thingification of thought*:
   a. "But soon there's a difference between 'I've forgotten' and 'I remember.' I don't kno·v where the forgotten is. Is the forgotten inside or outside? Is it in me or in them?" (Hunter, 1995, p. 97).
   b. "If delusion went away, what was it replaced by? When did it (pain, etc.) come from? When did it go? Into whom?" (private communication).

3. *The maximal and the minimal*:
   a. "In order to find out the smallest sound that they can hear, children listen closely to the soap bubble as they prick it or they click their nails with less and less force" (private communication).
   b. "We go about trying to make an even better best of a sadder job" (private communication).
   c. "How does one establish the difference and continuity between mini-

mal linkage and maximal splitting?" (Scott, 1984b, p. 154).

d. "We must study the greatest and least changes happening within both the longest and shortest periods of time, and when does oscillation become confusion" (private communication, 1994).

4. *The play of opposites*:

In conversation with Jones, Freud said that when he felt stymied in thinking out a problem, he recalled the counsel of his own private maxim: "Think of the opposite." On pages 185-186 of his autobiography Scott reported that piece of conversational exchange correctly; but elsewhere, a distortion in Scott's cryptomnesic account sheds insight into his own thought processes. Hence we read that Freud counseled thinking about as many opposites as possible when in difficulty (Scott, 1986c). In so giving the screw another turn, Scott (1987a) maximizes the opposite into the greatest number of opposites, a maximalization which he joins with klang association in another essay: "the problem is, which opposite is the most apposite?" (p. 4). In a still further turn of the screw, he sought uncommonly thought of opposites in asking about the opposite of experience and of intuition (*Becoming a Psychoanalyst*, pp. 185-186).

5. *Spatial distortion and discrimination*:

a. "When babies are frustrated, they try to get inside flatness, for example, a flat piece of paper. Then they can crumble up the paper and then get inside it" (private communication).

b. "How does the child know the difference between inside out and outside in? A certain child said: 'I was in the dream, but the dream is gone, and I am where am I now'" (private communication).

c. "The feeling that all is inside and nothing outside and one of its opposites—all is outside and nothing inside—are descriptions of maximal introjective and projective identification" (Scott, 1975c, p. 315).

d. "We grow to realize the difference between our backside and a world behind in contrast to learning about the difference between the world in front and our front-side. We did this all, helped by many sleeps and dreams, and by many wakings to use our senses to sort out insides, besides, and outsides and to sort out facts and fancies" (Scott, 1990b, p. 6).

6. *Spatio-temporal distortions*:

a. "We come to believe in growth and try to watch our hair and nails grow, but only believe our whole body has grown when we remember how much smaller it was then than now. The penis or clitoris may change in size and feeling and this may be confused with growth, as the child can wake to, or be awakened to the speed at which tumescence happens" (Scott, 1987a, p. 10).

b. "Another question is: Can I go everywhere? And when a child learns of space travel, discussion concerns whether, if he so travels, regardless of what he learns, will he be older or younger than his stay-at-home brother when he returns" (private communication, 1995).

7. *Quest to sustain paradox:*
a. "Over the years Milner struggled with the question of blankness of background, i.e., whether the basic idea is get back to the satisfied dreamlessness of the infant at the breast after a feeding, or whether this blankness of background is not also the conscious mind perceiving its own unconscious processes" (Scott, 1975c, p. 317). Scott added that it is not just A or B, but both; he then quoted Winnicott, who, referring to the paradox of the transitional object, suggested that the paradox be accepted rather than be resolved, with the resultant loss of its value as paradox.
b. There are various types of confusion: confusion between ego and object; good and bad objects; heterosexual and homosexual objects; and regressive and progressive depression. "These types of confusion must be carefully discriminated . . . . if confusion is not to be confounded" (*Mourning and Zest*, pp. 145-146).

8. *Incongruous measurements and incongruous sequencing of events:*
a. "Scientists publish so much that Oppenheimer has said that if the present rate of publication continues, this literature will outweigh the world within the next century. This points to limits" (Scott, 1964b, p. 3).
b. "Our hands handle, and our mouths mouth, our cocks and cunts piss, or with boys our pissers piss, but we are soon taught Latin" (Scott, 1986b, p. 10).
c. "As a boy I wondered about *amare*, the Latin word for *love*. The Bible story began with creation and I wondered why Latin began with love" (*Mourning and Zest*, p. 36).

9. *Totalities made by accumulated noises:*
"How many gigs make a giggle" (private communication, 1992)?

10. *Point of view projected into part objects*:
"Children soon argue about the immovable object and the irresistible force. In one way or another they soon discover how hard it is to be conscious of both aspects of a conflict—for instance, when they link their hands and start to pull them apart, and ask themselves: Can I be so strong that I can pull them apart, and yet so strong that I can hold them together?" (Scott, 1964b, p. 1).

11. *The limiting of the limitless*:
a. "Children later ask: 'Can I harness power that can counteract any power? Can I discover everything? Will it just take plenty of time?'" (Scott, 1964b, p. 1).
b. "I ask whether everything (God), or something (which we can give a name to), or nothing, for instance, sleep with a smile, is the most important thing to draw or to talk about. Or is it the link between all three: everything, something and nothing that is the most important" (1990b, p. 9)?
c. The U.S. Marines championed Whitehead's proverb, "The impossible just takes longer" (Scott, 1975c, p. 281).

12. *Combined reflexivity and recursivity*:
Repeatedly Scott spoke of our reflexivity (e.g., awake to being awake) which he combines—with a detectable enjoyment—with recursivity —(e.g., aware of awareness of awareness of forgetting of remembering and remembering it).
a. "We must heed remembering and forgetting, paying attention and reflecting (forgetting, forgetting and remembering, remembering)" (private communication).
b. "We can dream of daydreams, and daydream of dreams of day dreaming about waking and sleeping with or without dreams or remembering them but anticipating others" (private communication).

13. *Reversibility and controvertibility of experience*:
a. "The child breathes out and wonders if he can get it back in" (private communication, 1990).
b. "As a child, I often wondered about the caption in my picture book that read 'When there is nobody with me I am all alone,' and wondered if there were two stories, i.e., whether 'I'm all alone' is the same as 'there's nobody with me'" (*Becoming a Psychoanalyst*, p. 225).

Scott (1985) filtered much of his discourse through the above thirteen categories. Hovering above them is Scott's irony, even self-ironical posture, as when he refered to "the lover who looks at his beloved smiling in her sleep and asks himself, 'Is she smiling at me?'" (p. 33). The reader also meets with Scott's constant curiosity, wonderment, and a particular fascination with beginnings. The poem (*Becoming a Psychoanalyst*, p. 228) ending the first volume of his autobiography, for example, is about his first child's first waking and first movements: a stirring[26] and inklings of a smile. But no sooner had Scott mentioned those initial actions than he spoke of his awe, which he then maximalized in asserting that "there is no greater joy."

I see it fitting to terminate this section by referring to another striking passage that Scott wrote. Remarkable for about how much psychoanalytic wisdom and about how much of psychic life can be condensed into so short an expository space, the passage contains many thematic motifs and categorical matrices (the play of opposites, klang association, maximilization, recursive reflexivity) that are the trademark of Scott's discourse. The reader will also note the serendipitous use of klang associations (mad, sad, glad) in various sequences to portray the course of human experience. The shortness of the rhyming refrain is offset by the amplitude and central importance of its meaning—basic psychic states. And the superficial jingle of the rhyming sequence is undercut by the interaction of its meanings, the transformation of basic psychic states which comprises a crucial difference between healthy and unhealthy life. The one expository fault in the passage below is found in the last sentence, whose last dozen words should be rephrased as "in sharing the sadness rather than becoming potent in sharing the gladness of successful mourning":

> The patient who is sad at having been mad may by progression become mad at being sad. He works with the ambivalence of glad versus mad at being sad until he can tolerate and believe his loved objects can tolerate being glad at being sad on the way to being glad at being glad. Then he can test new reality in mourning without forgetting that the work being done is making reparation. This is perhaps maximally seen in glad sad potency, with tears and laughter mixed, without fear that the partner will become impotent sharing the sadness rather than sharing the potent gladness of successful mourning (Scott, 1984b, p. 154).

V. Scotsland: A Selective Collection of Clinical Vignettes

In his zestful awakenness, Scott was quick to notice unusual clinical phenomena and then to leave a record of them scattered throughout his abundant writings, lectures, and private papers. But he was also alert to the exceptional experience of others, including Winnicott's with a dead patient. It is fitting to begin this last section of the essay with Scott's write-up of his friend Winnicott's moribund surprise: Winnicott "heard that if you inject adrenalin into the heart muscles, the heart would start to beat again. The person would come back to life. He did it. The patient became alive. He looked at both Winnicott and the nurse and said, 'Oh, I thought I died,' and then he died again. Then Winnicott said, 'I'll have to be careful. I don't think I want to do that again'" (Hunter, 1995, pp. 205-206).

We turn now to Scott's own patients. As we journey through that mind scape, we hear many stories with varying unusualness in their subjects, incidents or dialogue, beginning with Scott's anxiety during his very first attempt at hypnosis when his female-subject had problems waking up (*Becoming a Psychoanalyst*, p. 68). We next follow Scott (1952) as he recalls that prior to 1952, he had two patients that somnambulated in the course of their therapeutic interviews (*ibid.*, p. 1). With equal bemusement, Scott further reminisced about naive patients who, when asked to lie down, did so on their stomach and looked at the analyst (Scott, 1970) or they laid with their head at the opposite end of the couch (*ibid.*). Bringing up a stranger case, Scott told of his only patient who could dream backwards and of another who tried with her own eyes to see underneath her own eyelids (private communication, 1992).

From the above short anecdotes we proceed to a series of short sketches which Scott wrote up for us to ponder and savor:

"I was intrigued by the patient using a cane who could not feel his hands on the cane but could feel the object touched by the end of the cane (*Becoming a Psychoanalyst*, p. 215) . . . . In one of my child patients, 'humming' was an attempt to control screaming; he began to ask people if they could 'hum' a scream" (Scott, 1958, p. 3) . . . . I had a child in analysis whose mother described him as being "excited without being excited" (*Becoming a Psychoanalyst*, p. 191) . . . . While strolling with a patient on the hospital grounds, I asked a patient to locate his complaint of his terrible pain, the patient pointed to the top of a flagpole and said,"There it is" (*Becoming a Psychoanalyst*, pp. 215-216) . . . . One of my patients at the Boston Psychopathic Hospital was proud of her capacity to achieve undetected orgasm during interview by sucking the inside of her lower lip (*Becoming a Psychoanalyst*, p. 10 and p. 152); I gave her 500 hours of therapy at the rate of five times a week (*ibid.*, p. 143). Years later she told me: "We tried to do too much too quickly" (*ibid.*, p. 156) . . . . A problem of a female patient was her belief that "Greta Garbo is me" instead of the reverse, "I am Greta Garbo," which interested me (*ibid.*, p. 210) . . . . Another patient said that his childhood dreams were between the armoire and his bedroom wall, but when he improved, he recognized that his dreams were in him (*ibid.*, p. 216) . . . . At the end of the war, I had the experience of trying to treat a war-neurosis in a man who was blind, deaf, and dumb, with the aid of a nurse who translated for me (Scott, 1976). . . . One patient said that she wanted to kill me. But I told her that I'd like to kill her first before she killed me. And then I cried" (private communication, 1980).

From the foregoing series we journey on to the mostly longer vignettes from Scott's fascinating clinical experience.

To read them quickly would cause a blurring effect that would undercut the reader's comprehension. In B.B.C. news broadcasting, let us note, a pause separating each news item enables the listener to better assimilate what he is hearing. Inspired by such sensible communicative practice, I have separated each of Scott's vignettes by linear spacings and end lines, thereby inviting the reader to reflectively pause for his own benefit:

The first patient I had under Jones was a man whose wife called because he was impotent when he was awake. But he began to play with her in his sleep and he had intercourse with her in his sleep (*Becoming a Psychoanalyst*, pp. 10, 201). Ella Sharpe supervised me as a student with a case of a man with the symptom of being potent only in sleep (Scott, 1975c, p. 309).

———••••———

I supervised Khan who had a patient who could read his mind; the case did not succeed because Khan was at a loss. I would have told the patient that he was anxious about submitting to my analyzing him (private communication, 1976).

———••••———

I once had a patient who wondered why people forget dreams. He felt he had always remembered all his dreams, but that they were private. From the beginning of analysis he was struck by my interest in everything, including dreams. His associations recurrently led to recent and old dreams, but rarely did he say "I dreamt last night" unless it was a dream he had been preoccupied with since waking. His analysis was the fastest I have ever experienced. We did not discover why he had not forgotten many dreams. The nearest we came to understanding this was to conclude that the continuity of memory of infantile dreams was a substitute for the discontinuity of memory of infantile waking experiences, but why both did not undergo early repression we did not understand (Scott, 1975c, p. 324).

———••••———

Once only during psychoanalytic treatment has a patient taken my photograph. I was bored, he was boring and ruminating about sleeping and not remembering dreams. Suddenly he sat up, turned around and said, "Doc, I am going to take your picture," and did so with his Minox. Later he gave me a print. The remainder of the interview dealt with his destructiveness in human relationships and his difficulty in maintaining an image of any constructive desire (Scott, 1975c, p. 329).

———————

A patient of mine dreamed of being in prison and eventually becoming able to climb up to a high window in the wall and look out onto a country landscape with wonderment. The dreamer woke to find himself leaning dangerously out of a window of a hotel several stories up looking at the landscape he had seen in the dream. He had arrived at the hotel in the dark the night before.

He was suicidal by day. In the dream the landscape was beautiful and he was in prison. He awoke frightened of the danger of falling. If he tried to fly over the beauty he would not fly long but fall and be smashed. He experienced the nothing between and death on waking. Between sleep and dream and waking the gap was filled with a memory of a dream of mother, of waking without mother being there, and the vague confusion of what was the transformation from the dream of mother to the nothing (Scott, 1986c, p. 27).

———————

A depersonalized spinster complained of never being awake like others. She felt most awake in pitch darkness. A male patient, on the other hand, complained that he could not wake as he used to—like snapping his fingers. Now the world was "spotted" with his dreams. In sessions he was sleepy but said he could not sleep unless I slept first (Scott, 1975c, p. 256).

———————

A female patient could never understand how anyone could ever be like anyone else. I pointed out that and related feelings "were partial memories of an infantile situation in which, while feeding, she felt that the balance of eating her way into her mother, in contrast to eating and taking her mother inside herself, had shifted in the direction of eating her way into her mother in order to find a nipple inside. Such fantasies of being inside extend to being inside the mother's nipple and breast" (Scott, 1975c, pp. 313-314).

———————

For a year and a half I watched a female patient who had tight lips, rounded tongue, with frequent movements of the tongue slightly out of the mouth, combined with anxieties about talking nonsense. When her fear of blathering now in infancy, due to her mother's rejection of it as a libidinal activity were interpreted, she pleasurably blathered three or four times. In my interpretation I did not speak the word blathering; I made the movement and sound which had a crucial effect. I said "You went (I blathered) to your mother and wanted her to blather (I blathered) to you." She smiled and blathered three or four cycles; she began to stammer; she was frightened lest she continue to stammer. Within two weeks she described the situation that had occurred in analysis, as she had wished it had happened in childhood. She said "I showed you something and you did it too." During the treatment it had only been after eighteen months that I was able to imagine that this was what she wanted to do (Scott, 1953b, pp. 3-4; 1984a, pp. 459-460).

Her other symptoms included longstanding fears of being alone and of vomiting or seeing anyone vomit. Toward the end of the analysis, the fear of vomiting abated and she had a pleasant dream of vomiting into a cupped breast; also toward the end of the analysis, the fear of being alone abated as I analyzed her omnipotent fantasies of being the whole world and of being inside her mother who herself was identified with the world (Scott, 1976b, p. 3).

Mr. B's problem was that of trying to express a great deal in very little and that little poetically. He had an earlier belief that the stars were holes in heaven and that one star represented the place from which he had come and through which he would return . . . . This feeling of his was related not only to fantasies of what it was like before birth, but in infancy, to the difficulty in solving the problem of where was mother—was she outside, was she beside, or was he inside, and was she multiple or single? After much analysis, this ended with a short poem:

The problem is not to find the needle
In the haystack
The problem is
Where to put it (Scott, 1977, p. 11).

After several years of analysis Mrs. G. was still depressed, especially because she could not have any feeling of union in her love for her husband. After several more years she overcame this difficulty and expressed the feeling that her love was so great that she wished to become the man she loved and wanted him to love her so much that he would wish to be her. These feelings preceded her discovery and fusion in lovemaking (Scott, 1977, p. 15).

———————••••••———————

One patient decided, as he put it, "Most of your patients are crazy and lie on the couch, I am going to lie on the floor." He did so with his feet a foot or so away from the foot of my chair. He continued so for two years until he eventually rose and sat facing me (Scott, 1970, p. 8).

———————••••••———————

From time to time I have collected individual responses to listening to white noise. The person talks without being able to hear what he is saying, as the white noise masks his own voice . . . . With my female patient (who had eleven personalities) I wondered how much her hate was of hearing her voice expressing hate and how much it was kinesthesia of the action of expressing hate vocally. In other words, when she was sadistic the pleasure may have been in the activity and the hate in the sound which she was putting in to the other person. The kinesthesia and the sound may be separated by masking the hearing of her voice with white sound recording speech which can be heard later (Scott, 1989, p. 19).

———————••••••———————

A patient became silent after discussing a newly acquired panoramic view of his childhood, feeling that there was much more than he could ever speak of. He then clicked his right thumb-nail on one of the fingernails of his right hand, but did not make a sound which I could hear. When it was interpreted that, as a defense against his inability to talk fast enough to say what he wanted to say, he had tried the opposite, namely, to discover how small a noise he could make with his nails, he quickly said that he was just about to describe a fantasy of bouncing on the couch like a baby but was afraid by my interpretation about something he couldn't control. His response showed the partial incorrectness of my interpretation, which should have included mention of the small controlled movement as well as the small controlled sound. He regressed to a bouncing baby instead of to a bouncing, yelling baby (Scott, 1958, pp. 3-4).

———————••••••———————

A patient who was a piano player told me that when playing with one hand and masturbating with the other, he felt that if he played with two hands, he would risk a spontaneous orgasm and would not be able to play with an éclat equal to the orgasm (Scott, 1987a, p. 13).

———••••——

I had a woman in analysis who undressed and tried to dance and sing triumphantly the song "I don't need psychoanalyzing, I'm just in love." I wondered if she would get dressed or was she going to embarrass me. She did dress before the end of the interview (Hunter, 1995, pp. 202-203).

———••••——

The youngest child I ever analyzed was the supervisory case of a 26- month-old boy I had with Klein: He came because he wasn't speaking, and I only analyzed him for nine months because he began to speak so quickly and so rapidly, though he never spoke to me. I carried the analysis on quite some time until he could speak understandably to others. He understood me, but he didn't speak (Scott, 1976a, p. 8). At the sixth interview the boy imitated the father humping in the primal scene (Scott, 1984b). The only words he spoke in analysis were "mum" and "Baba" (his teddybear); he yelled in rage once and made a few sounds during the sessions. Once he stood in the middle of the room, looked alertly about and yelled as loudly as he could. He then was silent for a moment, listening attentively and when nothing happened he broke into a beautiful smile. I did not discover how much his showing me his feelings about parental intercourse and not making a sound about what he showed, even though I talked about it; he was only showing me what he actually felt when he was observing parental intercourse and how much it was revenge at the parent-analyst of the parents not talking to him about their intercourse which he not only hated but also blessed (Hunter, 1995, p. 191; Scott, 1975a, p. 293).

———••••——

Under the analytic exploration of the effect of interpreting [Mrs. B's] fear of discovering a link, while awake or asleep, between the love she had discovered for her previous therapist and her inhibited orgastic activity she eventually dreamt, "I had an orgasm and shrieked with delight." . . . As we sought links between the dream and its functional and objectless pleasure on the one hand, and her transient pleasure with and for men and meanwhile depreciating them as not good enough, often because of their other commitments more or less secret to her, she began to become angry at me for having, as she said, stolen her dream. She said that analysis was dishonest . . . . Later her murderous anger at me led to my having to interpret and confront her with the fact, that if she murderously attacked me, I would defend myself and hope that I could control her, or kill her first, as I valued myself more than I valued her, but that I was very sad that all the work we had done which had accomplished so much for her, was in danger of being destroyed by her . . . . She could not tolerate distinguishing me from herself, her pleasure, her shriek, her talk, etc. Her dream was a turning point in her analysis and was more useful than had she spontaneously or in some response to an interpretation screamed orgasticallly with delight during an interview (Scott, 1986c, pp. 23-24).

———••••——

The intensity of feeling may spread to the secret joy of a noisy orgasm involving a patient who told of a famous singer falling more in love with her than he had ever been before. He told her he could not love her without being able to risk singing which would not be heard by more than them. She borrowed a house on a moor miles from anywhere. Not only did he sing but, as she said, bellowed telling the world defiantly "I love and I'm loved" but at the same time keeping all their love a secret to themselves on the moor (Scott, 1986c, p. 25).

———••••——

Another patient complained of not being able to be one with anyone she loved. The hope for this oneness was lost and she was depressed. The only hope she felt was in my hope. Eventually, she believed oneness could be obtained only if she loved someone she wanted to be. Nevertheless, this would not suffice unless he also wanted to be her. Then they could come together, become one, and separate later and tolerate the disillusionment . . . . In the background of memory was the fact that objects subjected her to being subjected at the same time that she, as a subject, had objected to objects being objects (Scott, 1986c, p. 25).

———••••——

Sometimes one of my male patients "relaxed so much that he snored so much when he was awake." Sometimes after snoring he would say immediately that he had been so relaxed and blank that he had snored, but had not slept. In other interviews we inferred that he had slept and dreamt that he had been awake blank, relaxed, and that he had snored as sometimes he told me he had snored when I had not heard him . . . . He was also either passive with regard to waking up (he woke immediately [after] I spoke) or unconscious of waking up. When I interpreted that the psychoanalytic situation was so allied to his feelings of the feeding situation that he was not separating them, he became conscious of the fact that he could neither have a phantasy nor a memory of the situation he was in (he had no sensations of his body on the couch when he became blank)—he began to realize how very blank the blankness had been . . . . I connected his talk of thinking (his thoughts are very much inside) and his talk of feeling (feelings to him are mostly something other people have) with the split he had made between thinking and feeling between the mouth and the nipple . . . . His associations were to his hiding breast memories behind his intellect—to wondering whether thinking is like a cow ruminating to anger at not being able to enjoy pleasure in psychoanalysis—to anger at my not giving him the pleasure he would have liked his mother to have given him—to his wanting me to make use of his productions as he would have liked his mother to have appreciated his sucking (Scott, 1952, p. 2).

Mrs. A was very depressed and could talk very little. She said there was something she wanted to say but she could not remember and could not understand why she had forgotten. Several decades ago, for the one and only time in my practice, I tried to see if this state of affairs would be changed by giving her a few breaths of nitrous oxide (laughing gas)—just enough to produce sleep . . . . On repeated occasions when she woke she began to smile almost childishly and as she woke to where she was she said two things: "I'll never tell you that . . . I'll never remember that." She then startled momentarily and became the depressed person she had previous been, forgetting what she had said.

The only other parameter I used during her treatment was one long interview, hoping that she might go to sleep in the interview. The interview lasted twelve hours. She did not sleep and it was no different from twelve consecutive hours. The interview was held in her own home (Scott, 1986c, pp. 22-23).

A female patient jumped up very suddenly from her stupor, intending to throw herself through the window, which was beyond the foot of the couch. Luckily, at that moment, I was alert enough to catch her leg. She fell on the floor beyond the couch and I fell on the couch. The only comparable experience I had was with a patient in analysis in hospital who was sitting up on the couch lighting a cigarette. Without warning, she set fire to her hair. I did not wait for her to put it out—I used my hands (Scott, 1970, p. 4).

A child I know said: "I do not want to die. I like it here." He spent several days testing people out to find out if he could find someone who would tell him that there was somebody in the world who had lived forever . . . .. It took him some time to believe that he could not go back; he had to go on and on, and try to make-up in some way for lost chances and for the loss of the belief that he could live backwards, or could go to sleep and wake up yesterday. He came to believe he would always wake up tomorrow (Scott, 1986c, pp. 20-21).

————•••••————

A drowsy patient in a drowsy way said: "I guess I'd better believe I am not everything" then he started and asked me in a clear voice: "Did I say, I guess I'd better believe I am not everything?" I said: "Yes" . . . he was giving up the belief in his omnipotent idealized wishes to be everything, to do everything, and to have everything done for him magically, just because he could wish. He could say, "I am what is inside me. I am not what is outside me." Perhaps the simplest way to put this disillusionment is to say that consciousness or waking are no longer identical with creativity (Scott, 1984b, pp. 152-153; 1986c, pp. 26-27).

I close this inventory of clinical vignettes with an excerpt from one of the periodic telephone calls that Dr. Scott and I have had together. He referred to his supervision of an aborted analysis in which the patient, a female stand-up comic, defensively used her talent to keep her candidate-analyst laughing anytime she wanted.

I replied: "What if a patient had the combined talents of a stand-up (or lie-down) comic and a telepathist who could read the analyst's mind?"

And he said with a laugh, "It's too much." And I then thought to myself, "By scot, it's much too much . . . ."

Notes

1. Two undated entries in the concluding bibliography merit mention here, as I shall have occasion to refer to them. Scott's lengthy monograph, *Mourning and Zest*, remains unpublished; on the other hand, the first volume of his autobiography, *Becoming a Psychoanalyst*, has been accepted by *Esf* Publishers (Binghamton, New York). At present, Scott is working on the other two volumes of his autobiographical project. Because Scott's syntactical control is often wanting, I have not hesitated to make silent minor changes in quoting him; in no case, however, have I dared to alter meaning.

2. I might add that Freud never used the term "fall-to sleep-work" (*Einschlafarbeit*). All subsequent footnotes continue my commentary on the main text.

3. Elsewhere Scott speaks of children's frustration about wanting to walk ahead alone and yet wanting simultaneously to talk about that experience to the person they have left behind (*Mourning and Zest*, 224).

4. You may wake up with a dream-high or a dream-over from having one too many dreams, all of those residues possibly containing anticipations of dreaming, waking

up, sleeping, remembering and forgetting.

5. *Wacharbeit* (G.W.: 2/3, pp. 578, 594), the German term for "wake-work," was translated by Strachey respectively as "the activity of waking life" and "waking activity" (Freud, 1900, pp. 573, 589).

6. It takes further wake-work to distinguish between a sleep-wake, a dream-wake, a dream-wake, a wake-up from hallucination, and an hallucinated wake.

7. We also need to know the bearing of that connection upon "wancies" or what might be labeled as fantasies about waking.

8. In that we are never fully awake, we're "awaking" during the day, mindless that part of our minds sleeps on: we go to sleep, then wake the other part of ourselves up to dream, then wake up but not to sleepwalk but to dream-walk and dream-talk. Day in and day out, thus we lead our awaking lives. Recalling his early technique with Miss Lucy, Freud (1893-1895) said that it was possible to "re-awaken, after an interval of twenty-one years," details of an experience in her "who, in fact, was in a waking state" (2, p. 114 fn.).

9. In this context we should know that in Sanskrit, Buddha means the awakened or illuminated one. It is quite to the point that it was he who founded the founder of the world's oldest mystical tradition. The Greek etymology of *mystic*, "to close the eyes," lends an interlingual aptness to the fact that statues of Buddha the mystic often present him in an awakened state, yet with his eyes closed.

10. Etymologically, dreaming in German means to deceive; and in Hebrew, to have orgasm; philologically therefore, in Hebrew, a wet dream is a tautology. The dream poaches wilfully on the reserve of our internalizations; while some of them are left to sleep, others are summoned to strut in the spotlight or strobe lights of our night mind. One could say that by thinking that dreams of neurotics do not differ from each other (Freud, 1915-1917, p. 456), Freud posits an incidental similarity between dreams and death, the great leveler. One is reminded of de Gaulle's sad relief at the burial of his Mongoloid daughter: *"Maintenant elle est comme les autres"* (She is *now* like the others).

11. Although monks in their solitude choose to withdraw from the world, their ascetic lack of sleep counters the withdrawal of cathexes upon the self.

12. In *The Interpretation of Dreams* Freud (1900) alluded to a special capacity of some dreamers: "There are some people who are quite clearly aware during the night that they are asleep and dreaming and who thus seem to possess the faculty of consciously directing their dreams" (p. 571). On the next page Freud quoted an author who had "acquired the power of accelerating the course of his dreams . . . and of giving them any direction he chose. It seems as though in his case the wish to sleep had given place to another preconscious wish, namely to observe his dreams and enjoy them." But as Freud privately admitted to Fliess, he himself could direct his dreams, but he dared not say that publicly for fear of undermining

the scientific stature of his Dreambook.

13. Dreaming occasions an awakening of consciousness, and secondary revision occasions a further awakening (cf. Freud, 1900, p. 575).

14. Since a dream aims not to be understood by its dreamer, it does not have a communicative function; and if successful, the dream has but a transitional representational function. The reporting of dreams, of course, can be enlisted as a defense against sleeping and dreaming in analytic sessions.

15. I am unfamiliar with anyone reporting an exact or telescoped anniversary phenomenon in remembering a sleep or dream from hours to years afterwards.

16. The manner of telling a dream may be mimetic of its symbolic form. At other times, the manner of narration, such as a dreamy drift into telling or a sleepy telling, may have more to do with the overall dream as an act that ended too soon.

17. To say it more poetically, in the ballet of diurnal and nocturnal chiaroscuro, the shadow of the daydream falls upon the dream, and the night light of the dream falls upon the daydream.

18. According to Freud's dispersed sartorial associations, when going to sleep, we undress both our body and mind (1917, p. 222) and strip ourselves of our morality garments (1915, p. 286)—to avoid hurtful redress, we might add as a punful condensation. Our dreams then take on a clothing disguise (*Traum-verklei-dung*, G.W., 2/3, pp. 519, 520, 618; Freud, 1900, pp. 515, 613). I have often observed that a prominent color in a patient's dream matches the color of his clothing, thus indicating that when dressing in the morning he is unconsciously continuing his dream. For another thing, nakedness, just like clothing, might also be a cover-up.

19. Accordingly, psychoanalysis "denaturalizes" dreams into being first remembered, and then understood. In that the best functioning dream is that which is not remembered, it is a dream-slip, a fall-out in mental ecology, that lies at the root at the discovery of psychoanalysis. Whatever its royalty, the road to the unconscious is a potted, defective one.

20. It would be more accurate to say that the patient's statement just prior to the reported dream is his first association to it.

21. Is there any study of the kinds of dreams of those people who dream with eyes open or half closed? Note that in Greek one can say, "I *saw* a dream." Such visuality is lost in other languages. Cf. English: "I *had* a dream"; French, "I *made* a dream" (*j'ai fait un rêve*); German: it has dreamt to me (*es hat mir geträumt*).

22. An example of Scott's own discriminatory perceptiveness of infantile behavior is found in an experiment that he urged Winnicott to carry out. The latter "watched babies of six to twelve months sitting on their mothers' laps while he sat across the corner of his desk from them. He placed a metal tongue depressor on the empty corner of the table and described the states of the baby's reaction to the new object;

from the various ways of taking the object, to the various ways of playing with it during mounting oral excitement, until it was played with enough and was dropped, and either retrieved or neglected. The modification I proposed was: as soon as the baby takes the tongue depressor one also takes hold of it and gently holds it until the baby lets go, and then immediately replaces it where it was before. Once can then observe whether the baby is frustrated or disappointed, and if disappointed, how he mourns the lost object or opportunity and makes up (reparation); (a) by using a new opportunity to play with it again or, (b) by seeking a substitute object" (1982b, p. 154). Scott called such an experiment a test of "micro-grief" and "the work of micro-mourning" (*Mourning and Zest*, p. 107).

23. In consultations I also question about minimal experience, e.g., when were you least guilty or how can you imagine becoming least guilty.

24. The constraints of Western social conventions being what they are, we should bear in mind that the less people know each other—and a fortiori on the occasion of their first meeting—the less will they resort to noise as a vocal exchange. Contrarily, the more people know each other, the more will they utter noises in informal settings, and most especially in circumstances both of erotic intimacy and of waking up together.

25. I suggest the term "otomization" for this phenomenon.

26. One of Freud's most principal technical terms is *Regung*, meaning stirring or the beginning of a movement; in Freud's original German texts, for instance, we come across hundreds of times such composites as wish-stirrings or instinctual stirrings. That fact that Strachey mistranslates *Regung* as "impulse" or "excitement" has caused it to be unfortunately unappreciated by English readers—unfortunately because usually we direct our clinical sensitivity not to obvious excitation but rather to the subtler stirrings. The phenomenon of firstness, of course, leads us into the problematic question of origins which baffled Freud all his life. I am reminded of the story told by Erikson about his being lost in Vermont, then asking a farmer for directions to a certain town and getting the reply: "If I wanted to go where you wanted to go, I wouldn't start from here."

References

Breuer, J., Freud, S. (1893-1895). *Studies on Hysteria. SE*, 2, 1955. In: J. Strachey (Ed.), *Standard Edition of the Complete Psychological Works of Sigmund Freud*, 24 volumes. London: Hogarth Press and The Institute of Psycho-Analysis, 1953-1974.

Flugel, J. (1953). The death instinct, homeostasis and allied concepts. *Int. J. Psycho-Anal.*, 34: 43-53.

Freud, S. (1900). *Interpretation of Dreams. SE*, 4 &5, 1953. [*Gesammelte Werke,*

2/3, Frankfurt a/M.: Fischer Verlag, 1942.]

Freud, S. (1901). *Psychopathology of Everyday Life. SE*, 6, 1960.

—— (1915). Thoughts for the times on war and death. *SE*, 14, 1957, pp. 275-300.

—— (1915-1917). *Introductory Lectures on Psychoanalysis. SE*, 15 & 16, 1961.

—— (1917). A metapsychological supplement to the theory of dreams. *SE*, 14, 1957, pp. 222-235.

—— (1925). Some additional noes on dream-interpretation as a whole. *SE*, 19, 1961, pp. 125-138.

—— (1940). *An Outline of Psychoanalysis. SE*, 23, 1964, pp. 141-207.

Garma, A. (1967). *The Psychoanalysis of Dreams*. London: Pall Mall Press.

Hartman, H. (1964). *Essays on Ego Psychology. Selected Problems in Psychoanalysis*. New York: International Universities Press.

Hunter, V. (1995). An interview with Clifford Scott. *Psychoanal. Rev.*, 82: 189-206.

Lewin, B.D. (1946). Sleep, the mouth and the dream screen. *Int. J. Psycho-Anal.*, 29: 224-234.

—— (1953a). The forgetting of dreams. In: Lowenstein, R.M. (Ed.), *Drives, Affect, Behavior*. New York: International Universities Press.

—— (1953b). Reconsideration of the dream screen. *Psychoanal. Q.* 22: 174-184.

—— (1954). Sleep, narcissistic neurosis and the analytic situation. *Psychoanal. Q.*, 23: 487-510.

Rey, H. (1992). Awake, going to sleep, asleep, dreaming, awaking, awake: Comments on W. Clifford Scott. *Free Assns.*, 3: 439-454.

Scott, W.C.M. (1948a). A psychoanalytic concept of the origin of depression. *Br. Med. J.*, 1: 1-9.

—— (1948b). Some embryological neurological psychiatric and psychoanalytic implications of the body scheme. *Int. J. Psycho-Anal.*, 29: 141-152.

—— (1952). Patients who sleep or look at the psychoanalyst during treatment: Technical considerations. *Int. J. Psycho-Anal.*, 33: 1-5.

—— (1953a). A new hypothesis concerning the relationship of libidinal and aggressive instincts based on clinical evidence obtained chiefly during the treatment of patients with manic-depressive illnesses. (Unpublished lecture, delivered at the International Psycho-Analytic Congress, London, July 29.)

—— (1953b). A note on blathering. *Int. J. Psycho-Anal.*, 36: 3-4.

—— (1958). Noise, speech and technique. *Int. J. Psycho-Anal.*, 39: 1-4.

—— (1960). Symposium on "depressive illness": III. Depression, confusion and multivalence. *Int. J. Psycho-Anal.*, 41: 497-503.

—— (1962). Symposium: A reclassification of psychopathological states. *Int. J. Psycho-Anal.*, 53, 344-350.

—— (1964a). Mania and mourning. *Int. J. Psycho-Anal.*, 45: 373-377.

—— (1964b). The limitations of science. *Canad. Med. Assn. J.*, 91: 700-703.

Scott, W.C.M. (1970). A review of the psychoanalytic situation. (Unpublished lecture, delivered at the Canadian Psychoanalytic Society, Montreal, November 19.)

——— (1974). Self envy and envy of dreaming. (Unpublished lecture, delivered at the Canadian Psychoanalytic Society, Montreal, May 23.)

——— (1975a). Comments on Freud's views about sleep. (Unpublished lecture, delivered at the Canadian Psychoanalytic Society, Montreal, January 23).

——— (1975b). Discussion of Dr. Knapp's paper(Unpublished commentary, delivered at the Canadian Psychoanalytic Society, Montreal, April 17.)

——— (1975c). Remembering sleep and dreams (title of the whole issue of *Int. Rev. Psycho-Anal.*, 2: 253-354, containing twelve essays by Scott).

——— (1976a). Discussion of Dr. Mahony's paper. (Unpublished commentary, delivered at the Canadian Psychoanalytic Society, Montreal, June 10.)

——— (1976b). Two recorded interviews. (Unpublished lecture, delivered at the Canadian Psychoanalytic Society, Toronto, March 10.)

——— (1977). Notes on conscious and unconscious conflicts in the transference. (Unpublished lecture, delivered at the Canadian Psychoanalytic Society, Montreal, June 16.)

——— (1978a). Common problems concerning the views of Freud and Jung. *J. Anal. Psychol.*, 23: 303-312.

——— (1978b). Discussion of Dr. Fayek's paper. (Unpublished commentary, delivered at the Canadian Psychoanalytic Society, Montreal, Nov. 23.)

——— (1981a). Discussion of Dr. Lakoff's paper. (Unpublished commentary, delivered at the Canadian Psychoanalytic Society, Montreal, February 19.)

——— (1981b). The development of the analysands' and analysts' enthusiasm for the process of psychoanalysis. In: J. S. Grotstein (Ed.), *Do I Dare Disturb the Universe?*, Beverly Hills: Caesura Press, pp. 571-577.

——— (1982). Melanie Klein: 1882-1960. *Psychia. J. Univ. Ottawa*, 7: 149-157.

——— (1984a). Primitive mental states in clinical psychoanalysis. *Contemp. Psychoanal.*, 20: 458-463.

——— (1984b). Psychoanalysis of a boy of 26 months with a 20 year follow-up. (Unpublished lecture, delivered at the Canadian Psychoanalytic Society, Montreal, October 24.)

——— (1985). Narcissism, the body, phantasy, fantasy, internal and external objects and the "body scheme." *J. Melanie Klein Soc.*, 3: 23-48.

——— (1986a). Mourning, the analyst, and the analysand. *Free Assn.*, 7: 7-10.

——— (1986b). The broken links between sleep and the unconscious and waking and the conscious. (Unpublished lecture, delivered at the Canadian Psychoanalytic Society, Montreal, May 22.)

——— (1986c). Who is afraid of Wilfred Bion? (Unpublished lecture, delivered to the

Canadian Psychoanalytic Society, Montreal, May 22.)

Scott, W.C.M. (1987a). Making the best of a sad job. (Unpublished lecture, delivered at the British Psychoanalytic Society, October 7.)

—— (1987b). Repairing broken links between the unconscious, sleep and instinct, and the conscious. (Unpublished lecture, delivered at the Queen Elizabeth Hospital, Montreal, November 3.)

—— (1988). Book reviews of Nini Herman's *My Kleinian Home* (Free Association Books, 1988) and *Why Psychotherapy?* (Free Association Books, 1987). *Free Assns.*, 13: 141-147.

—— (1989). Notes on an example of dissociated personalities without amnesia, with "further notes." (Unpublished lecture, delivered at the Canadian Psychoanalytic Society, Montreal, May 18.)

—— (1990a). Hypnosis, sleep and wake, conscious and unconscious. (Un-published lecture, delivered at the Canadian Psychoanalytic Society, Montreal, Jan. 18.)

—— (1990b). Pictures, music, dreams and creativity. (Unpublished lecture, delivered at the Queen Elizabeth Hospital, Montreal, October 2.)

—— *Mourning and Zest – Melancholy and Mania.* (Unpublished mss., 295 pp.)

—— (1998). *Becoming a Psychoanalyst.* Binghamton, NY: Esf Publishers, in press.

Winnicott, D.W. (1953). Transitional objects and transitional phenomena. In *Collected Papers*. New York: Basic Books, pp. 229-242.

Memories of Supervision with Dr. W.C.M. Scott

Michel Grignon

I first saw Clifford Scott in 1980, at the Allan Memorial Institute, when he was doing a live psychoanalytical consultation that we watched in another room on a television screen. I was astonished, puzzled, and excited about what I felt, heard and saw. I remember being struck by an awareness that I was attending the creation of something beautiful—some kind of delicate and complex embroidery. We could hear, feel and observe the moments where Scott and the patient emotionally touched each other both wandering unconsciously, in and out, regressively and progressively in various arabesques where links were done and undone with various knots of resistances creating a unique pattern of unconscious embroidery that both Scott and the patient were uncovering with fear, excitement, constant meticulous work and shared interest.

In 1984, I started supervision with Clifford Scott despite the fact that he was recuperating from a recent operation. While informing me about his failing health, he also wondered how this was affecting me. Trying to make the best of this news, I told him that I was happy for whatever time he could find for me. It took me a couple of years to realize that he had been introducing me existentially to one of his major concepts on the origin of psychic life, "the death bed scene." Scott felt that this phantasy was central, complementary, and in dynamic conflictual oscillation with the "primal scene" phantasy described by Freud. In our relationship, I always sensed the presence of death. I felt he was living every day as if it might be his last, courageously, not with despair but with zest and enthusiasm, painfully trying to create in the face of dark chaos. He shared with me his theory on dreaming, from the first imagined dream of the fetus to our hope of dying during our last dream. I never thought I would be at his death bed, seeing him fighting the mythic dragon for the last time. I was glad I could bid him good bye. It feels to me that Clifford is now within us more than ever.

He introduced me to the work of Paul Schilder and to his own conceptualization of the body schema. In fact, my interaction with Clifford always drew my attention to the sensory. When his hearing, as well as mine, became less acute,

I would sit quite near in order for him to hear me. This was uncomfortable at first since I was intimidated by his intelligent look, those lively eyes, challenging but never intrusive. He was a voracious reader, and it was with sadness that he shared with me the news of an operation to remove cataracts and the macular degeneration which came later. At times, he had tears in his eyes as he remembered painful and joyful moments in his practice. His hands, sometimes awkwardly expressing emotion, were gentle and reserved. On Thursdays, he often called me to accompany him to the scientific meetings. He would stand like a soldier awaiting my arrival and, at the meeting, was always ready to comment on the work of the person presenting. It was only recently that he accepted my arm back home because Eve, he said, would worry if he did not. One day, commenting on the smell in the house, he announced that he was making candy the same way his mother used to.

After I'd been in supervision for a year, I started receiving brief notes clipped to articles or book reviews Scott felt might interest me. I later discovered that many analysts and friends received those personalized notes. It was as if he carried all of us inside him and was constantly caring for us. I was always struck by his approach to the discussion of scientific papers. He rarely focused on critiques but tried to formulate questions that might open new avenues and enhance discussion.

Although he was in contact with many, many people, Scott was well acquainted with the profound solitude of the creative thinker. In his investigations, he often found himself where nobody else had been; many a time he talked without being adequately understood; finally, he wrote extensively often without being read or quoted. But he continued to think, write, and practice psychoanalysis all the while struggling not to make what he thought were compromises.

He and I discussed religion now and again, and he would urge me to write down my thoughts about the complex relationship of religion to infancy, idealization, and science. He was a dedicated scientist, but one always aware of the limits of the art of psychoanalysis which were also the limits of science. I am still struck by something Scott published in 1964 which neatly grasps the complexities of science:

> The limits of the scientist are seen in his faith in relativity which conflicts with his desire for absolute, his faith in uncertainty which conflicts with his desire for certainty, his faith in complementarity and multiplicity which conflicts with his desire for unity, his faith in reason which conflicts with his desire for authority. . . . Any one man's understanding is a small portion of what is understood by all living men. Understanding is limited by relativity, its uncertainty, its complemen-

tarity and its multiplicity but it is continually growing beautifully at an increasing rapid rate —toward an infinite limit which it will never reach (p. 4).

I learned from Scott an attitude of calm vigilance which keeps alive the internal struggle between a desire for the absolute and belief in the necessity for some degree of relativity and scepticism.

As I reported elsewhere in a paper focusing on the importance of child analysis for Scott, I once discovered in-between photocopies he had given me a small sheet of paper on which was written that saying:

> I know you believe you understand what I think I said. . . but I am not sure you realize that what you heard is not what I meant (Scott).

Scott was well aware of what he did not understand, but he tried to say something about what he did understand. He realized the words he used betrayed what he wanted to say because they were always inadequate to his experience. I came to share his hope that in dreaming about our thoughts and experiences we might gradually transform them and create new theories. Scott's gentle guidance led toward extending our capacity to tolerate our common ignorance. He wrote:

> When we overcome our anger and disappointment at ignorance, we may learn to appreciate it. We have so much of it that we should make the best of it. When we are able to love our ignorance from which all new good will come, life may become easier (Scott, 1981, p. 81).

In closing, I would like to quote from a poem by Samuel Beckett whom I discovered through Scott. I will quote this passage in French, remembering Scott's desire to speak the language of Moliere as well as his ironical laugh at the fact that he could only dream in French, but he did so wonderfully. Beckett (1978) wrote it in memoriam for a friend who had passed away.

Mort de a.d.

Et là être là encore là
Pressé contre ma vieille planche vérolée du noir
Des jours et nuits broyés aveuglément
À être là à ne pas fuir et fuir et être là
Courbé vers l'aveu du temps mourant
D'avoir été ce qu'il fut fait ce qu'il fit
De moi de mon ami mort hier l'oeil luisant
Les dents longues haletant dans sa barbe dévorant
La vie des saints une vie par jour de vie

Revivant dans la nuit ses noirs péchés
Mort hier pendant que je vivais
Et être là buvant plus haut que l'orage
La coulpe du temps irrémissible
Agrippé au vieux bois témoin des départs
Témoin des retours (p. 20).

References

Beckett S. (1978). *Poèmes*. Paris: Les éditions de Minuit.

Scott, S. (1964). The limitation of science. *Can. Med. Ass. J.*, 91: 700-703.

—— (1981). On positive affects. *Psychia. J. Univ. Ottawa*, 6(2): 79-81.

Did We Talk About Children
Or Did I Dream About It?
I Sure Know We Must Go On Talking More
About Children! And Children No More[1]

Michel Grignon

> Any one man's understanding is a small part of what is understood by all living man. Understanding is limited by relativity, its uncertainty, its complementarity and its multiplicity, but is continually growing beautifully at an increasingly rapid rate toward an infinite limit which it will never reach (Scott, 1964, p. 703).

> They may not believe what I talk about, but I am sure they will dream about what I talk about (S. Freud).

Introduction

Here is how Scott (1960) remembered his first analytic case 25 years after his supervision with Melanie Klein:

Dick, an inactive, non-talking first son of kindly parents, reared in a two-room apartment when in analysis at 27 months, 25 years ago, fondled a toy which represented his mother, after casually brushing another toy, which also represented his mother, from the table to the floor. Dick put his heel on the toy, which he had knocked to the floor, and continued to crush it, while he meantime continued to fondle the other toy, at the same time defecating into his pants. His coincident mouth activity varied from what might be called fondling behavior to crushing, biting behavior. The mouth, hand, heel and anus, the object in hand, the object under heel, the object in and about his anus were all interrelated and were more or less conscious. The anal activities being perhaps least conscious, the heel activity next conscious and the hand and mouth activities most conscious. The multivalent, coincident conflicts were seen in reparative fondling of a handful of mother substitutes, in coincident oscillating hate and love in mouth, in aggressive heel activity and in aggressive anal expulsion (p. 499).

In a later article on the use of the playroom, Scott (1961a) said: "Apart from my personal analysis I obtained my greatest stimulation both to observation and to learning during the psychoanalysis of the youngest children I have treated" (p. 8).

The main themes of Scott's later work could already be foreseen in these early observations. He noted the importance of early depression with the gradual elaboration of transformations of various affects oscillating between aggressive megalomania, depression, mania, reparation and zest. He also observed the complex involvement of various body parts with multivalent affects, objects and part objects. Finally, his allusion to various levels of consciousness announced the central concept of sleep as a primary instinct generating conflicts about waking up, eventually leading to problems such as somnambulism and multiple personalities.

Dr. C. Scott was trained in England both as a child and an adult analyst as was the tradition in British Psycho-Analytic Society with foreign students. Despite the fact that he reported only a few cases of children he himself analysed, I would like to demonstrate how child analysis plays a central role in his work as a child and adult analyst and in his observation, treatment and research of infants.

I. Child Analysis as a Catalyst

In 1950, Scott expressed his views on the training of psychoanalysts in the British Society in the following terms:

> Next to personal analysis no experience gives more conviction of the value of psychoanalytic concepts than analysis of a pre-latency child—and I would also say that no experience gives a more valuable background to psychoanalytic therapy of psychosis. As long as it will make future training I am convinced that the future training of psychoanalysts will most usefully be this sequence: first: neurotic adults, secondly: neurotic children, thirdly: psychotic adults and children (pp. 3-4).

Scott (1949) described the progress of psychoanalysis in Great Britain and pointed out:

> Work with children led to increased knowledge of unconscious mechanisms which are prominent during the first year of life. In particular the increased knowledge of introjection and projection mechanisms of infantile omnipotent fantasies and the almost lifelong importance of "object relationship" led not only to an increased

understanding of the child, but also to a realisation of the implications of these mechanisms in the neuroses of later life. The implications of such mechanisms for an increased understanding of adult and childhood psychoses, especially manic depressive psychoses may in the long run be a most important stimulus to further research in treatment (p. 33).

We could use, as Bion did, a chemical notation to describe the role of child analysis in the work of Scott. It could be written as follows:

CHILD

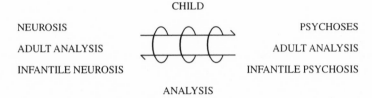

NEUROSIS	PSYCHOSES
ADULT ANALYSIS	ADULT ANALYSIS
INFANTILE NEUROSIS	INFANTILE PSYCHOSIS

ANALYSIS

For Scott the psychoanalytical experience could be diagrammed as a continuous dynamic interaction inside the psychoanalyst between his work with adult neurotics and psychotics. In this ongoing internal emotional reaction, child analysis acts like a catalyst. Equilibrium within the system depends on the achievement of quantitative and qualitative balance among the three elements. Like a catalyst, child analysis initiates interest, fosters the analytic work, maintains constant challenges in theory and technique, and finally permeates all the work of analysis without necessarily being mentioned (as often occurs for catalysts in chemical reactions).

According to Scott, all analysts during their personal analysis become interested in the child in themselves. Furthermore, because of its skillful attention to sequences of behaviors and its reliance on nonverbal material, the practice of child analysis transforms the thinking pattern of adult analysts. The great number of papers on technique in the analysis of neurosis in adults attests to the richness and creativity that Scott's child analysis introduced to psychoanalysis. To mention just a few, there are papers on the analysis of noises (1958), on the combination of noise and body movement such as blathering (1955), and on the importance of motor movement such as looking (1952b) or finger-licking and finger-flicking habits (1963).

Scott (1952b) feels that analysis of kinesics and noises deepens understanding and can sometimes accelerate the therapeutic process. He explained it in the following terms:

Just as technique developed in adult psychoanalysis paved the way for child analysis, so also aspects of technique brought into adult analysis from child analysis may create a situation in which oscillation between regression and progression can occur more rapidly little bits of experience to be worked through at a time. In child analysis body movements are allowed expression, made use in interpretation and furnish one of the ways we observe ego development during analysis. In adult analysis greater use of movements including eye movements may increase the speed and the depth of analysis. By such experiments we may become able to bring into analysis the implication of earlier and earlier problems and perhaps we may learn how to prevent the occasional long-term regressions which may occur during psychoanalytic treatment and which make further analysis difficult (p. 4).

However, referring to transference and countertransference issues, he pointed out that a change in "analytic attitude" is much more crucial than in technique:

Our attitude becomes extremely important when we talk about the treatment of children or of psychotic manic-depressives. Children and psychotics pay great attention to tone of voice and facial expressions and bodily movements and, if we are going to talk about these, we have to talk about the conflicts between the child's or psychotic's scenes, experiences, etc., and what he wishes and the difference between his own tone of voice, expression and movement, etc., and ours. This difference may be a matter of degree rather than kind. As far as we are concerned we will not necessarily be an unchanging mirror, not a blank face, not a monotone but some kind of calm serenity in the presence of changing affects of the patients whether child or psychotic (Scott, 1966, p. 272).

The rapport between the analysis of children and psychotics is, on the other hand, quite complex. Because of its games and abrupt changes of affect, child analysis introduces the psychoanalyst to the rapid oscillations in psychotic illness. Therefore, it brings us closer to the concept of oscillation of affects, so important in Scott's thought for the analysis of manic depressives and neurotics. He said:

In children's games. Pulling leaves of a rose. . . . She loves me, she loves me, no more. . . . In children's play and adult speech we come to understand in a longer time which took a very short time even a fraction of second, to occur first (Scott, 1954, p. 3).

Analysis of psychotics can improve our understanding of the early origins of some psychopathologies and will often give us the courage to offer early treatment to children who show what appear to be minor symptoms or signs but which are the first manifestations of what will later become severe disturbances.

Finally, I would like to mention a last aspect of the interaction between child analysis and adult analysis. Pearl, a manic depressive patient whom Scott analysed, asked him essentially the question "Where were you when I needed you?" (1960, p. 503). This woman taught Scott the importance of mourning the child analysis we would have liked to have had at different periods of our life when symptoms were present but analysis was not. The success of adult analysis is linked to the mourning of all those wished for earlier analyses that could have improved our lives as well as to the realization that adult analysis is the best we can do about this sad situation.

I would also add that, to develop both in theory and practice, child analysis has had to overcome a resistance that might be due to the absence of mourning by many analysts of their own missed child analyses.

II. The Real Child, the Real Analyst, and Science

Child analysis is central in Scott's thought and the motor for all his theoretical elaborations. However, Scott's interest in children was not only theoretical; he was interested in the real child's pain and contributed to the field of child analysis by promoting training and teaching in the field and by publishing numerous papers on the specifics of child analysis.

a. The Real Child

Scott was always talking about the infant but never did so in a theoretical or abstract way. He was communicating his deep desire to understand children in all their aspects. Two papers dealing with the war come to mind. The first one was written in 1948 and evaluated children's psychiatric care during and after the war. In this short article, he described psychiatric care given to children and criticized the complacent attitude of the British intelligentsia ("Everything will be alright"). He felt that "complacency too often hides resistances against dealing individually and specifically with severe symptoms in the child, for instance, depression and hate" (1948b, p. 174). The second paper came out 40 years later and dealt with the threat of nuclear war. Again, he expressed his concern over the complacency of adults and explained that children should be warned of danger in simple words and without idealization or denial. Care of children was always Dr. Scott's great concern, and he taught me that resistance to child analysis had to do with denying pain, affect and conflicts in very small children. Moreover, it had to do with denying our ability to feel, understand, and interpret in simple terms the complexities of their conflicts.

b. The Real Analyst

Scott dreamed about children, but he was a man who, upon awakening from his daydream, could make plans and work consistently with others to realize them.

He arrived in Canada in 1954 and very early on organized a study group for child analysts which held regular meetings in his office. Drs. E. Tétreault and J. B. Boulanger were part of that group when Dr. Gauthier first graduated in 1965.

In 1980, inspired by his example, a second group composed of Drs. I. Disher, E. Tétreault, J. B. Boulanger, G. Clark, L. Couture and J. Segal was formed. It established standards of training within the Québec English branch of the Institute. Today, training meets the standards agreed upon by the C.I.P. in 1980.

Recently, in 1990, Dr. Scott helped a group of 30 graduates in Canada to get together and organize their scientific interests. As a pioneer of child analysis, he has been inspiration to child analysts throughout Canada.

c. Scientific Publications: The Real Challenge

Dr. Scott's scientific publications testify to his constant efforts to show the dynamic complementarity of adult and child analysis. He also published on all major specific issues regarding child analysis alone. He was a courageous scholar and dealt in his papers with numerous controversial areas in child analysis, such as anorexia nervosa (Scott, 1948a), psychoanalysis for children with mental dysfunction (1961c), father-daughter incest (1962), infantile convulsion (1977), adoption (1981), psychosis and autism (1955). His clinical experiences and the way he discussed them in these papers demonstrate his desire to open new avenues by which to understand these disorders and to respect the complexities of child experience.

All these papers, as well as his teaching and seminars, reflect an ever-present preoccupation with the observation of detail and the importance of focusing on sequences.[2] The second preoccupation for Scott was the discovery of the early precursors of complex affects and ideas in the feelings and emotions of the preverbal child. Finally, what was always in the forefront of Scott's investigations was affect, the many defenses against it, the complex relationship between affects and their development early on during infancy and childhood as well as their relationship to adult psychopathologies.

III. Child Analysis and Infant Observation

a. Psychoanalytic Observations of Infants

Along with D. Winnicott, M. Klein and E. Bick, Dr. Scott observed babies and infants with their parents. He also used observation as a means of teaching students. Often these observations would repeat Winnicott's experience of letting the infant play with a plastic spatula but would creatively add new elements where the spatula would be removed and presented again after the child had interacted briefly with it (Scott, 1961b). Various reactions were carefully described and analysed with the students fostering their interest for early observations and introducing them to the early affective life of infants with their parents. He taught the students at the Montreal Children's Hospital for at least 10 years in this manner and continued to give his input through participation in various teaching opportunities at McGill. He also felt that the observation of infants should be an integral part of analytic training, and he repeatedly tried to stimulate the introduction of such an activity into the programme of the Institute.

b. Mother-Infant Therapy

In his comments on a paper by Berry Sandford, "Some psychotherapeutic work in maternity and child welfare clinics," Scott (1952a) provided a psychoanalytic framework which outlined his understanding of the mutual interactions between mother and infant in terms of complex combinations of introjective and projective identifications happening in both child and mother at the same time. To my knowledge only the French psychoanalyst M. Berger (1984, 1987) has written about the complexities of such interactions in families. Scott proposed a psychoanalytic way of listening using the concepts of introjective and projective identification to identify the best treatment approach for a given family that presents with its personal unconscious agenda. Part of Scott's technique of interviewing a family involved seeing the whole family together, subsequently in various pairs, and then individually, to sort out the complexities of their projective and introjective interactions and identifications.

c. Fetal Life

In 1948, Scott was already involved in what was to become a research area of lifelong interest, the relationship between psyche and soma. He was therefore interested in all the findings of Gesell (1946) concerning "the infant at birth.

. . [who] has experienced gravitational orientation, righting movement, respira-
tory movement and swallowing" (Scott, 1948, p. 4). He tried to include the
fetus in his new theory about body movement. Later on, when dealing with
narcissistic issues, he developed new theories about sleep (Scott, 1949a, 1975)
based on the hypothesis that psychic life originates from early fetal activity. In
1956, he said:

> How often has there been an oscillation between wakefulness and sleep before a
> state developed in which sleep first followed a pleasurable activity, such as pleasant
> feeding? This leaves out the question altogether of whether there are other causes
> of waking than pain (hunger pain or other pain) and whether there are types of
> going to sleep which are not a defence against pain or which do not follow the
> pleasure of hunger satisfaction. Here a hypothesis might be that intensities of what
> has been called muscle erotism may have a recurrent pleasant waking and sleeping.
> The prenatal movement of breathing, sucking, stretching, etc., when of a critical
> intensity may lead to waking followed by going to sleep. In all such theorizing we
> must remember that the genetic sequence is waking-sleeping and not sleeping-
> waking. The first event in an individual's life of the waking-sleeping series is being
> awake (p. 74).

His interest in foetal life was always marked by theoretical and clinical
analytic preoccupations which he constantly kept in mind in order to develop
hypotheses that could explain all new clinical realities. All his discoveries
regarding infant observation and fetal life did not deter him from continuing to
deepen his understanding of analysis. On the contrary, they stimulated him to
elaborate new theories and test them out by experimenting with new techniques.

Conclusion: Analysis is Analysis is Analysis

At first, my personal experience with Scott was marked by fear, curiosity
and worry. I feared that he would be intolerant of my ignorance which I myself
found intolerable. This fear gradually disappeared as I started to sense myself
awakening and eager to define with him our ignorance. My curiosity was at first
very superficial and then I became very keen to discover more and more, but at
the same time I felt that time was moving on too quickly. Finally, I was worried
that I would not understand what he was talking about since most colleagues
had told me they could not. Moreover, these new analysts never received
answers to concrete questions about their patients. This worry did not disap-
pear. What was first a worry was transformed into an attitude of acceptance and
openness; I became curious as to how many new ways Scott would find to
understand today's material; I became used to traveling into the world of Alice

in Wonderland.

He would often say "Think of the opposite. Think of many opposites. Think of the most opposite of all the opposites." I learned the difficult task of constantly looking for something else, something that I did not see, feel or hear right away. I learned to differentiate between simpleness and the search for simple words to express complex realities. Looking through my notes, I found a sheet of paper he gave me along with a few reprints I had asked for. It read: "I know you believe you understand what you think I said. . . . But I am not sure you realize that what you heard is not what I meant" (Scott).

I think I started to calm down when I realized that Scott was aware that he did not understand it all but was trying to communicate a little of what he thought he understood. He realized that the words he used betrayed what he wanted to say and that I would be misled if I thought these words were the sum of what he experienced. The only hope we shared was that we could continue talking and dreaming about what we felt had happened with a patient we were trying to understand.

Finally, Scott taught me an attitude of calm vigilance toward the constant internal struggles we face as we are torn between our conflicting wish for faith in relativity and uncertainty and our desire for absolute certainty, our faith in complementarity or multiplicity and a desire for unity, our faith in reason and desire for authority. The only way I can best conclude this homage to Dr. Scott is with a quote from his paper on "positive affects." It clearly demonstrates that our task in analysis, supervision, and theory consists mostly in continually extending our capacity to tolerate our ignorance in order to foster new discoveries:

> When we overcome our anger and disappointment at ignorance, we may learn to appreciate it. We have so much of it that we should make the best of it. When we are able to love our ignorance from which all new good will come, life may become easier (Scott, 1981, p. 81).

Only then will we be able to listen to the unconscious that constantly evades us, hiding behind new disguises, always leaving us unsatisfied, but at the same time stimulating us to listen more for the unheard, the unspoken, and the unthought child inside of us.

Notes

1. For Dr. C. Scott's 90th Birthday.
2. His first psychological paper is about the importance of sequences in drawings of children (Scott, 1937).

References

Berger, M. (1984). *Entretiens familiaux et champ transitionnel.* Paris: PUF, 1984.

—— (1987). *Pratique des entretiens familiaux.* Paris: PUF, 1987.

Scott, W.C. M. Note on adopted children. (Unpublished.)

—— (1937). Discussion: E. Guttman and W.S. Maclay's "Clinical observations on schizophrenic drawings." *Brit. J. Med. Psychol.*, 16: 184-185.

—— (1948a). Notes on the psychopathology of Anorexia Nervosa. *Br. J. Med. Psychol.*, 21: 241-249.

—— (1948b). Psychiatric problems amongst evacuated children. *Br. J. Med. Psychol.*, 11: 171-174.

—— (1948c). Some embryological, neurological, psychiatric and psychoanalytic implication of the body scheme. *Int. J. Psycho-Anal.*, 29: 1-15.

—— (1949a). The body scheme in psychotherapy. *Br. J. Med. Psychol.*, 22: 139-150.

—— (1949b). Progress of psychoanalysis in Great Britain. *Brit. Med. Bull.*, 6(31-35): 33.

—— (1950). Evolution and present trends of psychoanalysis (in contribution to a symposium at the International Congress of Psychiatry, Paris, proceedings). *J. Psychothérapie, psychanalyse, médecine psychosomatique*, pp. 3-4.

—— (1952a). Discussion of a paper presented by B. Sandford, Some psychotherapeutic work in maternity and child welfare clinics. *Br. J. Med. Psychol.*, 25: 9.

—— (1952b). Patients who sleep or look at the psychoanalyst during treatment. *Int. J. Psycho-Anal.*, 33:1-5.

—— (1954). A new hypothesis concerning the relationship of libidinal and aggressive instincts. *Int. J. Psycho-Anal.*, 35:1-4.

—— (1955). A note on blathering. *Int. J. Psycho-Anal.*, 36: 348-349.

—— (1956). Sleep in psychoanalysis. *Philadelphia Association for Psychoanalysts*, 6: 72-83.

—— (1957). Discussion of a paper by Dr. Kanner on Autism. (A.P.A. Reg. Research Conference, 1955.) *Psychia. Reports*, (7).

—— (1958). Noise, speech and technique. *Int. J. Psycho-Anal.*, 39: 64-68.

—— (1960). Depression, confusion and multivalence. *Int. J. Psycho-Anal.*, 41: 497-503.

—— (1961a). Difference between the playroom used in child psychiatric treatment and in child analysis. (Presented as part of the Child Psychiatric Program at the Annual Meeting of the Canadian Psychiatric Association, Banff, 16 June 1960.) *Can. Psychia. Assn. J.*, 6(5): 281-285.

—— (1961b). The demonstration of object relation in a set situation in infants of 6 to 12 months. *Proc. Third World Congress Psychia.*, Montréal, pp. 58-69.

Scott, W.C.M. (1961c). The psychotherapy of the mental defective. *Can. Psychia. Assn. J.*, 8(5): 293-315.

—— (1962). Psychodynamics of father-daughter incest. *Can. Psychia. Assn. J.*, 7(5): 250.

—— (1963). A finger-licking finger-flicking habit. *J. Amer. Psychoanal. Assn.*, 11(4): 832-835.

—— (1964). The limitations of science. *Can. Med. Assn. J.*, 91: 700-703.

—— (1966). The mutually defensive role of depression and mania. (Special Supplement, part IV: On the psychoanalytic concept of depressive illness.) *Can. Psychia. Assn. J.*, 14: 272.

—— (1975). Remembering sleep and dream. *Int. J. Psycho-Anal.*, 2: 253-354.

—— (1977). Au sujet de la convulsion. D.W. Winnicott. *L'Arc*, Paris: Gallimard, (69): 84-93.

—— (1981). On positive affects. *Psychia. J. Univ. Ottawa*, 6(2): 79-81.

On Learning to Talk and Learning to Mourn: Remembering Clifford Scott

Costas E. Benierakis

> The stream has reached the sea, and once more the great
> mother holds her son against her breast (Gibran, 1966,
> p. 113).

Emil was about seven years old when one evening he went to the theater with his parents. The performance had just ended and they were walking home, himself between his parents holding their hands, when his father and mother started to argue again. This was very painful to him but he could not tell them to stop; instead he began to feel a pain in the back of his knee and only mentioned this to them, managing to divert their attention to whether he could walk or take a taxi, which they did. Thus, he once again averted a disaster in the family but at the cost of his becoming a "cripple." Avoiding arguments became a pattern by choosing an adult life of self-immolation, adapting his lifestyle to those of others, supporting and helping them to fulfil their lives but never living his own. Upon his father's death, he resolved to be courageous, but behind his bravado lurked a chronic depression. In analysis, he would often be silent or have difficulty free associating.

Pavlos was a young adult obsessional patient who, in childhood, had been emotionally abused by his brother from whom their parents had been unable to protect him. He became overwhelmed by doubt and inaction which spread to his speech, and he developed a severe difficulty expressing himself. He was extremely bright, but his life came to a standstill as he could no longer study or work. He became totally isolated away from home because he was unable to maintain any social contacts. For a period in the analytic transference, his emerging rage culminated in despairing suicidal thoughts while at other times he would doze off in the protective safety of the analyst's presence in the session (Benierakis and Dongier, 1977). A basic wish of his was to wipe out everything from his past and to have his life begin again from scratch.

Damon, a six-year-old boy, began his treatment sessions by frenetically playing with toys or acting in disruptive ways, avoiding speaking to the analyst and ignoring him completely, or demanding that the analyst also cease to talk. A repetitive action of his was to suddenly touch the analyst's penis. It seemed that the boy was searching for his identity and for his non-existing father, who had shown no interest in Damon and never saw the boy since his birth when the parents divorced. The continuous ignoring of the analyst made the latter face the anxious feeling of his "non-existence" in the sessions and the boy's re-enacted predicament. Damon's acting out and projective identification were badly tolerated by his borderline mother, who herself had difficulties with the development of her reflective capacity.

All three cases were known to Clifford Scott who had some impact in their lives through supervising their treatment and/or seeing them in consultation.

How early does a problem start and how early should analysis start? In most adult analyses, Scott brought attention to the wish of the analysand to have started analysis earlier in childhood. How early (postnatally or prenatally) do the memory traces we carry in our body become ingrained in its various parts? Bion (1989 edition) reminds us of Freud's (1926) statement that "there is much more continuity between intrauterine life and earliest infancy than the impressive caesura of the act of birth would have us believe" (p. 138). Bion asks, "How is one to penetrate this obstacle, this caesura of birth? Can any method of communication be sufficiently 'penetrating' to pass that caesura in the direction from postnatal conscious thought back to the pre-mental in which thoughts and ideas have their counterpart in 'times' or 'levels' of mind where they are not thoughts or ideas?" (p. 45). He says that in psychoanalysis we are concerned with the translation of what we do not know into something we know or can communicate, and also in the opposite direction from what we do know to what we do not know, and are not aware of it because it is unconscious and which may even be prenatal. Occasionally, we may detect a primitive vestige in a psychosomatic experience. Bion rephrases Freud's statement as follows: "There is much more continuity between autonomically appropriate quanta and the waves of conscious thought and feeling than the impressive caesura of transference and counter-transference would have us believe" (pp. 53-56).

Before birth, the baby leaks its internal contents into the maternal tissues in the womb which, together with the fetus, form one unit. The separation into two bodies at birth requires skin contact to minimize the dread of sensory discontinuity and experience of dissolution. Ogden (1988) refers to the relief provided by snugly wrapping in sheets a hospitalized patient experiencing the terror of impending dispersal of the self into unbounded space. Perhaps the old practice in some cultures of tightly wrapping new-born babies in sheets of clothing had the same meaning. Klein's idea that the infant, shortly after birth, has the omnipotent phantasy that it can split off what it does not want and evacuate it, represents a continuation of what the infant actually does in the mother's body before birth. When words begin to be expressed as communication, as opposed to words used as things for evacuation, there is a movement from the paranoid-schizoid to the depressive position with the loss of omnipotence, and this shows itself as a sense of loss when the patient begins to speak (Bion, 1962) (and use non-psychotic verbal thought).

Progressing, therefore, from body sensation and muscle movement to making noises with meaning in play, to eventually finding words for feelings, is to allow the mourning process to unfold and to go through the stages of learning gradually how to overcome frustration and disappointments and how to be glad to be sad remembering the disappointments and that one cannot have everything. Then, finally, one can be glad about being glad until the next sadness or disappointment with all the intricate relationships which Scott (1980) elaborated on, including learning to face the finality of things and to love with zest the infiniteness of ignorance in ourselves and others, and learning to mourn faster lost objects and opportunities so as to be ready for new ones. A new opportunity with the same or a new object may give the satisfaction missed in prior lost opportunities or relationships (Scott, 1955). Scott said that Winnicott's finding that a baby satisfied with playing with a tongue depressor or eating food is not upset at their disappearance is so because they are felt to be inside the baby (Winnicott, 1941; Scott, 1961). Scott took this theory further and demonstrated that when a baby's play with the tongue depressor was frustrated before the baby was satisfied with it, anger or sadness appeared at the missed opportunity. When Scott returned the depressor, the baby was at first inhibited but then often took it and had another opportunity with the same object. In life (and in therapeutic work), there may not always be opportunities with the same object to repair damage done. We need to mourn missed chances and try to make up as much as possible with new objects with which experiences will be different but could also be better. Overcoming our envy of others and our self-envy will give a boost to our mourning efforts and our development. Scott (1975) said that envy of somebody else's achievements may stop one from sharing in the enjoyment of the other's achievements or from finding substitute enjoyment, e.g., envy by the child of the way the father can please the mother. In self-envy, the self-critical part of the ego envies the part that has achieved progress and blocks it from developing further by interfering with mourning, e.g., the idea that progress did not occur sooner and it is now too late. In psychoanalytic therapy, the envying part of the self may attack the working alliance between the helpful part of the self and the analyst, and endanger treatment (López-Corvo, 1992).

His paper, "Making the best of a sad job," was read by Scott to a gathering of the British Psychoanalytic Society on Wednesday, October 7, 1987. Ann Marie Sandler had given her place to him as this was to be Scott's last visit to London. He was visibly moved by the warm reception and applause of his former colleagues.

With children and adults, often more work is done with what is said in analysis after a lot of work has taken place with what is done in analysis, while more exposure of the facial expression by the patient and watching it by the analyst occurs later in analysis (Scott, 1974). Scott stresses the potential meaning or communicative value of movements, especially in a silent patient. He says that we learn to observe in detail, and eventually we learn that no matter how much we observe, there is always more to observe. In discussing with Scott the value of observation in analysis, I thought that a mirror in front of the patient would show him or her the expressions that the analyst saw. Scott said that he had had a mirror in his old office and added that two cameras and two screens could help show the expressions of both analyst and analysand to each other, much like Scott had made periodic use of the mirror. Scheduling two-hour sessions at certain times might be another way of encouraging experimentation in the interest of advancing psychoanalysis. Scott himself had had daily two-hour analytic sessions in the summer of 1931 with Melanie Klein as her first training analysand (Grosskurth, 1986). Occasionally doing something, such as making a sound, as part of an interpretation may convey what the analyst means better than the use of a word (Scott, 1955, 1974). In child analysis, when the child gives up free play for free speech, the analytic process may be sped up except when speech is used as a defense against noise and then analysis is slowed down (Scott, 1958). Scott often encouraged his analysands with inhibition of speech to try to make a noise or sound in an effort to reach the infantile origin of the block and analyze the defenses against the unconscious wish to make noise. Immense satisfaction may be felt upon overcoming the anxiety for the wish to make a noise and making the noise, and attempts to put various sounds into words may lead to connecting affects with words.

Winnicott (1949) has written that a mother is not a good mother until she can tolerate hating her baby, i.e., she allows herself to be aware of this feeling of hers without expressing it to the child. I think that this allows the mother to be more tolerant and accepting of the child's anger and hatred toward her as well as the child's sexual feeling toward her. Inhibition in talking in analysis derives often from childhood inhibitions and prohibitions to talk or be spontaneous. Scott has said that there is a need for a book to be written about how parents should handle their children who (say they) want to fuck them, and a book for parents whose children (say they) want to kill them.

Klein (1927) wrote that it is always progress when a child in analysis acknowledges the reality of objects through use of his own words. This bridge to reality may be avoided by the child who brings his phantasies only through wordless play. She (1930) also showed how excessive defense, to allay the anxiety due to sadism against the mother's body, blocks phantasy-life and the development of speech. In her analytic work with a four-year-old boy, Klein initiated play and communication by using her general knowledge from clinical experience to make interpretations and help this psychotic boy establish contact with reality and develop his language.

It has been proposed that one way of facilitating free association is the use of "distancing" in a number of ways: a) by the use of Freud's analogy of sitting in a moving train and describing what one sees outside, the observing part of the ego being the passenger; b) the anxiety of a sexual or aggressive attack felt against the analyst in one session may be lessened by speaking about it at a later session (this, of course, is a postponement of free association); c) the anxiety is lessened if the analysand makes a connection between the attacked analyst and a parental figure of his; and d) the anxiety is lessened also when the attack on the analyst is linked to a similar attack on oneself. I have found that immediate verbalization without postponement to a later session is possible if the attack on the analyst is expressed toward him or her in association with the link established by the analysand to his father, mother or to the analysand's self. Gray (1973, 1987) has emphasized the importance of the analyst's effort to demonstrate to the analysand the use of the latter's defenses in blocking the expression of a feeling related to the analyst in the course of the analytic session. This helps to develop the observing part of the ego and to increase the range and effectiveness of the ego in the management of the id impulses, which gradually will be allowed more access to consciousness. This, in turn, enhances the self-analyzing function of the patient, a subject very dear also to Scott who encouraged some of his analysands to practice self-analysis during holidays or other periods of interruption of psychoanalysis with him. He also, on occasion, used part of a session to encourage the practice of self-analysis while he would step out of the office for a number of minutes, with the opportunity to discuss the results upon his return. Scott said that by speaking loudly during self-analysis one may surprise oneself by hearing something which might otherwise have gone unnoticed. Self-analysis is like talking to the internal mother after having talked to her in external reality.

I would now like to present the following vignette from an analytic session with Emil (referred to above). This patient often had difficulty talking and the analyst here intervened to facilitate free association which led to some mourning: Emil made an attempt to start talking but suddenly stopped in order to think how to proceed.

Analyst: That is repression. . . you were told many times (in the past) to stop talking.

Analysand: How do you know it's repression?

Analyst: I don't, but it's a possibility.

Analysand: It feels idiotic to talk about the same things over and over.

Analyst: Repetition could be defensive or one repeats until a solution is found. Defensive in order to inhibit. . . . When you don't talk, I have to observe your movements, touching your face, your head. . . there is little movement in your face.

Analysand: How do you know you free associate rather than just talk a lot?

Analyst: If you talk a lot and don't need to listen to yourself, you may say things which I will hear and let you know what you said. . . . You don't talk and think instead because you must check what you are about to say.

Analysand: I am afraid of pouring abuse on you. . . am feeling like shaking you and saying "go to hell" or "stop talking about the same things."

Analyst: You could make use of me by pouring abuse which could be directed at your father or mother.

Analysand: When I was a child, I was doing more things than talking, bumping into people or kicking people in their legs.

Analyst: If your foot could speak, what would it say?

Analysand: I want to get into you. . . .

Analyst: Go back in from the place I came out with feet first?

Analysand: . . . or go in the opposite way from the way I came out.

Analyst: The last thing to come out will go in first.

Analysand: Or shove my penis in. . . .

Analyst: Then your mother might tell you, if you told her this, that there is a little girl somewhere in the world for you to love; like your mother fell in love with your father and gave birth to you, and like your grandfather and grandmother fell in love and gave birth to your mother. . . . Would you have liked to have been able to talk like this with your mother?

Analysand: Yes, like I would have liked to have been able to talk to her before her death about her dying.

In a later session, Emil, continuing the mourning for his mother, described the following dream:

I was in a large room with beds and people. I asked my sister if they had brought Mother and if they had given her something to eat. I was answered "yes" to both questions. Mother was sitting on a bed in a far corner of the room near a window, and as I went near she was turning her head from side to side and opening her mouth, and I thought she was waiting to be fed as if they hadn't really given her anything to eat. I went near and greeted her and she smiled and called my name, being pleased to see me.

Emil, at this point, became aware that he was stroking his face. This immediately elicited the memory of a forgotten part of the dream in which he held his mother's hands and then he stroked her face.

Epilogue

Scott's uniqueness as a psychoanalytic theorist and clinician is extensively surveyed in Mahony's (1997) recent essay. Reflecting upon my own experiences with Scott, I recall his ability to reduce anxiety in people so that they could talk about any topic and any feeling; he would often bring problems back to the child in the adult and encourage the use of words used in one's childhood. He would reduce a seemingly complicated concept to simple basic questions. He said jokingly that analysts who use obscure jargon probably do not know themselves what they mean. He believed that all experiences can be understood in terms of one's ontogenesis and the relation between the body and the inner and outer world (Scott, 1949). He emphasized the possibility of learning to be increasingly more wakeful to one's behavior and unconscious motives. Becoming freer to analyze the conflict between the wish to sleep and the wish to be awake would lead to being able to sleep and dream in the analytic session with the possibility of analyzing a dream at the time it is dreamt before it is altered or forgotten. He said that analysis offered the chance to discover a new potential in ourselves, something which did not exist before, or recover something which we had forgotten that we forgot.

Psychoanalysis has captured the imagination and the antagonism of man because it searches for the truth. Man is curious about himself and asks questions about his origins, the meaning of his existence and his death, but man is also intolerant of frustration and may wish to fill in too soon the vacuum of ignorance. We must therefore always consider that our theories may be only space-fillers (Bion, 1977). Bion believed, along with Maurice Blanchot, that, "La réponse est le malheur de la question," i.e., that the answer is the misfortune of curiosity—it kills it (Grinberg, 1985, p. 185). If a question is answered, it must not be answered as if that is the only answer because this will block all further curiosity for alternative possibilities. "Say not 'I have found the truth,' but rather, 'I have found a truth'" (Gibran, 1966, p. 66). Scott (1952) loved to play with a myriad of possibilities. A dream could be known it was a dream only after the dreamer woke up. But then, did the dreamer really wake up? Or did he only dream of waking up? Perhaps he woke up in another dream. A child might dream of waking inside mother. What is the relation of this to waking inside mother before birth?

Scott's body is no longer with us but his spirit is, and we who worked with him shall remember his enthusiastic urging of our curiosity. As the poet (Gibran, 1966) says, "It was but yesterday we met in a dream. . . . And if our hands should meet in another dream, we shall build another tower in the sky" (pp. 113-114).

> I rejoice to hear that your soul has set sail, like the returning Ulysses, for its native land—that glorious, that only real country—the world of unseen truth (Plotinus, in Bucke, 1901, p. 121).

References

Benierakis, C. & Dongier, M. (1977). Before and during analysis. Two videotaped interviews with an obsessional. Presented to the Quebec English Branch, Canadian Psychoanalytic Society, Montreal, March 1977.

Bion, W.R. (1962). *Learning from Experience*. New York: Basic Books.

—— (1977). Emotional turbulence. In: P. Hartocollis (Ed.), *Borderline Personality Disorders*. New York: IUP.

—— (1989 edition). Caesura. In: *Two Papers, The Grid and Caesura*. London: Karnac Books.

Bucke, R.M. (1901). *Cosmic Consciousness. A Study in the Evolution of the Human Mind*. New York: Dutton.

Freud, S. (1926). Inhibitions, symptoms and anxiety. *SE*, 20: 75-175. In: J. Strachey (Ed.), *Standard Edition of the Complete Psychological Works of Sigmund Freud*, 24 volumes. London: Hogarth Press and the Institute of Psycho-Analysis, 1953-1974.

Gibran, K. (1966). *The Prophet*. London: W. Heinemann.

Gray, P. (1973). Psychoanalytic technique and the ego's capacity for viewing intrapsychic activity. *J. Am. Psychoanal. Assn.*, 21: 474-494.

—— (1987). On the technique of analysis of the superego – An introduction. *Psychoanal. Q.*, 56:130-154.

Grinberg, L. (1985). Bion's contribution to the understanding of the individual and the group. In: M. Pine (Ed.), *Bion and Group Psychotherapy*. London: Routledge and Kegan Paul.

Grosskurth, P. (1986). *Melanie Klein. Her World and her Work*. Toronto: McClelland and Stewart.

Klein, M. (1927). The importance of words in early analysis. In: *The Writings of Melanie Klein*. Vol. 3: *Envy and Gratitude and Other Works, 1946-1963*. London: Hogarth Press, 1975, pp. 314.

—— (1930). The importance of symbol-formation in the development of the ego. In: *The Writings of Melanie Klein*. Vol. 1: *Love Guilt and Reparation and Other Works, 1921-1947*. London: Hogarth Press, 1975: pp. 219-232.

López-Corvo, R.E. (1992). About interpretation of self-envy. *Int. J. Psycho-Anal.*, 73: 719-728.

Mahony, P.J. (1997). An introduction to Clifford Scott: His theory, technique, manner of thinking and self-expression. *J. M. Klein Object Rel.*, 15(1):5-50.

Ogden, T.H. (1988). On the dialectical structure of experience: Some clinical and theoretical implications. *Contemp. Psychoanal.*, 23(4):17-45.

Scott, W.C.M. (1949). The "Body Scheme" in psychotherapy. *Br. J. Med. Psychol.*, 22(3-4): 139-150.

—— (1952). Patients who sleep or look at the psychoanalyst during treatment – Technical considerations. *Int. J. Psycho-Anal.*, 33: 465-469.

—— (1955). A note on blathering. *Int. J. Psycho-Anal.*, 36: 348-349.

—— (1958). Noise, speech and technique. *Int. J. Psycho-Anal.*, 39:108-111.

—— (1961). The demonstration of object relations and affect in a set situation in infants of 6 to 12 months. In *Proc.Third World Congress Psychia.*, 1: 56-59.

—— (1974). Non-verbal communication in psychoanalysis. Paper presented at the First International Symposium on Non-Verbal Aspects and Techniques of Psychotherapy, Vancouver, July 29-31, 1974.

—— (1975). Self-envy and envy of dreams and dreaming. In: Remembering sleep and dreams. *Int. Rev. Psycho-Anal.*, 2: 333-338.

—— (1980). The development of the analysand's and the analyst's enthusiasm for the process of psychoanalysis. In: J.S. Grosstein (Ed.), *Do I Dare Disturb the Universe? A Memorial to Wilfred R. Bion*. Beverly Hills: Caesura Press, 1981, pp. 571-577.

Winnicott, D.W. (1941). The observation of infants in a set situation. *Int. J. Psycho-Anal.*, 22: 229-249.

—— (1949). Hate in the counter-transference. *Int. J. Psycho-Anal.*, 30: 69-74.

Fig. 22. Clifford Scott with Monique Meloche, September 1988.
Credit: The Estate of W.C.M. Scott

Memories about My Analysis with Scott

Monique Meloche

M y first encounter with Dr. Scott goes back to 1960, during a conference of the American Psychosomatic Society in Montreal. Dr. Engels presented a paper entitled "Is Grief a Disease?" to which Dr. Scott was commentator. Dr. Engels thought grief was a disease while Dr. Scott considered that uncomplicated grief and mourning were achievements of healthy development, the healthy reaction to the discovery of the ambivalence of instincts, our own and that of our loved ones, and that of mortality of men. This divergence of views led to a heated exchange between them, both of them strongly holding on to his view; Dr. Scott intervened quickly, many times, talked rapidly and was very red in the face. When the chairman told him he could make only one last comment, he came to the microphone and said: "Is grief a disease? No." I guess I felt restored to normality and decided that if I ever went into analysis, I would go to him.

His boundless curiosity and his kaleidoscopic mind left us sometimes bewildered; he could extract meaning out of the plainest of words and, believe me, in analysis he left no stone unturned, no word, sigh or silence unanalyzed; when words were inadequate, he thought new ones should be invented. To a declaration of powerlessness, he asked: What would happen if? The famous "WOOF" question. He taught me to think, to analyze, to write. He even taught me basic English and succeeded in teaching me the difference between "can I" and "may I," where years of schooling had failed. His knowledge of French was better than he made it to be, and so was his hearing. One could not mutter something in French and expect it to go unnoticed.

In supervision he wanted to find out what had not been said, or interpreted, or thought, which sometimes induced an overwhelming feeling of ignorance in the supervisee.

"We are always in the situation of watching the unexpected and having to be prepared for it. . .," he said in 1985, and ready he was, delighted when we could share his enthusiasm.

In his comments to Dr. Engels' paper, one could find most of his favorite topics: early affective development, mourning and depression, his famous "from bad to mad to sad to glad." During my analysis and for the long years of our friendship afterwards, every time he started this kind of terse argumentation— inside, outside, beside—I had the same fantasy; I saw him as a magnificent juggler, playing with concepts embodied in a few one-syllable words like as many balls or better, like flaming torches, to which he kept adding and sending them higher and higher in the air. We admired his verbal skills, the fireworks of his mind, but sometimes the full impact of their meaning only hit us later on.

He enjoyed being a psychoanalyst, practicing psychoanalysis, thinking and talking psychoanalysis. By his constant marveling at things, he was the youngest of us and usually the one to point to the nakedness of the emperor. He was always ready to re-examine some of his "impermanent certainties" as he put it. When we discussed my translation of one of his papers, some of my questions led him to change or add a few lines to the paper he had written forty years before. His constant preoccupation with new discoveries made him a prolific writer; he was an encouragement to us all: "Why don't you write a paper about it, just a page, just a paragraph."

He gave great importance to the irreversibility of time: "You can't wake up yesterday." But we keep on wishing we could. Waking up last year, when he was still among us, when we could ask him the questions we have not had time to ask, and tell him our love.

Doctor Scott, we miss you.

Notes and Comments about a Videotape Done for the 90th Anniversary of W.C.M. Scott (1993)

Monique Meloche

Perhaps offering Clifford Scott a *Portrait of W.C.M. Scott, Psychoanalyst*, as a birthday present is a bit peculiar at first, because he only has to look at himself in mirrors, psychic ones and others, to see himself. He does not need them, he knows. However, it appears that several "Portrait of a Gentleman," by Rembrandt, Frans Hals and other famous painters have been tokens of love and gratitude. We have made this portrait out of his own life and works.

The original idea of the videotape we are about to see came from Pierre Drapeau, together with Henri Rey, Paul Lefebvre and Jean Baptiste Boulanger, in an effort to record on film some of Dr. Scott's contributions to psychoanalysis and particularly to Canadian psychoanalysis. The first meeting of interested parties took place at Bruno Cormier's residence in December 1988 and consisted of Bruno and Ruby Cormier, Henri Rey, Paul Lefebvre, Pierre Drapeau and myself. A sketchy outline of interviews was made, first chronologically: Dr. Scott in Canada, in the USA and in the United Kingdom, then Dr. Scott and Melanie Klein, then some of the ideas of Dr. Scott.

The first session was recorded at Dr. Scott's home in January 1989 by Roland Duchesne. We soon realized that we were tackling a major project, involving a great deal of time and efforts than we had originally imagined. What started as a 2 or 3-hour project developed into 12 hours of videotaped interviews, 6 hours in Dr. Scott's home, 6 others in Ste-Justine Hospital, extending over 3½ years. The interviewers were Henri Rey, Paul Lefebvre, Pierre Drapeau and myself. We had greatly underestimated Dr. Scott's generosity and his endless capacity to make links between memories, metapsychology and clinical material. He never failed to tire the interviewers out, while he was always ready to—and sometimes did—do 2 hours sessions without a break.

But if 12 hours of taped sessions is a Thesaurus of knowledge and wisdom, it is hardly a document that can be shared by all, at a given time. A "montage" operation had to be done and many hours of viewing were necessary to bring out a clear picture of him. Although basically the outline remained close to the original one—Dr. Scott's childhood and education in Canada, his psychiatric training in the United States and psychoanalytic training in the United Kingdom, his analysis with Melanie Klein, his leading ideas, his usual generosity had contributed a great deal more, and a lot had to be left out: some of his ideas on the body-scheme and the psyche-soma regression and progression, reparation and creativity, splitting, doubling and projective identification, as well as memories about colleagues and many pearls of wit or wisdom had to be left out. I have to take full responsibility for this painful process—perhaps others would have selected other excerpts. I can only invite you to see the 12-hour tapes and select what you want or need. There is plenty for everyone.

This video would never have been possible without the financial backing of the Société Psychanalytique de Montréal and Le Département de l'Enseignement de l'Hôpital Sainte-Justine as well as the support from Jean Baptiste Boulanger, Bruno Cormier, Ruby Cormier, Charles Levin, Sidney Perzow and Evelyn Scott and the secretarial staff, mesdames Gatien, Lalonde and Légaré. However, the main contribution came from the cameramen Roland Duchesne and Jacques Viau. Jacques Viau has transformed into a real audio-visual document what could have remained tape-recorded interviews that we could have listened to with our eyes closed.

I sincerely hope that the complete transcripts of the interviews can be published in book form with a good index, to keep Clifford Scott's contribution alive and well, and be the source of many more papers to come.

Portrait of W.C.M. Scott, Psychoanalyst, is our birthday gift to him as well as his gift to us. Many happy returns to all.

A Portrait of W.C.M. Scott[1] was presented to Dr. Scott on the celebration of his 90th birthday; it is a selection from 12 hours of interviews conducted with Dr. Scott from January 1989 to May 1992. It includes material from his autobiography, his training, his reminiscences of colleagues and his own contribution on depression, sleep and dreams and clinical analysis, envy and reparation and aging.

Note

1. This video can be rented or purchased from: Le Service Audio-visuel Hôpital Sainte-Justine, Centre hospitalier universitaire, 3175 Chemin de la Côte Sainte-Catherine, Montréal, Québec H3T 1C5, Canada. The complete tapes can be borrowed from the Société Psychanalytique de Montréal.

Memories of Dr. W.C.M. Scott[1]

E.G. Debbane

D r. W. Clifford M. Scott died on the 19th of January, 1997, in Montreal, after a brief illness. He would have been 94 in March. On December 31, 1996, he wrote to me, "Today is bright and cheery, the day before New Year's Day. I found a book of poetry and pictures selected by someone I didn't know, nor had I heard of, but it had a peculiar fascination and stimulation for me, and I am sure I will see more of it." I had written to him earlier, wishing him good health. In that same letter, he said, "Thanks, indeed, for your hopes that I am in good health. I am, but only moment to moment, and hour to hour, and not day to day, as I would like to be."

These words are precious to me. They are the last I received from him, also, they represent my experience of him and reverberate into so many memories.

Beauty and the awed relationship we could have with it fascinated him. You could feel the excitement in his voice as he reflected on it. He liked to play with sounds; awe, oh, O. He wondered why Bion selected O. He was fond of repeating the well-known opening song of Oklahoma—noticing "en passant" the O of Oklahoma—Oh, What a Beautiful Morning—and I felt that every time he saw a different version of the beauty of that morning, as I imagine he saw it on December 31, 1996 and, upon reading his words, I could see it, too.

He was curious about the transitions that weave themselves in the back and fro of regressions and progressions. He was extremely visual with a keen sense of light and space. It could be experienced in his living room, which he used as an office in the last few years. He was curious about what I saw and mindful of the difficult and, at times, frustrating transition from pictures to sounds, particularly, those sounds that modulate the pictures of our feelings as they lapse into singing. Why wouldn't I sing, he wondered? He wanted to know how I heard my voice, reminding me of our fascination and intense pleasure at hearing our earliest utterances as they developed into our baby babble, and that became a language; our baby's tongue that wishes to express its wonderment about our incessant discoveries in the Ah! Oh! Eh! and their modulations.

The baby's language for Dr. Scott was the source of our creativity but, then,

Fig. 23. C. Scott (left) with Elie Debanne (middle) and Austin Lee (right) (1994).
Credit: The Estate of W.C.M. Scott

it had to be given up. The babble had to give way to the words of the mother's tongue through an act of love. Dr. Scott felt that the way that happened was very important as we give up the "every thing" and its boundlessness for a sequence of "some" things, hoping to recapture, in these attempts, a picture, a re-presentation of the "every thing." He felt that remnants of that time could be found in those short words that try to capture the "whole" picture, like the Oh of awe. They could be found in the silence between the words and in the evocative power of tonality and punctuation. They also could be in the evanescent beauty of poetry and its pictures. Poetry—I wanted to tell him—is always by someone one does not know. It is the manifestation of that flicker of eternity, our creativity, our genius, that does not want to die despite our repeated attempts to do away with it, to "grow up," more likely, to "grow away."

On December 31, 1996, it was with him, and he was with it. He felt excited by it, and wanted to meet it again, and I felt happy, and sad. I could hear him ask, "Were you sad to be sad, or happy to be sad, or sad to be happy at your sadness?" and that would throw me back to my reflections. I felt my sadness brought me closer to the experience he was conveying to me, and his sadness at the realization of the constriction of time which he so eloquently expressed in the rhythmic punctuation, "moment to moment. . . and hour to hour" and the evanescent "day to day." It was "contained" in the tolerance of the problematic of the ultimate loss, "It is only. . . and not as I would like it to be." I felt he was not about to engage in a futile battle with time, but in the exquisite acceptance of the reality of the moment he was going to experience moment to moment, to the last moment he could tolerate, asking himself and whoever was there, the question that the moment brought, and he would only stop when he would run out of breath, and of the time breath punctuated.

Another circle in the ripple of memories. . . after I moved to Vancouver in 1994, I took advantage of my frequent visits to Montreal to see him and we would talk. He was always interested to find out what I had been thinking about, all the while keeping me informed of what he was reading, wondering if I had read it, and, if I had not, he thought I might find it interesting to read. I remember at the end of such meetings walking away, exhausted, amazed, and full of all kinds of sensations which would eventually germinate into thoughts.

Talking with Dr. Scott was an unusual experience. I could try to illustrate it with the memory of some of our interchanges and what I imagine to be his notion of the creative exchange. The organizing principle that I gathered was in an expanded notion of "free associations." I could not find a substantial difference in the way he talked during analysis or during the course of a conversation or a clinical presentation. In analysis, he used to ask, "Why do you want to think about what you are going to say or about what you are saying?" He was aware that old habits died hard, if ever. He used to say, "As a child you are told to think before you talk, why don't you try to talk before you think?" At other times, he would inquire, "Why are you trying to understand what I am saying?" obviously aware of my efforts at understanding. He also wanted to know why I stopped talking while he was talking, and why it could not take the form of a duo in some form of mutual projective identification which elicited the dread of those moments of comm-union. He referred to the fear of getting lost and not being able to find one's way back into oneself. His was a particular way of talking about transformations which outlined to me an aspect of projective identification, related to a fundamental trust, the capacity to trust with abandon.

I realized that the common thread that ran through these comments, and that I could detect in his conversations with others, as well as my later conversations with him, had to do with the urges of possessiveness, the desire to capture a thought, an idea, a meaning, and, in so doing, to immobilize it, to suffocate it, to prevent it from breathing. The kind of transitionality Dr. Scott was advocating used breathing as a memory/metaphor, a function that represented ongoing transitionalities, and which sustained life. He used to remind me, "You do not have to think about your breathing." Here, he was emphasizing the possessive, controlling, omnipotent phantasy about thinking, our illusions about our consciousness, and our intolerance about our unconsciousness. He frequently preferred to use the notion of awake, or aware, and invited me to think about the differences and implications of these terms and their relationship to consciousness.

With Dr. Scott, there was hardly any small talk; he felt ill at ease with it, and somewhat at a loss. Talking presupposed a desire to question, exchange, and a free exercise of curiosity, and then one had to let oneself be guided by the moment, available to the thoughts that might become available, that he might stimulate, or that might be stimulated in him, all the while trusting that meaning was being exchanged which might only manifest itself later, at times, much later, maybe never. This required a particularly generous disposition, one that had mourned its greed and its envy, and was sadly glad and maybe, later, gladly glad of the opportunities the moment offered. I felt he had achieved such a disposition and, as a result, exuded an intense sense of freedom that allowed for the deployment of a particular mixture of curiosity and enthusiasm. He liked to use the word "zest," which he elaborated as a "notion." His enthusiasm was contagious, he was like a breath of fresh, invigorating air, whose memory remained long after it has been expired.

He was extremely generous with his colleagues and his students. He had the quality of genuine interest. I always felt that his door was open to me, and this feeling was shared by a number of colleagues. He was always available to review or discuss papers, texts, and presentations. His comments were abundant, thoughtful and encouraging. Some of us would ask him to discuss their presentations at the Society's meeting, secretly hoping that he would be presenting that part of the text that was not written, the unthought thoughts of the writer. It frequently turned out to be the case and he did it with humility and a lively sense of pleasure.

I remember our last meeting, and as he was ushering me out in the light of a sunny summer afternoon, he paused for a moment and, with a wistful smile, said, "So, you think you're going to live forever?" his last contribution to my self-analysis. During that meeting, he had been more preoccupied with his thoughts. He had asked me earlier, "Have you ever considered giving up your most important beliefs?" I had the sense of his awareness that some element of possessiveness was interfering with his curiosity and he was left to consider the possibilities of new beginnings. His hesitation might have been his sense of the time that was left to him. He wished to keep alive his fascination with beginnings and how far back their boundary could be extended.

He always wanted to know what was before, what was the first manifestation of a phenomenon, and what was there before it? What was there before the primal scene? What were the phantasies of where that before was? He was equally curious about the end, and the beginning signs signaling the transition between life and death. He encouraged me to think about my own death, as he had been thinking about his for many years. It heightened his realization every morning that he was still alive, another day full with the promises of its realizations, and he reconciled himself every night with the possibility of not waking up again, but waking up again joyful at the prospect of still another day. At a more conceptual level, he felt that there was an important primal phantasy which was not discussed. He referred to it as the death bed scene. He felt it to be an organizing phantasy, at the same level as the primal scene, or the oedipal phantasy, and believed that we live our lives in accordance to the way we have come to terms with our death.

Dr. Scott lived a long and fruitful life. We are left in awe as we imagine his life and the richness of his experiences that spanned this century. With his death, a whole era of psychoanalytic pioneering comes closer to its end. For the many of us who have been fortunate to cross his path, the memory of his extraordinary humanity, the infinite richness of his mind, and his untiring generosity at sharing both, will remain with us, together with the emerging reverberations of the memories of the times spent with him.

Note

1. Published previously in *Correlations*, Seattle. Reprinted with permission.

W.R. Bion – The Individual and the Group: Some Reflections

E.G. Debbane

B ion's work on groups tends to be relegated to his pre-analytical period and segregated from the rest of his contributions. It reflects an ongoing dichotomization between individual and group which has been intro- duced by Freud and questioned by Bion. For this author, these texts seem to inaugurate Bion's psychoanalytical period and contain, in their earlier version, many of the concepts that will be developed later, as well as some that have remained undeveloped. These texts illustrate the freshness of Bion's approach which starts from his experience of the clinical situation and his ongoing obser- vations unfettered by preconceptions. It shows his tolerance of his ignorance and his capacity to be surprised by the phenomena he encountered, both being a stimulus for his thinking, leading to the gradual elaboration of a number of hypotheses that eventually assume the shape of a conceptual framework.

His later notion of "without memory or desire" could be seen at work through his clinical vignettes. They also emphasize the importance of "truth as a criterion." His experience of the clinical phenomenon of projective identifica- tion is vividly illustrated, as well as its impact on his capacity to think. The fear of the possibility of lapse in a psychotic set of part object relations is constantly underlined and energizes the basic assumptions. It previews his later interest in the psychotic mind and his notion of bizarre objects.

Finally, we are left with some preliminary thoughts about psychoanalysis viewed from the perspective of his group dynamics which we might find useful to explore at this point in the history of our profession.

In the course of my meetings with Dr. Clifford Scott, questions about Bion and my interest in his work surfaced many times. In October 1985, he was invited to present at the Los Angeles Psychoanalytical Society at a two-day meeting on Bion's work, and, in May, 1986, at the Canadian Psychoanalytical Society in Montreal, he presented a text entitled, "Who's Afraid of Wilfred

Bion?" in which he said, "One answer is those who fear the truth. . . the naked truth, what babes would say, could they speak. . . could we learn some of their invented language. . ." (Scott, 1986, p. 1) and later, he asked, "When do we begin to lie instead of telling the truth to babies?" (*ibid*). He was also curious about my interest in groups and spoke to me about Trigant Burrow (1875-1950) whose experience with Clarence Shields about mutual analysis led to the development of group analysis "in which members oscillate between being analyst and analysand" (*ibid*, p. 7). The question of mutual analysis is a complex and extensive one. A sense of that complexity could be gathered from Freud's comment in a letter to Foulkes in May, 1932, "To me it appears to be the greatest disappointment in analysis that it does not effect a greater change in the analysts themselves. No one has yet made a subject of study the means by which analysts succeed in evading the influence of analysis on their own person" (Campos, 1992, p. 6). It might have been somewhat disingenuous on Freud's part to have ignored his own contribution to it and the kind of model of the analyst that is portrayed in the technical papers. Nevertheless, this issue is as relevant today as it was in 1932.

Commenting on Bion's contribution to groups, Scott (1986) said, "Bion in his work with 'leaderless' groups made very insightful inroads into group analytic work, but did not continue with groups larger than two" (p. 8). Indeed, we are left mining the richness of his texts on groups. This essay is a further effort in that direction.

I have quoted Bion extensively in this text. I do not believe that my quotations from Bion represent his thinking. He might have said, as he did, "I had no idea what it might be like to be the reader of my books, or, at most, a very imperfect idea" (Grinberg *et al.*, 1975, p. 7). Indeed, these quotations represent my thinking as stimulated by his texts. I have found that as I rearranged some of his statements I was able to see a representation of what I had in my mind with a kind of ongoing reverberation. Bion's capacity to construct sentences in such a way as to allow for ongoing reverberation is unique.

Many authors have alluded to the difficulty inherent in reading Bion's texts. He shares that difficulty with Clifford Scott. Both have offered us texts that do not convey a sense of familiarity. They appear to present us with a language that is difficult to comprehend through the usual language of psychoanalysis. We are not offered interesting variations along familiar thematic lines. We are not given to understand what we have already understood. Scott (1986) believed that the difficulty in reading Bion, and I suspect his own texts as well, could be found in "being stimulated so much that you tolerate being confused before the confusion becomes the simplicity of tolerated complexity" (p. 4).

Reading Bion's clinical seminars and similar texts where transcripts of his interactions with professionals in a quasi group supervisory structure are available, the same phenomenon appears to occur with disconcerting regularity, a question is being asked, an answer is expected, and Bion appears to be attempting to deal with the question as thoroughly as possible. Inevitably, the outcome is more questions about questions that were not raised in the original question. The result is a sense of frustration that is much better masked in a professional audience than in a lay one. This resonates with his statement, "The exasperation. . . is dictated, not so much by the frustration of a legitimate aim, as by the exposure of difficulties the patient has not come to discuss" (Bion, 1949b, p. 297). We are thus invited to consider and reflect upon issues we "have not come to discuss." The new state that appears as we are about to discover the unexpected is the equivalent of waking up to realize that we were under "the dream hallucination of a wish fulfilling object" (Scott, 1986, p. 5), and we are now confronted upon waking with the discovery of a no-thing. The intolerance of that state of affairs is compared by Scott to "the baby go(ing) to pieces to some degree in anger at the new state of affairs and destroy(ing) the beginning of symbolization, destroy(ing) the symbol of the thought of, or experience of, no-thing" (*ibid*).

Indeed, the reader has not come to be confronted with the creative potential of a no-thing. Like in the group illustrated by Bion, the reader is full of "desire," desire to be authoritatively told something about something, which might preclude any further need to think about it. Bion was fond of quoting the French author, Blanchot, "la réponse est la mort de la question" (the answer is the death of the question) (Bion, 1978, pp. 21-22). Meltzer (1978) suggested that ". . . For the stressfulness of reading his work. . . is to be found in identification processes, that is, identification with members of the group he is treating (and in later papers with his patients in analysis) and in failure of identification with Bion himself" (p. 7). Identification with Bion would require a position of being without memory or desire in order to be available to the possibility of an experience. Later, in his writings, Bion (1967) would elaborate on the difficulties inherent in the position of "without memory or desire" and its experiential concomitant that might make it intolerable for the analyst, thus, illustrating the difficulties in identification with him and the possibility of identification with his patient as an alternative and a regressive solution. Likewise, the nature of the difficulty presented by these texts might stimulate an attempt at a regressive solution which precludes the possibility of learning from experience. Bion is not particularly interested in the "learning about" which he characterized much later in terms of our capacity to mimic or imitate, both of which do not necessitate development. For Bion, development is the outcome of "learning from," essentially, learning from experience. The reader then is not

going to learn from Bion about groups, psychoanalysis, etc. He might learn
from his experience and the ongoing reflections on his experience as stimulated
by Bion's texts. This whole process is not unlike the analytical process with
Bion providing elements for self-analysis as well as elements for reflection on
psychoanalysis.

My comments are reflections on Bion's texts, particularly "Experiences in
Groups" and "Group Dynamics: A Re-view." Meltzer (1978) viewed these
texts as pre-analytical. He contrasted them with his later analytical work when
he said, "to distinguish it from the technique and mode of thoughts he developed from the special experience of psychoanalysis" (p. 6). He concludes the
chapter on these texts by saying, "the aim was to draw a baseline of the pre-
analytical Bion" (*ibid*, p. 11). While I find a great deal to agree with in these
statements, I tend to favor Grinberg (1975) who talks about rediscovering "the
conducting thread of his [Bion's] original concepts through his writings and
early papers on group dynamics" (p. 9). I shall allude to some of these threads
while struggling with the complexity of Bion's conceptualization of the reciprocal relationship between the individual and the group.

The issue of the individual and the group might be viewed as an esoteric
one or, at best, a theoretical issue that pertains more to philosophy or sociology
than to psychoanalysis. As analysts, we have been reticent to consider the
relationship of the individual to the group as pertinent to our field. At best, we
have viewed it as an instance of applied psychoanalysis. This has been consistent with Freud's impetus. Although he devoted a number of major texts to the
elucidation of group behavior, he presented that aspect of his work either as a
validation of insights that became available to him from the analytical situation,
or as further proof of their applicability. Bion (1955) characterizes Freud's
ambiguous position by stating, "He postulates an individual outside the primitive group who possessed his own continuity, his self-consciousness, his tradi-
tions and customs. . . (and) that, owing to his entry into an unorganized group,
the individual had lost his distinctiveness for a time" (p. 462). Freud's particular perspective, as outlined by Bion, has left its imprint on psychoanalysis as a
practice, as a theory, and as an organization. It was mentioned earlier in
reference to Freud's comment to Foulkes and will be elaborated further later in
this text.

We might, at times, entertain the phantasy of unimpeded individual distinctiveness that remains unaffected in spite of our inevitable membership in different groups. It could be found in the notion of the "self made man." Bion does
not agree with the postulate of an "individual outside the primitive group,"
indeed, it begs the question, where does he or she come from? is he/she self
made? In fact, contrary to Freud's query whether group psychology antedates

individual psychology, Bion (1951) proposes a totally different perspective, "The apparent difference between group psychology and individual psychology is an illusion produced by the fact that the group provides an intelligible field of study for certain aspects of individual psychology" (p. 225). His first account of that "illusion" is phenomenological, "This congregation of the group. . . has no significance whatsoever in the production of group phenomena. The idea that it has, springs from the erroneous impression that a thing must necessarily commence at the moment when its existence becomes demonstrable" (*ibid*, p. 224). His dynamic account of that "illusion" is both complex and revolutionary, "In his contact with the complexities of life in a group the adult resorts, in what may be a massive regression; to mechanisms. . . typical of the earliest phases of mental life" (1955, p. 440). He further states that, "The belief that a group exists, as distinct from an aggregate of individuals, is an essential part of this regression. . ., substance is given to the phantasy that the group exists by the fact that the regression involves the individual in a loss of his 'individual distinctiveness,' indistinguishable from depersonalization. . ." (*ibid*).

The notion of "contact" appears to me as a precursor of his later notion of "links" and "linking." There is an assumed relationship between the ability to "contact" and the perceived capacity to tolerate and contain "the complexities of life in a group." The incapacity to tolerate the complexity of that situation leads to a regressive solution through con-fusion and its concomitant un-linking activity. Hence, the individual not only feels disconnected from other individuals, but also from himself. This situation is fundamentally different from the individual in a cooperative relationship with other individuals. The group that the individual constructs in his regression can be made to assume a variety of relationships to the individual, from the narcissistic omnipotent to the schizoid, to the paranoid, to the depressive. Thus, sitting in the group, the individual might feel alternatively helpless, recourseless, isolated like an island in the midst of a congregation of islands, or the object of relentless and potentially devastating intrusions, or in the grip of unfathomable losses.

The novelty and boldness of Bion's formulation elicits a sense of disbelief as he seems to assert that:

1. the group is an illusion created by individuals who, when confronted with the complexities of life in a group, regress
2. there is no such thing as a group that would be distinct from an aggregate of individuals except as a phenomenon produced by the regression of individuals.

To compound the difficulty, Bion reverses the perspective and raises the possibility of "individuals composing a 'group'. . ., (individuals all in the same state of regression). . . (who). . . become threatened by awareness of their individual distinctiveness, then the group is in the emotional state known as panic" (*ibid*, p. 441). To share the illusion of the group through regression requires the abandonment of "individual distinctiveness." Its re-emergence is a clear threat to the groupishness shared by the individuals and threatens the very existence of the group. So, there could be such a thing as a shared illusion called a group, but then "individual distinctiveness" is a clear threat to its stability and its existence. In fact, individuals as part of a group attribute little value to the individual, "the individual feels that in a group the welfare of the individual is a matter of secondary consideration" (Bion, 1949a, p. 16) and, "individual distinctiveness is no part of life in a group acting on the basic assumption" (1951, p. 226). This may be due to the fact that the individual cannot dispense from membership in a group, and again Bion (1949b) provides both a descriptive and a dynamic explication when he states, "In the group, the individual becomes aware of capacities which are only potential so long as he is in comparative isolation" (p. 302). He then elaborates, "An individual in a group is more than an individual in isolation. The additional potentialities activated by membership in the group are. . . best adapted for function in the basic assumption group" (*ibid*).

But then, what is meant by basic assumptions, a group suffused by basic assumptions or a basic assumption group, and are basic assumptions a characteristic of the individual or of the group? Although Bion refers to basic assumption groups, one might be misled into believing in the existence of such an "aggregate of individuals" constituting a "group." One is reminded that in each case it is about a mentality, frequently unconscious, about an emotional drive seeking satisfaction. Regarding whether basic assumption mentality is a function of the group or of the individual, Bion (1955) states, "Basic assumption group functions are active before ever a group comes together in a room, and continue after the group has dispersed" (p. 463). Again, the gathering of the group is only necessary to demonstrate the existence of these functions in the individual which remain at the level of potentialities as long as he is in relative isolation. As to what basic assumptions might be, at a descriptive level, basic assumptions could be said to be emotional states that become revealed as a tacit, shared understanding about the existence of wishes that have taken the shape of a need about to be fulfilled. At a more abstract level, Bion describes them as. . . "mental activities which have in common the attribute of powerful emotional drives" (*ibid*, p. 444). This is a puzzling statement, namely, what is the relationship between a mental activity and an emotional drive? We are more familiar from the dualistic perspective initiated by Freud to consider mental activities as separate from emotional drives, even though never free from their influence. This follows what Bion described as Freud's assumption of an "individual outside the primitive group" or as an ego structurally separate from the primitive group, i.e., the drives. Bion allows for a much more complex relationship. Here, to extend Bion's comment to its limit, it appears as if an emotional drive would, at times, take the disguise of a mental activity. Bion proposes a sequence which will be more fully elaborated in his later work, "Ideas existed, invested with reality by force of the emotion attached to them" (*ibid*). The strength of the emotional drive invades and subverts the idea from the inside, it precludes the development of the idea, as an idea, i.e., the required transformation of the dream elements through alpha processes. It has only preserved the external presentation of an idea. It might sound like an idea, be phrased like an idea, but it is not an idea. It is one of those elements that are not suitable for elaboration through "reverie," but are only suitable for discharge, what Bion later described as beta elements. He says, "The basic assumption can only be understood if the words. . . are taken as literal, not metaphorical" (*ibid*).

Bion (1949b) illustrates a particular aspect of the function of emotional drive that could be summarized in terms of "the drive knows" or, in Bion's words, "arriving fully equipped, fitted by instinct to know without training or development. . ." (p. 302). In the arrangement of this particular sequence Bion offers the juxtaposition of instinct and knowledge. Instincts for their expression presupposes the unfolding of a sequence that includes their object. It could be said that the instinct minds its object, i.e., that it has a preconception which, given certain conditions, will sequentially unfold. That sequence itself would require a certain amount of mentation (thinking) for its execution. Bion contrasts this kind of knowledge, i.e., without training, with the knowledge that develops out of experience (subsequent to the vicissitudes of "contact" with reality, and the reality of objects, i.e., training). That statement also represents the saturation of the mind by its desire, and, by the same token, its unavailability to know through learning, as it already knows what there is to know. It would stand to reason that there is an "inability of the basic assumption group to tolerate development" (Bion, 1955, p. 451). This is in keeping with the classical notion of the drive as seeking discharge. Development as presented in these texts implies the ability to learn from experience. "Arriving fully equipped, fitted by instinct" preempts the possibility of learning, as, again, emotional drive is constrained in the linearity of stimulation/discharge. Bion's use of the notion of emotional drive is more in keeping with Melanie Klein's view of instinctual development than Freud's, and is close to Isaac's notion of the phantasy as the mental representative of the drives. Although at the time of "Experiences in Groups", Bion does not assume any evident Kleinian affiliation, the theoretical

perspective that he expounds is essentially so. Klein has described the fundamental importance of the object in the interplay between drive and object, but
also for the modulation, combination and potential integration of different
opposing and contradictory part object relationships. In Freud, this integration
is the outcome of a relatively successful resolution of the oedipal constellation
and the establishment of the superego. In Klein, it is to be found much earlier
in the emergence of the depressive position and the concomitant change of
balance between projective and introjective processes.

There is a fundamental difference between Freud and Klein in their understanding of projection. With Freud, the destiny of what is projected is not
theorized in its objectal ramifications, only in its subjectal one. Klein introduces
the notion of projection into an object, but also the projection of the part of the
ego linked to what is projected. She unwittingly provided an expanded definition of the individual; however, she did not elaborate it beyond its implications
in the transference situation. It was Bion's contribution that vastly modified and
redefined projective identification. The foundation of his later notion on projective identification could be found in "Experiences in Groups" with their characteristic malleability and pervasiveness. The differentiation between self and
object becomes less clear cut, less stable and more fluid than usually described.
One of the effects of the regression that accompanies membership in a group
"involves the individual in a loss of his individual distinctiveness indistinguishable from depersonalization" (*ibid*, p. 440). Thus, to the introjective identifications elaborated by Freud, Klein, and, in particular, Bion, have added the
projective identifications. To the extent that projective identification implies the
projection of a part of the ego with its functions, there is a part of the individual's mind that lies somewhere in the other, or in the group. This notion is
further elaborated in Bion's subsequent work. At this point in Bion's theorization, it is expressed in terms of "There is a matrix of thought which lies within
the confines of the basic group, but not within the confines of the individual"
(1949b, p. 303). Hence, the individual viewed solely "in isolation," that is to
say, from the perspective of his introjective identifications, is incomplete. The
missing parts are to be found in his projective identifications that are located in
his "group," the progressive extension of the original pair. The totality of the
individual then has to include both his introjective as well as his projective
identifications. This introduces a central and fundamental difference in our
description and definition of the individual. This difference has not been
sufficiently appreciated and although the concept of projective identification has
gained much wider acceptance and has been the object of many discussions, its
implications from the perspective of the individual's relation to the group have
not been fully explored. This includes Bion's statements about the "additional

potentialities activated by membership of the group" (*ibid*, p. 302).

In his discussion of the basic assumption group, Bion presents projective identification innocuously enough in terms of the "individual's anonymous contributions" (1948b, p. 492). All the members of the group contribute anonymously. These anonymous contributions are pooled to constitute a group mentality, a kind of group mind. As these contributions are anonymous, they are disavowed and split from their owners, it is as if they have a separate existence. Indeed, the belief that they might have had a separate existence is to be found in the notion of the herd instinct or in what Jung formulated as the collective unconscious. For Bion, this is an illusion, a proof of the successful disowning of the individual of parts of his emotional drives. The notion that part of the individual's emotional drives are disowned and located in the group provides an important perspective for the understanding of the individual's relationship to the group.

A related belief is that the anonymous nature of these contributions renders their effect negligible or becomes somebody else's responsibility. Bion tries to demonstrate that these anonymous contributions are not only ever present and active, they also form the basis of what the individual is complaining about. The therapist is recruited to take responsibility of these anonymous contributions and get blamed for their activity, but this, too, is a blind alley; nevertheless, it afforded Bion the opportunity to experience their impact and might have been at the origin of his reflections on projective identification. Bion (1948a) suggests that, as a member of the group, "we are constantly affected by what we feel to be the attitude of the group to ourselves, and are consciously or unconsciously swayed by the idea of it" (p. 315).

Another aspect of Bion's notion of anonymous contributions is that they are constituted of the individual's drive aspects which are evacuated in the group situation. Thus, the drive configuration of the individual is a split one, one part is anonymously contributed, disowned, and evacuated in the group, and another part is acknowledged by the individual with the constant possibilities of conflict between the two. The group then is an essential structure for the individual that allows him to come in contact with those aspects of drives that have been split off and deposited in the group.

The notion of the impact of the patient on the analyst, although widely accepted at present, was quite novel at the time. It signaled a major shift from Freud, introduced by the realization of projective identification and its consequences. Freud's early definitions of transference and countertransference and his particular definition of neutrality, emphasized the position of the analyst as, "an individual outside of the primitive group," relatively immune from contamination or suggestion. In Bion, the focus has shifted. Neutrality is not in identifying with a reflective surface, but in a position that is as close as possible to "without memory or desire" (Bion, 1967). Indeed, the analyst provides the space created by "without memory or desire" where the patient's projections could lodge. Thus, frequently, the analyst encounters what the patient has deposited through the fluctuating awareness of what he feels or the way he is being affected. The notion that the evidence is frequently to be found in the countertransference, which Bion (1955) mentioned with some trepidation in "Group Dynamics: A Re-view," becomes much more clearly established later on in his analysis of psychotics. The reservations that he expressed then when he said, "It can be justly argued that interpretations for which the strongest evidence lies, not in the observed facts in the group but in the subjective reactions of the analyst, are more likely to find their explanation in the psychopathology of the analyst than in the dynamics of the group" (p. 446) seems to have been attenuated by his realization that "the analyst in the group. . . is at the receiving end of ... projective identification" (ibid).

Bion attempts to describe the experience of being at the receiving end of projective identification, "the analyst. . . feels he is being manipulated so as to be playing a part. . . in somebody else's phantasy" (ibid). He further divides this experience into "two closely related phases; in the first there is a feeling that. . . one has certainly not given a correct interpretation; in the second, there is a sense of being a particular kind of person in a particularly emotional situation. I believe ability to shake one's self out of the numbing feeling of reality that is a concomitant of this state is the prime requisite of the analyst in the group" (ibid). Here, Bion refers to the subjective experience of being at the receiving end of projecting identification. He also alludes to the ease with which one can slip into it and its effects, i.e., "a numbing experience," reflecting the inability to think through, to transform what is intrusively projected, and, instead, feel immobilized by it. Bion also raises the question of how to manage the situation of "being at the receiving end." He subtly alludes to the analyst's valency in the dependent assumption mentality, i.e., the analyst's underlying belief in his curative abilities, superior wisdom, and knowledge about how the individual should conduct his/her life. It indicates the necessity of drawing a difference between receiving, i.e., partaking on the one hand, and becoming aware of on the other. This is described by Bion through the notion of "shaking oneself out of. . . ." This is abstinence in relation to projective identification. It relates to what will later be described in the notion of "without memory or desire." It is from this position of without desire that the analyst can make the observation of what is happening to him, what is done to him, and its origin in the individual or in the group. It is the working through of these observations that lead to interpretations.

The group mentality, the caldron of disavowed emotional drives, is constantly active in a kind of subterranean turmoil, but also constantly shifting, a rather unstable entity. It represents the coalescence of the individual's disavowed anonymous contributions. "It is thus a machinery of inter-communication which is designed to ensure that group life is in accordance with the basic assumption" (Bion, 1949a, p. 16), that is to say, the fulfillment of "powerful emotional drives." This is the beginning of Bion's later development of the notion of projective identification as a "machinery of intercommunication" but also as a way to manage "powerful emotional drives." Also, the group mentality represents "the unanimous expression of the will of the group, contributed to by the individual in ways of which he is unaware. . ." (ibid., p. 13). Its predominance always poses a danger for the individual for his individualness, but also for his perception of reality.

We are already presented with a multifaceted conception of projective identification which, at this pre-analytical (Meltzer) period of Bion contains on one hand all the basic ingredients of his further elaborations and is both an extension of Klein's description and includes diverging elements. The novel elements introduced by Bion include: a) the notion of projective identification into a group and its impact; b) the effect of these anonymous contributions on the individual and their possible expression through symptoms; and, c) the numbing effect of projective identification and its effect on the capacity to think. These different aspects might have drawn his attention to the vicissitudes of thinking for the members of the group and his awareness of his own difficulty to think when he was too much at variance with the mentality of the members of the group. The question of whether an individual can think "outside" of a group, is answered by Bion (1951) in the negative, "No individual, however isolated in time and space, can be regarded as outside a group or lacking in active manifestations of group psychology" (p. 224). The numbing effect described by Bion affects the capacity to represent and symbolically elaborate. There is the constant risk of the introjection of projective identification, versus the capacity to make use of them as an experience of the other or of a situation, i.e., as one of the most intimate modes of communication and a particularly powerful one in the communication between one unconscious to the other.

In the first chapters of Experiences in Groups, we are privileged to observe glimpses of Bion's working through of the emotional situation in the group. These texts are much less condensed than his subsequent writings. Indeed, the members of the group develop the idea that Bion is mostly preoccupied with himself and, although they expect everything to come from him, they also resent the fact that he analyzes it as such, i.e., transferentially.

Experiences in Groups is essentially a clinical text. Its beginning illustrates the function of preconception, starting with the simplest one, namely, that Bion is an "expert" in group psychotherapy. This preconception is followed by subsequent ones, namely, that his "expertise" would correspond to the unstated and unformulated belief by the members of the group about what group therapy ought to be, and, although they could not state what, in fact, that is, it appears that Bion's notion does not correspond to theirs. He says, "The group is not concerned to understand the point of what I say, but rather to make use only of such parts of my contribution as they can conveniently weld into what appear to be an already established corpus of belief" (1949b, p. 298). The situation that he presents at the beginning of his text is an illustration of saturation by desire. From his clinical illustrations, one can gather the limited capacity that the members have left to themselves for the apprehension of the new situation, as their desire that is represented by a corpus of belief only wishes to be re-cognized and real-ized, even though, and at the same time, it is perceived that the wished for realization of that "corpus of belief" could have disastrous consequences. Bion appears to have been impressed by the extent to which desire is represented by beliefs that obliterate the possibility of thinking about something that is not oriented to the realization of that desire.

The situation as described is not particular to individuals starting a group therapy. It also permeates other situations and, as well, the group of analysts in their practice of psychoanalysis, who might be analogous to the members of Bion's group, i.e., saturated by their preconception of what should develop within the psychoanalytical situation. At that stage, Bion appears to differenti-ate knowledge that represents the concretization of a wish from the knowledge that is derived from the experience of the emotions and their reflective elabora-tion. Later, he would develop his conception of knowledge as part of the context love, hate and knowledge (L, H, K) (1962). Bion's ability to direct all his attention to the observation of a situation as it unfolds, while withholding his own preconceptions, is remarkable. It is also fundamental to the unfolding of the reflective elaboration of his observation. The abstractive elaboration of these observations lead to the beginning articulations of a model.

The gradual establishment of the functions of the depressive position brings an increased awareness of the object. The depressive position is essential in the process of learning from experience as it brings the realization of the dual nature of the object (i.e., the good and the bad object are one and the same) but also of its separate existence and its vital importance for the subject. Its preservation becomes paramount and the attacks on the object have to be mourned and repaired to prevent its loss for the subject and something has to be created out of what has been destroyed. "Learning from Experience" is a feature of the depressive position as it implies contact with reality and the capacity to differentiate internal from external and be present to both. It is minimal in the paranoid-schizoid position characterized, among many things, by a predominance of projections and projective identifications, with an ego that has not yet been structured by the experience of its losses. The essential "Learning from Experience" is a function of what Bion described as the work group, which is based on cooperation, an outcome of the depressive position. The work group is aware of the passage of time, it is reality and task oriented, scientific in its approach, and based on cooperation among the members of the group. Bion likened the work group to Freud's description of ego functions. The work group mentality is a necessity. Because of its capacity to apprehend the reality that is not obliterated by superimposed wishes and desires, it can accept the difference between the two realities. It protects both the individual and the group from action that would be based on the direct expression of the basic assumption mentality. Bion (1950a) says, "It is almost as if human beings were aware of the painful and often fatal consequences of having to act without an adequate grasp of reality, and therefore were aware of the need for truth as a criterion in the evaluation of their findings" (p. 7). Acting on the basic assumption mentality requires taking one's wishes for reality, that is to say, obliterating one's perceptual field by the projections of one's desires, falsification and the belief in a lie. I suspect that this is the first use of the notion of "truth as a criterion." These particular aspects of Bion's conceptualization, "truth as a criterion," and "lying," were greatly expanded in his subsequent work. Some have suggested that Bion's later use of the notion of truth was somewhat mystical. His subsequent work on the understanding of psychosis alludes to the psychotic's hate of reality and the truth that it reveals which is resolved by his attack on the apparatus that allows him to perceive it, that is to say, his mind.

Truth, here, is presented in the context of an optimal balance between the part of the group that is oriented to the reality of the situation and the part that is oriented to the reality of the emotional drive and under the sway of the basic assumption. There is some resemblance to Freud's notion of the ego as a mediator between reality and the id; however, in Bion, the configuration is fundamentally different. It already prefaces his later elaborations on the relationship between container and contained.

The relationship between the basic assumption and the work group is both complementary and problematic. It is complementary as long as the basic assumption remains in the background of the work group mentality and serves to provide its drive. This is not unlike the Freudian formulation of the ego deriving its cathexis from the id. However, in the context of continuous movement between foreground and background, there is the possibility of different configurations of basic assumption and work group. It is problematic, as the coexistence of basic assumption and work group mentality is, at the same time, essential, unavoidable and conflictual. Essential, as when Bion (1948b) says ". . . group mental life is essential to the full life of the individual. . . satisfaction of this need has to be sought through membership of a group" (p. 493). "Powerful emotional drives" require a group, whether actual or phantasmatic, for their satisfaction. Unavoidable, as when Bion (1949b) says, "Man is hopelessly committed to both states of affairs" (p. 302), that is to say, basic assumption and development through the work group. It is conflictual when he says, "The individual. . . as being in some way opposed to the group mentality although a contributor to it" (*ibid*, p. 493). In a more humorous vein, he says, "Liberal thinkers of recent times have been disposed to argue that emotions and reason are easily harmonized" (1951, p. 223).

Bion appears to have restated Freud's notion of the relationship of the ego to its emotional drive, whereby, Freud views the ego as a mediator, Bion sees it more in a reciprocal transformational relationship with the drive, as in the relationship of container/contained, both being transformed by their interaction. The danger that Bion identified in *Experiences in Groups* is the possibility of acting on the basic assumptions. It is the main fear of the members of the group. The danger exists because the "powerful emotional drives" are in no position to appreciate the external reality and to differentiate it from the internal one. They confuse them. Appreciation of reality is a function of the work group mentality. Its central ingredient is its experience in and its capacity to tolerate absence and losses, allowing for the exercise of its capacity to think.

The connection between absence and thinking was expressed in reverse by Freud when he referred to thinking as trial action; however, it implied the successful resolution of the "absence" of gratification. The capacity to think requires a particular relationship to "memory and desire," a state of temporary suspension that is neither its destruction nor its obstruction, thus allowing the thinking apparatus to become available to the perception of thoughts. This later led Bion to postulate the autonomy of thoughts from the thinker and his description of thoughts without a thinker. In this perspective, the thinker provides the container and, according to the state of his relationship to his "powerful emotional drives," the capacity to think. Thus, the thought, as expressed by the thinker, is a composite container/content and a function of their relationship. It is only one of the possible presentations of the thought and there remain thoughts awaiting a thinker with the capacity to think them.

Although Bion's discourse in these texts is about the group situation, he affords us the opportunity to reflect on the earliest elaborations of his understanding of the analytical situation and its dynamics. He appears to be interested in continuities between different situations, and their capacities to reveal varied and complementary aspects. The group situation could then reveal certain aspects of the dyadic situation that are only potentially present in the latter. As well, the dyadic situation reveals aspects of the individual that could not be otherwise available. Bion's notion of reverse perspective and his advice to "see the reverse as well as the obverse of every situation" (1949b, p. 300) should allow the analyst to constantly shift perspective and focus. The therapeutic relationship is full of both unknown and desire. The unknown brings with it the possibility of something new, something that cannot be recognized as having been there before, and that cannot be dealt with by using one's memory of previous instances. In the context of the work group, the individual would have to admit it doesn't know as well as the feelings connected with the state of ignorance. Because of his difficulty to tolerate an empty space, the individual might endeavor to fill it by any means. Ignorance can then be replaced by false knowledge and this is amply illustrated by Bion. This situation exists for both members of the analytical dyad. Applied to ourselves as members of the group, it should lead us to question our use of "wishful" knowledge and how much of it permeates our conceptions and beliefs. Bion suggested the necessity to consider the possibility that "our theories are a kind of space filling elaboration ... indistinguishable from a paramnesia" (1976, p. 229). Thus, the unknown can be short lived and be replaced by paramnesias. Another possibility in the face of increased or intolerable frustration, vis a vis what is unknown, is the individual's acting on the wish to get rid of the unknown and the apparatus that makes him aware of it. The unknown has become a bad object that can only be dealt with through evacuation. Bion noticed that the members of the group appeared to be concerned about the realization of something that they energetically tried to prevent.

In the therapeutic situation, the unknown is immediately filled by desire waiting to be fulfilled. It is filled by phantasies, ideas, which, when saturated with desire, assume the strength of a fact, not the kind of fact from which the observer can take some distance, but the fact that constitutes belief. Bion makes this point when he says, "It has been difficult for an individual member to convey meanings to the group which are other than those which the group wishes to entertain" (1948a, p. 318). The same holds true in the analytical situation where the analyst might find it difficult to convey meanings other than those which the analysand wishes to entertain (and vice-versa). This sheds a different light on the notion of resistance, indeed, Bion might have assumed that the individuals in the group were resisting interpretations, which they were. He might have looked for a different way of tackling the resistance; instead, he became interested in their beliefs and the underlying compulsion to hold on to them, as if they were aware of some potentially catastrophic outcome were they to abandon them. He illustrates this when he says, "They are determined to believe that experience of a group taken by myself is valuable, in spite of their observations so far" (*ibid*, p. 316). This belief seems to structure a protective fence against a kind of free fall into the chaotic world of part object relationships, leading to object disintegration and no-thing-ness. Bion (1955) seems to conclude that the basic assumptions operate against the fear of spiraling regression into the world of part object relationships. In the classical psychoanalytic situation, this kind of regression exists only potentially. It is more clearly available in the analysis of borderline disorders and in the analysis of psychotics. It follows that Bion's next interest turned out to be the psychoanalytic understanding of the psychotic's mind.

Bion views the psychoanalytical situation as not only related to individual psychology, but also to the psychology of a pair. He says, "Psychoanalysis. . . can be regarded not only as taking part in the investigation of one mind by another, but also of investigating the mentality of a pair" (1949a, p. 15). The first part of Bion's statement excludes the consideration of the inevitable regressive movements that occur in a group. It only refers to his notion of an "aggregate of individual," in this case, two individuals. It encompasses the classical view that accounts for the development of the transference by an individual, its analysis by the other who remains aware of the influence and the impact of the former through continuous self-analysis. This implies that regression affects only one member of the pair. The necessity to take into consideration phenomena that develop within the context of a pair and affect both parties is stated by Bion in terms of "but also investigating the mentality of a pair" (*ibid*).

Bion (1955) has suggested that Freud's understanding of groups has evolved from his experience of psychoanalysis. He offers a preliminary view from the reverse perspective, ". . . and psychoanalysis, in the light of my experience of groups, can be regarded as a work group likely to stimulate the basic assumption of pairing. That being so, psychoanalytic investigation, as itself a part of a pairing group, is likely to reveal sexuality in a central position, further, it is likely to be attacked itself as sexual activity" (*ibid*, p. 466).

The relationship between the predominant basic assumption mentality and the work group one is constantly oscillating. Thus, the basic assumption can at times provide the work group with its drive and, at others, obstruct the work group through contaminating its aim or proposing itself as the aim, as in the idea of continuing to meet in the hope of keeping hope as a hope or, as Bion suggested, "Only by remaining a hope does hope persist" (*ibid*, p. 448). The lack of psychological "work" is explained away, as it might endanger the overall atmosphere of "hopeful expectation," (*ibid*, p. 447) which is the main affect of the pairing basic assumption. This also alludes to another feature common to all basic assumptions, namely, their disregard for the passage of time.

The interconnectedness of all basic assumptions suggest an ongoing state of relationship between them where they could either act as a precursor to or a defense against each other. The pairing assumption that is stimulated in the psychoanalytical situation is, according to Bion, both "a precursor of sexuality and a part of it" (ibid). It allows for the exploration of sexuality in its central position but also keeps at bay elements of the other's basic assumptions, particularly the fight-flight mentality. Bion has implicitly indicated a relationship between the pairing and the fight-flight assumptions when he suggested that the pairing mentality implies "a person or idea that will save the group—in fact, from feelings of hatred, destructiveness, and despair" (ibid, p. 448). Freud might have implicitly recognized this underlying dynamic when he delimited the classical indications of the psychoanalytical method to the so called transference neurosis, excluding from that situation those who did not seem to readily develop a transference relationship with a predominance of sexual themes. To the extent that the classical understanding of transference emphasized these themes, it excluded the conditions which were under the sway of the fight-flight assumption and where other themes predominate, particularly, "hatred, destructiveness, and despair" (ibid). In that context, "emotional support is obtained of such proposals as express hatred of all psychological difficulty or alternatively, the means by which it can be evaded" (ibid, p. 449). This covers the whole spectrum of the borderline conditions which have come to represent today's problematic condition the way hysteria represented it a century ago (Green, 1977). The borderline patients constitute an ongoing challenge in our attempt to involve them in a psychoanalytical or even a psychotherapeutic endeavor. The consideration of borderline conditions for analytical therapy have forced upon us a reconsideration of the psychoanalytical situation and the problems raised by the predominance of a fight-flight mentality with the concomitant difficulty of establishing a pairing assumption that is not contaminated by "hate, destructiveness, and despair" (Bion, 1955, p. 448). It has reoriented our emphasis on the person of the analyst and his ongoing relationship with himself, which has become the focus of the sustaining pairing assumption mentality that hopes to eventually contain the hateful and destructive attacks of the analysand.

Bion has emphasized the importance of the underlying pairing assumption in sustaining the psychoanalytical enterprise, particularly the affect of "hopeful expectations" but also of the "messianic idea that occupies a central position" (ibid, p. 466). The specialness of each member of the pair permeates the analytical situation. The analyst is in the position of an "exalted parent" (ibid, p. 455). While the "individual patient is worth the analyst's very considerable devotion" (ibid, p. 467), together, as a pair, they function as an aristocratic sub-group. Bion suggests that "In the pairing group, the aristocratic sub-group allows exalted parents wedlock and palatial crib, but the child is notable only in being one of us" (*ibid*, p. 455). However, in the course of analysis and because of the working group function of the analytical situation, "we also indicate (and provoke, albeit unintentionally) primitive behavior" (Bion, 1980, p. 12) which might stimulate a shift in the direction of "hate, destructiveness, and despair" (Bion, 1955, p. 448).

Bion seems to suggest an ongoing, uneasy relationship between pairing and fight-flight assumption in the psychoanalytical situation. As analysts, we prefer to work within the boundaries of an underlying pairing assumption. We might choose to exclude from our practices these conditions that are more suffused with a fight-flight mentality or, more frequently, utilize the pairing assumption to placate the fight-flight mentality. Alternatively, we might develop technical modalities that prevent regression and/or attempt to superimpose a pairing mentality. Finally, we might deny the continuous existence of a potentially destructive situation and allow ourselves to be lulled by the quietness of our setting. This is underscored by Bion when he suggests, "When two personalities meet, an emotional storm is created" (1979, p. 247) and then, "The problem is how to make the best of it, how to turn the adverse circumstances ... to good account" (*ibid*). This particular definition of the psychoanalytical situation takes more into account its potential disruptiveness for both parties. To illustrate the challenges of psychological work in the context of a fight-flight mentality, Bion uses a war analogy, "In war, the enemy's object is so to terrify you that you cannot think clearly while your object is to continue to think clearly, no matter how adverse or frightening the situation" (*ibid*, p. 248). He might have added a new parameter to the "impossible profession" by emphasizing its dangerousness. Indeed, as we set up an analytical situation, we implicitly accept to make ourselves vulnerable and exposed to unforeseen dangers, "Analyst and analysand are alone in the same room. . . they are still dangerous animals" (1980, p. 12). The consequences to the analyst of such an ongoing exposure have only been peripherally addressed, or addressed within a limited context. Bion has provided a more general framework when he said, "None of us can be free from hatred of analysis and the analytic experience, whether it is engendered by our own knowledge and experience or whether by the sort of thing which is said to us by a patient who wears his id outside and his ego and superego tucked away inside" (*ibid*, p. 28). This comment addresses some aspects of the previously quoted comment by Freud in his letter to Foulkes. It also highlights the extent to which our perspective of the analytical situation has been dominated earlier on by the notion of "an individual outside the primitive group" which became translated into an analyst "outside" (i.e., independent of) the analysis of his analysand, and later as we came to consider the analytical pair and their relationship, our focus has been dominated by the pairing and dependent basic assumption mentalities to the exclusion of the fight-flight one, its emergence signaled a fault in the procedure or a contra-indication to it. Thus, while it is inconceivable in theory to imagine an analytical situation that does not deal with the individual's "hatred of all psychological difficulty and/or alternatively the means by which it can be evaded" (Bion, 1955, p. 449), such eventuality is seldom discussed as an ongoing aspect of the analyst's difficulty in the analytical situation.

The implications of Bion's statement regarding the "hatred of analysis and the analytical experience" (1980, p. 28) should concern the group of analysts organized as "societies." The fact that it has seldom been discussed suggests either a collective disbelief of its existence or its attribution to only certain cases or certain instances. It highlights the difficulty of taking some distance from the idealizing potentialities provided by the dominant pairing assumption. This is reinforced by the fact that the dyadic situation provides an easy exit from the difficulties of the "society" group so that the difficulties experienced in the "society" group can be avoided by a sustained and enforced idealization of the dyadic situation. This leaves no "place" where the difficulties in the dyadic relationship could be explored. For individual analysts, there is the question of the nature of the shifts that take place as he/she moves from the dyadic clinical situation to the larger group situation of his/her "society" and comes in contact with a variety of different dynamics that belong to the larger group and where the ongoing manifestations of pairing mentality assume a different form than in groups of two. It frequently takes the form of subtle, ideological differences that serve to structure and separate the different sub-groups. Ideology is frequently linked with filiation which brings into existence a number of "aristocratic" sub-groups, some closer to the ascending ideology, others in a position of exile, and still others in relationship to a more illustrious past. The underlying pairing assumption mentality that is activated in the sub-groups is manifested in each of them by their allegiance to a "messianic" idea that carries with it the belief that it represents the future, the coming of the new order, that will ensure the survival of the group, provide the solution to its difficulty, and win widespread acceptance. Ideas other than the dominant one in each sub-group is perceived as an obstruction that has to be fought vigorously and hated for its deviance, thus, the pairing basic assumption is frequently infiltrated by the fight-flight mentality which expresses itself in the form of the threat of a schism which has to be contained by an emphasis on loyalty, unity and other attributes that belong to the dependency mentality. From the perspective of the work group, we can refer to the diversity within the analytical community and the different ways of articulating the links between the different sub-groups. From the perspective of the basic assumption group, "the schismatic group attempts to resolve its problem by internal war" (Bion, 1951, p. 222). The particular dynamics of groups composed of psychoanalysts might favor the uneasy relationship between the pairing mentality and the fight-flight one, whereby, the "aristocratic" sub-group is always under the potential threat of becoming a schismatic one. These dynamics that develop in the group are contributed to anonymously by individuals. They, in turn, affect each one of them, contributing to their individual sense of isolation. The dynamics that are specifically inherent to groups of analysts and the intricate relationships that develop between the clinical dyadic situation and the large society group, with its multiple possibilities of projections and displacements from one to the other and vice-versa, would need a great deal of further exploration and elucidation. It might be a fruitful way to explore some of the aspects of the present malaise in psychoanalysis as we re-appropriate some of what we might have unwittingly and anonymously projected, and which faces us, namely, the "hatred of analysis and the analytical experience" (1980, p. 28).

References

Bion, W.R. (1948a). Experiences in groups I. *Human Relations,* 1: 314-320.
—— (1948b). Experiences in groups II. *Human Relations,* 1: 487-496.
—— (1949a). Experiences in groups III. *Human Relations,* 1: 3-22.
—— (1949b). Experiences in groups IV. *Human Relations,* 2: 295-303.
—— (1950a). Experiences in groups V. *Human Relations,* 3: 3-14.
—— (1950b). Experiences in groups VI. *Human Relations,* 3: 395-402.
—— (1951). Experiences in groups VII. *Human Relations,* 4: 221-227.
—— (1955). Group dynamics: a re-view. In: Melanie Klein, Paula Heimann, R.E. Money-Kyrle (Eds.). *New Directions in Psychoanalysis.* Reprinted 1985. London: Karnac Books, pp. 440-477.
—— (1962). *Learning From Experience.* London: Heinemann. Reprinted in 1984 by Karnac Books, London.
—— (1967). Notes on memory and desire. *Psycho-Anal. Forum.,* 2: 272-280.
—— (1976). Emotional turbulence. In: Francesca Bion (Ed.). *Clinical Seminars and Four Papers.* Abingdon: Fleetwood Press, 1987, pp. 223-233.
—— (1978). *Four Discussions with W.R. Bion.* Perthshire: Clunie Press, pp. 21-22.
—— (1979). Making the best of a bad job. *Bull. Br. Psycho-Anal. Soc.,* 1979. Also in: Francesca Bion (Ed.) (1987). *Clinical Seminars and Four Papers.* Abingdon: Fleetwood Press.
—— (1980). *Bion in New York and Sao Paulo.* Perthshire: Clunie Press.

Campos, J. (1992). Burrow, Foulkes and Freud: An historical perspective. *Lifwynn Correspondence*, 2(2): 2-9.

Grinberg, L. et al. (1975). *Introduction to the Work of Bion*. London: Karnac Books. Reprinted in 1985.

Green, A. (1977). The borderline concept. In: P. Hortocollis (Ed.). *Borderline Personality Disorders*. New York: International Universitiesd Press, 1977. Reprinted in: *On Private Madness*. Madison, CT: International Universities Press, 1993, pp. 60-83.

Meltzer, D. (1978). *The Kleinian Development. Part 3. The Clinical Significance of the Work of Bion*. Pertshire: Clunie Press.

Scott, C. (1986). Who's afraid of Wilfred Bion? (Unpublished lecture delivered to the Canadian Psychoanalytic Society, Montreal, May 22.)

The Emergence of Thinking: Bion as the Link Between Freud and the Neurosciences[1]

Guy Da Silva

> It is a matter of the greatest possible urgency that the human animal should discover what sort of animal he is before he has blown himself off the earth (Bion, 1978, p. 10).

> Noise [in the body] links us as adults to infancy as well as to the animal kingdom (Scott, 1958, p. 111).[2]

The paper deals with Freud's old dream of unifying brain and mind and therefore with the emergence of thinking. Bion, inspired by Freud, went further with his own creativity. Certain aspects of Bion's theorization are juxtaposed with some recent findings of neuroscience particularly those of Edelman regarding the embodiment of the mind. Bion's idea of the mental digestion of the emotional experience is examined; it is a concept at the very center of Bion's theory of thinking which describes the transformation from corporeity to humanization. It is suggested that Bion's intuitive ideas about thinking may provide a linkage from Freud's instinct theory and Freud's old dream to modern neurosciences. This linkage should encourage cooperative efforts between psychoanalysis and neuroscience to investigate the very beginnings of hominization, an urgent task recommended to us by Bion in order to better comprehend the woes and discontents of our times.

I. Introduction

Freud's old dream that one day brain and mind will be unified is expressed as late as 1926: "We may look forward to a day when paths of knowledge. . . will be opened up leading from organic biology and chemistry to the field of neurotic phenomena" (p. 231). And in 1921 he wrote that analysts "instead of waiting for the moment when they will be able to escape from the constraint of the familiar laws of physics and chemistry, they hope for the emergence of more extensive and deeper-reaching natural laws, to which they are ready to submit" (p. 179).

My intention is first, to remind you briefly of some of the Freudian concepts about the emergence of thinking, concepts which, I feel, have inspired Bion; secondly to juxtapose some of the ideas of Edelman and Bion about the embodiment of the mind, memory and consciousness; thirdly, to relate Bion's "digestive model" with its usefulness in the clinical situation and with recent findings of neuroscience about the enteric nervous system.

II. Freud and Bion about the Emergence of Thinking

Three works of Freud have particularly influenced Bion's theory of thinking: the *Project*, the seventh chapter of the *Book of Dreams* and the 1911 "Two Principles of mental functioning." In these three works, Freud (1895) returns to the account of the "experience of satisfaction." In it, Freud came closest to formulating the part played by object relations on the emergence of thinking, that is in the transformation of a somatic animal into a thinking human being. Indeed the screaming of the infant not only expresses primarily the discharge of an instinctual impulse due to the sensations of pain and hunger but, to quote Freud: "when the attention of an experienced person is drawn to the child's state, this path of discharge acquires a secondary function of the highest importance, that of communication" (p. 318).

It may have been this remark of Freud along with his own work with psychotics which prompted Bion, by imprinting his own creativity, to modify Klein's idea of pathological projective identification into a normal way for the infant (or the psychotic) to communicate his distress to the experienced person. The term "experienced" is important in Bion's work (the experienced officer, the emotional experience, learning from experience); it should be taken in its etymological meaning: *ex-perire*, someone who has encountered a peril to his life, physical or mental, and has survived. Clearly for Bion thinking emerges from bodily events (beta elements) and the experience of satisfaction is the matrix of new mentation.

In the *Project*, after mentioning the dissimilarity between the wishful cathexis of a memory and the cathexis of a perception, Freud (1895) writes: "The coincidence between the two cathexes becomes a biological signal for ending the act of thought and for allowing discharge. Their non-coincidence gives the impetus for the activity of thought which is terminated once more with their coincidence" (p. 328). Compare this with Bion's idea of the preconception mating with the presence of a realization to produce a conception, while its mating with the absence of and a realization will bring the emergence of a concept. And compare this also to chapter 12 of *Learning from Experience* in which Bion (1962) elaborated further on the emergence of thinking in the absence of the realization of the breast: "if there is no 'thing,' is 'no thing' a thought and is it by virtue, of the fact that there is 'no thing' that we recognize that 'it' must be thought" (p. 35). Therefore, for Bion, all new nascent thought in the clinical situation would follow a similar pattern from its prototype in the experience of the "hungry baby" (Freud, 1900, p. 565).

Again in the *Project*, Freud (1895), while discussing cognition, writes: "It is in relation to a fellow human being that a human being learns to cognize" (p. 331). Compare this to Bion's reverie of the mother to do the thinking for the infant and to the similar task Bion assigns to the analyst of "doing the dreaming" for his patient recycling the mental confusion of a previous emotional experience never before comprehended (etymol.: *cum prendere*, to take with) with the necessary mental assistance of a fellow human being.

In *New Lectures*, Freud (1933) went even further suggesting a progressive transformation from body to mind stating "the source of an instinctual impulse is a state of excitation in the body, its aim is the removal of that excitation; in its path from its source in the body to its aim [which is satisfaction by the appropriate object] the instinct becomes operative psychically" (p. 96). The remarkable thing here is that Freud has moved considerably since 1915 and the metapsychology papers when he referred to the instinct as a conflict on the frontier between the mental and the somatic, sometimes placing it on the side of the mental and sometimes on the side of the somatic, but not telling us about the crucial passage from one to the other. Here in 1933, Freud implies a progressive transformation of something somatic and sensory which becomes operative psychically through the satisfaction of its aim by an object.

Here again, inspired by Freud, Bion borrowed from Klein in recognizing the importance in the epistemophilic impulse of the emotional link with the object. But he went further than Freud and Klein by establishing the basis of his theory of thinking on the centrality of the "digestion" of emotional experience, with the assistance of the reverie in the mind of the object, therefore suggesting a physiological process in progressive relation to a psychological process.

III. Bion and Edelman: The Embodiment of the Mind and the Question of Memory and Consciousness

Just as Freud (1901) who referred to "the great Darwin" (p. 148), both Bion and Edelman have been inspired by the evolution theory and the passage from animality to hominization. Edelman's[3] whole book (1992) dedicated to both Darwin and Freud is an attempt to answer the question "How is the mind embodied" (p. 265). And no other analytic theory of mentation is more embodied than Bion's theory. Edelman's theory is strongly inspired by Darwin's work on evolution and natural selection, and Bion's theory proposes many philogenetic and ontogenetic connections: protomental apparatus, prenatal or unborn parts of the personality, basic assumptions derived from primitive groupings which could be linked to the survival of the animal in us during evolution: dependence on food, fighting or fleeing an aggressor, and sexuality for reproduction of the species.

Edelman's first work was in immunology. He studied the body's capacity at the cellular level to distinguish self from non-self. He went on to prove that the body produces a vast repertoire (perhaps millions) of antibody molecules. When a foreign antigen (non-self) from the environment enters the body (self), it selects only those specific molecules with which it has a "good enough" fit. Then the cells that produce these specific antibodies multiply rapidly giving the body the immune response that eliminates the intruder. In this way, he confirmed that the immune system functions by selection not by instruction, a theory of immunity now widely accepted and for which he received the Nobel Prize in 1972. Later, Edelman realized that the system of recognition in the immune system might be a model for what happens in the brain, where there exists an enormous diversity and therefore an open field for a process of selection. So he turned his attention to neuroscience and proposed that both brain and mind develop and function by selection, one of the conditions for selection being great diversity. This condition is well fulfilled in the brain which contains at leas twelve billions neurones (there are reports of many more billions) and each of these neurones may have several thousand synapses.

Metaphorically speaking, brain development sounds like a neuronal free-for-all in which the fittest neurones prevail. Indeed, it seems likely that the "fittest" neurones are the ones that are in the right place at the right time to be stimulated by both the internal and external environment. The others do not survive or do not develop synapses as a result of lack of stimulation. Therefore for Edelman, at the level of brain development, it is the stimulation of new experiences that makes a difference, just as well as for Bion, for whom the stimulation of new emotional experiences will make a difference in psychic growth.

To quote Gibbard (1995): "Edelman's theory of neuronal group selection [TNGS] is beautiful in its simplicity and awesome in its complexity; beautiful because it is simply an extension of Darwin's theory of natural selection; awesome because a thorough understanding of the theory of neuronal group selection (TNGS) demands more than a passing knowledge of evolution theory, molecular biology, immunology, genetics, neuroembryology, and philosophy"

(p. 350).

Edelman's concept of memory as categorization or recognition is very similar to a theory of memory that Freud proposed in a letter to Fliess (December 6, 1895) in which Freud mentioned that he has been working on the idea that memory traces are being subjected to a rearrangement in accordance with fresh circumstances, to a retranscription (*Nachtraglichkeit*); memory therefore would be present not once but several times over, then laid down in various kinds of indications. Edelman (1992) came to a similar conclusion: memory is not permanent, not isomorphic with experience, "Memory in the nervous system is a dynamic property of populations of neuronal groups. . . . Memory emerges from continual dynamic changes in the synaptic populations within global m-appings . . . . In such a system, recall is not stereotypic. . . [but] result from a process of continual recategorization. . . unlike computer-based memory" (p. 102) which is exactly repetitive. Memory is present not once but several times over; every time a memory is recalled, it is recalled differently. The degree of difference depends upon the context in which it is remembered. As memories change, so the past is changed.

Compare this now to some of Bion's ideas. For Bion, the development of the mind is also a complicated process which has to be structured every step of the way. Bion's concepts of the selected fact and of mental digestion are, it seems to me, at the very center of the question of memory and consciousness. As early as 1959, Bion wrote in his private notes published under the editorial care of Francesca Bion (1992): "Obviously what is needed is to consider what 'digesting' facts consists of in detail" (p. 52). Already he was embarking on a most important task.

For Bion, the "undigested facts" or beta elements are stored in the form of bodily sensory traces. They are raw elements of sensuous and affective impressions in which psychic and physical are yet indistinguishable. As such they can only be dealt with by projective identification as a form of primitive communication. It has been one of his main contributions to remind us, that much of our lives is lived without thinking outside significant emotional experiences. And that we often busily go about our daily activities without thinking about its meaning, surrounded by a mass of "undigested facts."

Bion (1962) insists: "It is important to distinguish between memories and 'undigested facts'" (p. 7). Because they are not genuine memories, they are unavailable for thought and consciousness until they are transformed by alpha function that is by the interpretation of the "selected fact" in order to become "recycled" as genuine memories which can then acquire the possibility of retranscription and be forgotten or recalled. *Learning from an emotional experience is indeed a retranscription* so that "the mind builds itself, bit by bit, by 'digesting' experiences" (Meltzer, 1984, p. 42), and the Grid will graphically describe the whole progressive process going from corporeity to levels of greater abstraction. But when the "undigested facts" are not transformed (or metabolized), they remain in the words of Alvin Frank (1969) "The unrememberable and the unforgettable" and may correspond in the words of Edelman to the "remembered present" (p. 120) characteristic of the "primary order consciousness."

This primary consciousness may be at least 300 million years in evolution, a consciousness which we share with chimpanzees and most mammals. In this state of "remembered present" even though the animal can act on long term memory, it is unable to be aware of that memory at the moment of its action and it cannot plan an extended future based on that memory. Edelman (1992) gives this example: "An animal with primary consciousness sees the room the way a beam of light illuminates it. Only that which is in the beam is explicitly in the remembered present; all else is darkness" (p. 122).

Is this mental image of Edelman similar to Bion's alpha element or dream thought? This absence of an usable inscription in the temporality, this state in which the mind is not aware of past and of future is reminiscent of the clinical situation with borderline and psychotic patients and may correspond to Bion's "psychotic part of the personality" present in all of us. Aren't we, at these moments, functioning at the level of Edelman's "primary order consciousness"? Bion's injunction "to be without memory [past] and without desire [future]" seems pertinent here. Before reaching mentalization and being in a position to give an interpretation, it may be appropriate to remain first in the state of the primary consciousness of the "remembered present" that is, in the presymbolic state of a sensory and affective experience (Daniel Stern's affective attunement? or, as I prefer to say: a state of "sensory and affective attunement") before eventual transformation in higher conceptual abstraction.

For Edelman, the tyranny of the "remembered present" of primary consciousness will be broken by "higher order consciousness" which arises from primary consciousness but does not replace it even though there may be oscillations philogenetically or ontogenetically. (These oscillations, in my opinion, are beginning to resemble Bion's SP↔D.)

The higher order consciousness will come from several developments of new neuronal maps and then mapping of the maps, mutually interacting and propelling one another. The end result will be:

   a. An emerging consciousness of self and non-self in social communication. And then with the brain, mapping an awareness of its own processes, there will emerge the capacity for consciousness of being conscious, a momentous step in evolution comparable to the ontological development of the child beginning to think about thinking.

Here again we can think of Bion's (1962, p. 21) statement about consciousness often quoting Freud (1905): "What part is there left to be played in our scheme by consciousness. . . . *Only that of a sense organ for the perception of psychical qualities*" (p. 615). And we can think of Bion calling our attention to the fact that we live in a sort of "altered states of consciousness" or of vigilance or of awareness in relation to the "emotional experience" of the moment whether we are asleep or awaken.

b. New forms of memory capable of modeling a past and a future and a brain repertoire in the frontal cortex stimulated by affective rewards for delayed responses enabling the capacity to wait for gratification.

Here, we are reminded of Bion's (1962) statement on the capacity to wait for gratification: "The choice that matters to the psychoanalyst is one that lies between procedures designed to evade frustration and those designed to modify it. That is the critical decision" (p. 29).

c. Evolution of the vocal tract and brain centers for articulated sounds and eventually language but before language, the capacity for metaphor which should not be overlooked by considering it only as a figure of speech. (This point has been elaborated by Arnold Modell [1995] and Edelman refers, in his book, to a discussion between them.)

As we know, metaphoric communication is not limited to words as it is ever present in gestures and mimetic actions. That metaphors are used to describe bodily sensations is well known to analysts. One familiar metaphor is that of the body as a container filled with affects, as if affects were a concrete substance within that container. Klein's (1946) "memories in feelings" are experiences stored without verbal content and we know in our work how appropriate interpretation of Bion's "selected fact" may act as a container of affect. The linkage here with Bion's container-contained is evident.

IV. Bion's Theory of Thinking: the Digestive Model, a Metaphor, an Analogy, or More?

In the analytic literature, it is possible to find before Bion hints of a digestive model for the thinking apparatus: Rado's (1926) "alimentary orgasm" (p. 408) and Simmel's (1944) "intestinalization of the process of thinking" (p. 129). But, it is Bion (1962) who for the first time in psychoanalysis has proposed an integrated theory for the construction of a thinking apparatus based on the alimentary system "as a model for demonstrating and comprehending the processes involved in thought. . . certain patients [being] influenced by the belief that they digest thoughts and that the consequences of doing so are similar to the digestion of food" (p. 62) ". . . the mental component, as distinct from the somatic requires a process analogous to digestion" (*ibid*, p. 35) and "the effect on the personality of such deprivation [of truth] is analogous to the effect of physical starvation on the physique" (*ibid*, p. 56). Accordingly, the mind having constructed itself by the observation of the alimentary system, the model that the psyche would have of itself would be one of a gastro-intestinal-sensory-emotional-conceptual system. This system would have the task to digest, that is to metabolize, to transform the "emotional experience" finding its sustenance in truth and having to recognize and to reject lies to avoid being potentially intoxicated by them.

To summarize: Bion's formulation about thinking is that thinking commences with the observation of the emotional experience and the emotional experience is right there in the body, it is absolutely apprehended first as a bodily event which may then be processed through symbol formation and becomes available in dreams and therefore may become available for transformation into thought and so on (see: the grid). . . . We see it in the clinical situation, people first experience a somatic state and then it began to be apprehended as a conscious emotional experience. What alpha function works upon is in the body, there is no body-mind in this model of the mind. Emotional experiences that are not worked upon by alpha function are thus evacuated into the body. And this is Bion's theory of psychosomatic, the most clinically usable framework of reference for psychosomatic illness as well as somapsychotic manifestations.

a. Observations in Clinical Practice

In Bion, it is clear that mental development depends on the efficient working of a mental alimentary system. I was inspired by these ideas of Bion when I began noticing gurgling sounds of patients and of myself, occurring at very specific moments during the analytic session. In previous papers (Da Silva, 1990, 1992), I have presented extensive reports and observations inside and outside the clinical situation which, in my opinion, sustain Bion's proposal that the mind, during evolution, may indeed have employed the digestive model as an analogy for its development. And I have become convinced that *borborygmi* (gurgling sounds) *of both analysand and analyst at certain moments of the analytic session may be seen as markers of psychic work and witnesses to the transformation from soma to psyche*; at these moments of truth, patients experience a fantasy and at times an hallucination of an alimentary gratification by a feeding object as if they were "rewarded," so to speak, for their newly acquired capacity to tolerate the absence of the concrete gratification.[4]

The idea of a "mental digestion" presupposes a transformation requiring time and space,[5] time to accomplish a task and space to contain whatever should be worked over with an expenditure of a quota of energy. But with the presence or the absence of borborygmi, there were other fantasies about the intestinal tract as well as other sounds and noises involving the alimentary system such as demonstrated in the following vignettes:

1. A psychotic woman had the conviction that her anus was in the back of her neck. She was deprived therefore of the length of time necessary for the task of digestion requiring that food goes through the space of a long intestinal tract. As a consequence, she treated both food and experiences of life in the same manner, they were gobbled up and immediately evacuated; she remained starved physically and mentally.

2. A young boy whose mother worked as a prostitute and whose father had committed suicide after his release from jail was admitted to a residential house. Other boys of the residence had immediately named him "Prout" because he made this sound going about farting continuously. On evaluation, his behavior was two-fold. He farted constantly but he also constantly pointed to objects asking "What is it?, What is it?" When given the name of the objects, he could not remember and continued pointing: "What is it?, What is it?" After months of therapy, interpretations were often followed by belching, his farting had ceased and he began to draw. I was encouraged to work with him by his intelligence which he demonstrated by playing with the double meaning of the word rapport in french: *avoir un rapport* may signify either I am having a belch or these two things are related, there is a rapport between them. When my interpretation was followed by his belching, which happened often, he would look at me with a teasing eye and say with a mocking smile: *Il n'y a pas de rapport*, that is: It's not related. I became convinced that a mental digestion of his mental confusion was taking place, very analogous to the process of physiological digestion.

These observations, it seems to me, are very close to the work of Geneviève Hagg (1991) working with autistic patients and signaling in the development of the early ego what she has called *les fantasmes de Moi-tuyau non sphinctérisés* in patients incapable of mental digestion.

b. Observations Outside the Analytic Situation

We can find in animal life and in cultural practices many examples pre-figurating the situation of a experienced person doing the mental digestion for the benefit of a less capable partner: as we know, many birds do this for their fledglings still in the nests. The Inuits, known in the past as Eskimos, that is "eaters of raw meat" had a ritual of hospitality in which they would welcome a visitor in their igloo for a meal of friendship sharing food and conversation and having previously chewed the raw meat before offering it.

The medieval monks considered that in order to reach the deepest spiritual meaning of a sacred text, it was necessary to internalize it by a process which they compared to digestion, absorbing the words in a state of devout tranquillity, ruminating them in some way in order to extract a more spiritual meaning; the plain-chant was approached with this state of mind as recommended by the Abbess Hildegard Van Bingen (*Harmonia mundi*, 1982).

c. Observations from Biology, Embryology and the Neurosciences

Ontogeny teaches us that the two most primitive layers of cells forming the embryonic plate will detach themselves, one the layer of endoblast to form the endoderm from which the alimentary canal will be formed, the other, the layer of ectoblast to form the ectoderm which will develop into the neural tube and the brain. It appears that enteric neurons are the descendants of cells that emigrated from the neural crest and have migrated to colonize the bowel. It is likely that precursors able to give rise to each type of neurons found in the mature enteric nervous system are present among the earliest neural crest emigrés to reach the bowel (Gershom, 1983).

On the other hand, phylogeny indicates that there exists a remarkable similarity between primitive organisms and more advanced mammals in the chain of evolution in the form in which the alimentary canal traverses the interior of the body from mouth to anus; in certain organisms, for instance in the ascarid and in the earthworm, the alimentary canal, surrounded by a ring of nervous web, occupies most of the bodily space, as if this "tube" serving for the ingestion of food, the digestion and the elimination was the main if not the sole organ of survival (*Atlas de biologie*, 1994, pp. 127-128).

The modern neuroscientists have been so impressed by their recent findings that they have started to call the gastroenteric nervous system a third division of the autonomic nervous system referring to Langley's (1903) classic description or even as a "third brain." In summary here are some of their findings:

a. Over the past ten years, many peptides (cholecystokinin; vasoactive intestinal polypeptide; insulin, glucagon, etc.) which were believed to have their sole origin at the level of the gastrointestinal tract, were found to have also their synthesis at the level of the central nervous system in the vertebrates; these peptides seem to have a function of neurotransmission or neuromodulation at the synapses, and a function of regulation of the homeostasis; at least fourteen gastrointestinal peptides are found in the central nervous system; the locus cereleus is one possible central nervous system area having both afferent and efferent connections to the gastrointestinal tract that might constitute what Walker (1990) called a "missing link." In the invertebrates, before the development of an endocrine or a neural system, these peptides seem to serve as primitive elements for the intercellular communication (Krieger, 1983).

b. The enteric nervous system has been called the third division of the autonomic nervous system, structurally resembling the central nervous system more than the peripheral nervous system. It is unique: structurally, chemically and functionally. It has a blood myenteric barrier analogous to the blood-thymic barrier and the blood-brain barrier. Like in the cortex it uses glial cells for support rather than Schwann cells.

All these findings can only reinforce one's conviction about how much brain and mind but most especially the alimentary system and the nervous system have been enmeshed in the course of evolution.

V. Conclusion

In his "Project for a scientific psychology" Freud (1895) wrote: "The intention is to furnish a psychology that shall be a natural science" (p. 295). He later abandoned the Project but he never abandoned his position that psychoanalysis, a human science, shall also be part of natural science.

From the perspective of the theory of neuronal group selection, mind and brain compose a seamless web. If the theory of neuronal group selection is proven to be correct, Edelman will have succeeded in creating a monist theory of brain and mind and he would have succeeded where Freud failed no doubt because the necessary basic neuroscience was not known at the time and could not have been anticipated either during the last years of Bion's life. However, Bion (1978) called our attention to the necessity of investigating the prenatal parts of the personality and their lasting effects on human existence (p. 26) and in *Memoir of the Future* (1991) he returned to his earlier interests in group life but exploring it within the individual person in whom the prenatal parts of the personality do their thinking with the body and obey laws closer to neurophysiology than to psychology.

We will not be able to advance in this investigation which entails the early beginnings of hominization without the cooperative efforts of psychoanalysis and neuroscience. Both Bion's theory of the mind and Edelman's theory of neuronal group selection have put aside Descartes' dualism and replaced it by monism. As we have seen, Bion has intuitively suggested that the process of mentation develops by analogy to the process of digestion. Are these recent observations in neuroscience suggesting, at least in some ways, an homology of function if not of structure?

Obviously many questions remain and much work need to be done by psychoanalysis and by neuroscience which is now exploring the problem of intentionality, consciousness and meaning. Will the gap ever be closed between natural science and human science? Whatever the course of events, Bion's theory is, in my opinion, the most interesting analytic theory as a linkage between the propositions of Darwin and Freud and the recent findings of modern neuroscience.

As I have indicated in exergue, Bion has summoned us to the urgent task of discovering what sort of animal we are, before we blow ourselves off the earth. This exhortation reminds me of another one attributed to Konrad Lorentz who apparently would say half-jokingly and half-seriously: "We should stop searching for the 'missing link' between animality and humanity because we are the 'missing link'!"

Notes

1. This paper is an enlarged version of the one presented at the Centennial Conference on the work of Wilfred Bion in Turin, Italy, July 1997.
2. Scott, who often referred to Bion's work, insisted on the importance of sounds and noises coming from the body during the analytic session as witnesses of our animality.
3. I have been introduced to the work of Edelman by Bruce Gibbard. Gibbard has presented in meetings of the Canadian Psychoanalytic Society the parallels that he and Arnold Modell see between Edelman's neuroscience and some psychoanalytic ideas. Hearing him I was immediately impressed by the rapprochement one could make between Edelman's neuroscience and Bion's own theorizations. It prompted me to read Edelman's work.
4. I have not found in Bion's work any written allusions to borborygmi even though Scott mentioned in personal communication that Bion had referred to them. Surprisingly while it is a common occurrence during the analytic session and while

many literary writers (Ferdinando Camon, 1984, p. 103; Milan Kundera, 1984, p. 53; Albert Cohen, 1968, p. 701) have been sensitive to borborygmi as signaling a very intimate merging in relationship, there has been no mention of their possible significance in the analytic literature except for one notable exception namely Scott (1958, p. 110) who suggested that "countertransference reactions to borborygmi might well lead to cooperative research amongst analysts." Scott strongly supported my interest in these investigations and encouraged me to include all sounds and noises of the body in my observations as well as fantasies about them.

5. No one has written more extensively and more convincingly from a psychoanalytic point of view than Henri Rey (1994) about the construction and the transformations of the concepts of time and space in normal development as well as their mishaps and vagaries in neurotic, borderline and psychotic states.

References

Atlas de biologie (1994). Translated from German into French by Vogel G. and Angermann, H. Paris: Librairie Générale Française, pp. 127-128.

Bion, W.R. (1962). *Learning from Experience*. London: Heinemann.

—— (1978). *Four Discussions*. Perthshire: Clunie Press.

—— (1991). *Memoir of the Future*. London: Karnac Books.

—— (1992). *Cogitations*. Edited by Francesca Bion, London: Karnac Books.

Camon, F. (1984). *La Maladie humaine*. Paris: Gallimard.

Cohen, A. (1968). *Belle du Seigneur*. Paris: Gallimard.

Da Silva, G. (1987). Un appareil à digérer les pensées: Exploration d'une réaction psychophysiologique (Borborygmes) au cours du processus analytique. Scientific Meeting of the Société Psychanalytique de Montréal, February.

—— (1990). Borborygmi as markers of psychic work during the analytic session. A contribution to Freud's experience of satisfaction and to Bion's idea about the digestive model for the thinking apparatus. *Int. J. Psycho-Anal.*, 71: 641.

—— (1992). Le modèle alimentaire dans la théorie de la pensée de Bion. Suivi d'une application de ce modèle dans l'analyse d'un patient. Symposium of the Société Psychanalytique de Montréal, Spring 1992.

—— (1996). La supervision collective dans l'enseignement de la psychothérapie psychanalytique: Enveloppe groupale et contenant pour une rêverie à plusieurs. In: Doucet and Reid (Dir.), Gaétan Morin (Ed.), *La psychothérapie psychanalytique: Une diversité de champs cliniques*. Montréal, 1996.

Edelman, G.N. (1992). *Bright Air, Brilliant Fire: On the Matter of Mind*. New York: Basic Books.

Frank, A. (1969). The unrememberable and the unforgettable: Passive primal repression. *Psychoanal. Study Child*, 24: 44-77.

Da Silva

Freud, S. (1895). Project for a scientific psychology, *SE*, 1: 283-397. In J. Strachey
    (Ed.), *Standard Edition of the Complete Psychological Works of Sigmund Freud*,
    24 volumes. London: Hogarth Press and the Institute of Psycho-Analysis,
    1953-1974.
Freud, S. (1896). Letter to Fliess, December 6, letter 52. *SE*, 1: 233.
—— (1900). *The Interpretations of Dreams. SE*, 5: 509-625.
—— (1901). *The Psychopathology of Everyday Life. SE*, 6.
—— (1911). Formulations on the two principles of mental functioning. *SE*, 12: 213-
    226.
—— (1921). Psycho-analysis and telepathy. *SE*, 18: 177-193.
—— (1926). The question of lay analysis. *SE*, 20:179-258.
—— (1933). *New Introductory Lectures in Psychoanalysis. SE*, 22: 81-111.
Gershom, M.D. (1983) Development of the enteric nervous system: *Fed. Proc.*, 42:
    1620-1625.
Gibbard, B. (1995). *Bright Air, Brilliant Fire*: On the Matter of the Mind by Edel
    man. Reviewed in *Canad. J. Psychoanal.*, 3(2): 347-351.
—— (1996). Dreaming, metaphor, symbolism and psychoanalysis. (Paper presented
    at the Canadian Psychoanalytic Society's Annual Meeting.)
Hagg, G. (1991). Contribution à la compréhension des identifications en jeu dans le
    moi corporel. (Paper presented at the International Congress of the I.P.A.,
    Buenos Aires, July 1991.)
Harmonia Mundi (1982). Text with production "Ordo Virtutum" Hildegard Van
    Bingen, Deutsche Harmonia Mundi.
Klein, M. (1946). Notes on some schizoid mechanisms. *Int. J. Psycho-Anal.*, 27: 99-
    110.
Krieger, D.T. (1983) Brain peptides: What? Where? and Why? *Science*, 222: 975-.
Kundera, M. (1984). *L'insoutenable légèreté de l'etre.* Paris: Gallimard.
Langley, J.N. (1903). The autonomic nervous system. *Brain*, 26: 1-26.
Meltzer, D. (1984). *Dream-Life.* Pertshire: Clunie Press.
Modell, A. (1995). Metaphor and mind. Presentation at the American Psychoana
    lytic Association Meeting (December).
Rado, S. (1926). The psychic effect of intoxicants. *Int. J. Psycho-Anal.*, 7: 396-413.
Rey, H. (1994). *Universals of Psychoanalysis in the Treatment of Psychotic and
    Borderline States.* Ed. Jeanne Magagna, London: Free Association Books.
Scott, W.C.M. (1958). Noise, speech and technique. *Int. J. Psycho-Anal.*, 39: 108-
    111.
Simmel, E. (1944). Self presentation and the death instinct. *Psychoanal. Q.*, 13: 160-
    185.
Stern, D. (1985). *The Interpersonal World of the Infant.* New York: Basic Books.
Walker, (1990). Irritable Bowel Syndrome. *Amer. J. Psychia.*, May 5, 147: 569.

Fig. 24. Copy of C. Scott's edition of *Alice' Adentures in Wonderland*, given by his mother who wrote, "For into my heart you have stolen as sunbeams to shadows creep" (1908).
Credit: The Estate of W.C.M. Scott.

Memorial Gathering for Dr. W.C.M. Scott (May 25, 1997)

Clare Coulter

L ast night, I was looking at a video that myself and two actors took of Doctor Scott a couple of years ago, and we were asking him questions, all of them very solid and boring, and his face revealed someone of such sweetness and gentleness and accepting our boring questions and answering them with as much interest as he could and then waiting to see if anybody had caught anything that he had said, anybody coming along? anybody want to take that up? anybody? anybody?. . . no. . . . All right, what's the next question then. And he went on and on and on, never tiring of our attempts to talk to him and our inability to follow anything that he had to say. In 1954 he taped a patient in London as an experiment for teaching, he said, and these tapes became the basis of a performance which with his help I presented in a Theatre. In the last interview that he records this woman he is asking her to speak to the Doctors at the Maudsley who will be questioning her about her experiences with him and she says. "Yes it is so sweet to speak to someone, but for strangers, I don't know. . ." and he said, "Well. . . you can imagine you are speaking to me, and other people are listening. . . ."

One of the books that I disliked the most when I was a child was *Alice in Wonderland*. I did not like the horrible adventures she had, and I did not like the rude ways that people talked to her, the way they teased her and this turned out to be one of the most important books in Doctor Scott's life and how I began to see as I was seeing him, this is how he worked, in that same way. It was a book that he was given when he was five and his mother inscribed it, "For into my heart you have stolen as sunbeams to shadows creep."[1]

Well, I would like to tell you what it felt like to go to his house to be a patient for the first time. I had a number of names of people in Montreal and against his name was "An older man, very unusual." I thought, I'll try that one. So going to his house first of all, was a stop to Laura Secord's for a piece of fudge to get over the first couple of moments if I needed to, and then the bus up the Côte des Neiges in the blizzard and the snow and feeling it was a metaphorical journey to a spot of wisdom far away. And then if you had not broken your neck on the way down the hill to the house, you rang the bell and the door was opened by the most solid human being standing there, with a warm smile on her face, and the sense that she was open to you but the keeper of secrets. And then the interview itself which began, and I would like to read a few pieces from *Alice* just to say what it was like. Monique [Meloche] said it was like jugglers, to me it was like a trapeze artist. . . . He would set off with a couple of words and a huge swoop, over the silence and then he would turn to see if you were. . . . "Get that? No. . . ." If you could not come along he would swoop all the way back to where you were and say, "Well here, let's start again then. . . ." Then whoosh! Indeed you might be dissolving in tears with frustration and he would say, "Never mind, next time we will try again."

This one is from the Chapter called "The Pool of Tears":

> "Curiouser and curiouser, cried Alice. She was so much surprised that for the moment she quite forgot how to speak good English. Now I am opening out like the largest telescope that ever was. . . . Good-by feet!" (Carroll, 1989, p. 19).

And then there was one from *Through the Looking Glass*:

> "Can you row?" the sheep asked, handing her a pair of knitting needles as she spoke. "Yes a little, but not on land and not with needles" Alice was beginning to say when suddenly the needles turned into oars in her hands and she found they were in a little boat gliding along in between banks so there was nothing for it but to do her best (Carroll, 1986, pp. 90-91).

And then there was one more piece. . . . He. . . . It seemed to me that everything was riddles, everything was a confusion of language, at first and for a long time I had no way of understanding why he was doing that. And in this the Duchess says:

> "I quite agree with you" said the Duchess "and the moral of that is, be what you would seem to be, or if you like to put it more simply, never imagine yourself not to be other than what it might appear to others that what you were, or might have been was not otherwise than what you had been would have appeared to them to be otherwise" (Carroll, 1989, p. 91).

He always seemed to be the person who was ready for an exploration. He used to tell that story of how he had watched this patient whom he had taped in England for a year and a half, looking at her face to see what it was she wanted to do and finally deciding after a year and a half that she wanted to go "blblbblb," and then he did it first for her and then she followed. It was always, he would try whatever you were afraid to do and then you could follow if you wanted to. Well then we started on these tapes, to put them onto the stage, and when we were waiting for permission from the patient in England in order to do this, and we thought what would we do if the patient said no. . . . And he said, "Well, we could do our own analysis. . . ." "Or," I said, "we could do our own analysis and you would analyze me, and we would tape it and that will be the play." And he said, "Yes, fine, but what would your symptom be?" and I thought he is asking me to pretend, I do not know how to do that! And then when we were trying to decide who would play Doctor Scott, I asked him would he possibly agree to play himself? "Oh no," he said, "I could never remember my lines!" And he said he had once wanted to be an actor when he was a student at Hart House, and he was put into a play, the nativity play, and I think he was asked to play God. That may be my invention, anyway, he found that he could not remember his lines, and instead he just invented anything he could think of. And in the end they said, "We're very sorry, you're going to have to just do the lighting." So the last thing I wanted to say, was these games at first as Alice sees them, are very insulting, almost confusing and distressing, and you think is this all my life is to this person? A chance to play with words and make fun of me? But there was always the sense that behind this all as you were saying, was this sense of darkness. He had been through two world wars, and seen an enormous amount of destruction, and been part of the Physicians Against Nuclear War. And I wanted to read a piece from Carlos Williams (1962), that is about the bomb, and the imagination, and it is from "Asphogel":

> Do not hasten, laugh and play in an eternity. The heat will not overtake the light, that's sure. That gelds the bomb. Permitting that the mind contain it. This is that interval, that sweetest interval, when love will blossom, come early, come late, and give itself to the lover. Only the imagination is real, I have declared it time without end (p. 178).

Thank you.

Note

1. This was the dedication written by his own mother in the book *Alice's Adventures in Wonderland* given to Dr. Scott. A reproduction of this dedication can be seen in the book.

References

Carroll, Lewis (1865/1986 edition). Chapter 5. Wool and water. In: *Through the Looking Glass and What Alice Found There*. Illustrated by Justin Todd. London: Victor Gollancz.

—— (1872/1989 edition). Chapter 2. The pool of tears. In: *Alice's Adventures in Wonderland*. Illustrated by Peter Weevers. London: Hutchinson.

—— (1989). Chapter 9. The mock turtle story. In: *Alice's Adventures in Wonderland*. Illustrated by Peter Weevers. London: Hutchinson.

Williams, Carlos (1962). Asphogel, that Greeny Flower. Poem from the section "Coda" in the book *Pictures from Brueghel and Other Poems*, New Directions Books.

Introduction to *Sessions*

Michel Grignon

Father	We are in search of an author.
Director	An author? What author?
Father	Any author, sir.
Director	But there is no author here. We are not rehearsing a play.
Stepdaughter	All the better, so much the better, sir. We can be your new play [...].
Director	You people must be joking.
Father	No. What on earth are you saying sir? On the contrary, we bring you a serious and painful play [...].
Director	All this is fine, but what is it that you want here.
Father	We want to live, sir.
Director	For eternity?
Father	No, only for a moment. . . in them [...]. Look, look! The play has to be made but if you wish, and your actors are willing, we can soon work it out among ourselves.
Director	[...] Here we do plays: drama and comedies.
Father	Precisely, we have to come to you precisely for that.
Director	And where is the script?
Father	It is inside of us. Drama is in us. We are it; and we are anxious to play it. The passion in us drives us to this.

(Pirandello, *Six Characters in Search of An Author and Other Plays*, pp. 11-14).

At the memorial for W.C.H. Scott in Montreal on May 25, 1997, the actress Clare Coulter remembered her collaboration with Dr. Scott in the early 1990's which led to the play called *Sessions*. While listening to her, I felt that the story of this theatrical event, itself a tribute to Scott's creative and innovative spirit, had to be included in the celebration of his life and work. *Sessions* was a very important experiment, the first to my knowledge to offer a theatrical presentation of the psychoanalytical experience as much as a demonstration of the skills and technique of Scott himself.

The play *Sessions* was developed from nineteen hours of audio taped analytic meetings held in the 1950's between Scott and Mrs. J.R., a writer. This woman had been hospitalized at the Maudsley, a psychiatric institution in London, England, where the tapes were made. From 1953-1954, she continued to be seen by Scott at his London office (49, Queensgate Gardens).

The tapes were used as teaching tools and were kept personally by Scott. Unfortunately, they were not well preserved. In May 1977, Scott published a transcript of two sessions from those tapes in the *Journal of Psychiatry of the University of Ottawa*. In giving her permission for the publication of these transcripts, some twenty years after the termination of treatment with Scott, Mrs. J.R. wrote,

> I was tremendously pleased to hear from you—to know that the actual you is alive and well, and working and real. The fantasy you, of course, has been with me ever since you gave me what now feels to have been a second childhood. I have such strange memories of it! Some real, some quite dreamlike—there wasn't sunshine, was there? Or a wide beach with only sea and sand, nor a wall dripping with milk, and trailing honeysuckle. . . . No, obviously not. But I shall be very pleased if you can use any of it, whatever it was. It is good to think of other people having the same chance to be helped (silly word, I want to say reborn) (Scott, 1977, p. 21).

The inspiration for *Sessions* came from a psychoanalytic consultation that took place in 1990 between Scott and Clare Coulter. The idea became reality when the husband of Mrs. J.R., now deceased, gave his permission for the use of the transcripts.

Clare Coulter is a very well known actress who has been associated with the Tarragon Theatre in Toronto for over twenty-five years. *The Globe and Mail* (April 1995) describes her as having "national stature." Playwrights from Judith Thompson to John Murrell have written specifically for her. She has premiered English language productions of plays by Michel Tremblay. She had roles in *1837: The Farmers' Revolt*, *Them Donnelleys*, and *Under the Greywake*. At the Tarragon Theatre she was the first woman to perform *The*

Fever, a one woman play written by the New York playwright Wallace Shawn. It played at the Edinburgh Festival in 1996 and in the Royal Court Theatre in London in 1997.

Sparking Coulter's project with Scott was her special interest in creating plays out of everyday material. *The Seaford Tapes* (1989), a play that premiered at Theatre Passe Muraille, is really about memories and some of these memories were the experiences during the war. The English couple on the tape were not friends but neighbors of Coulter's aunt who had died and with whom she was staying while taking care of her things (Letter of C. Coulter to M. Grignon, August 15, 1997).

During her psychoanalytic consultation with Scott, Coulter discovered him to be "a trapeze artist." Scott asked her if she would be interested in putting some tapes into performance as she had done with *The Seaford Tapes*. In the introductory note to *Sessions*, Scott (1977) wrote that in the new spirit of the last three decades, "senior psychoanalysts have become more willing to say something of their work and to make public their audio recordings or transcripts for teaching purposes" (p. 20).[1] However, he was also curious about the public's reaction to his work. I, myself, realized the importance of his project when, as an interpreter between Scott and Mrs. E. Rudinesco,[2] I struggled to translate the essence of this artistic performance and its significance for Scott. He explained that this experiment was about a new way to communicate the nature of analysis to the public through a direct and powerful medium, theater. In looking for an alternative to the case history, theoretical exposition, or written transcript, he was curious if theater could familiarize the public with psychoanalysis through something approaching an actual experience of a series of sessions.

He insisted that *Sessions* should be as faithful as possible to the transcripts and respect the unfolding of the dialogue in real time. This theatrical project was another expression of Scott's struggle to share the incommunicableness of the analytic experience. He believed that the patient and analyst together create a script about the internal and external realities of the patient, one that unfolds itself in emerging conflicts and emotional oscillations as they are lived in the actual relationship of the patient with the analyst, either as a defense against or an enactment of unconscious phantasy.

When asked how he could ever imagine that someone listening to *Sessions* would understand or have a glimpse of the drama of his patient in the ways he did, Scott's answer was his usual, "Let's wait and see." His vision of the analytic drama was of an unbounded interpretive experience similar to the confrontation with any great work by Shakespeare or Molière; the interpreting public were expected to discover meanings in *Sessions* beyond what he and his patient had created or perceived.

Sessions first played at the Theatre Centre in Toronto from December 1 to 5, 1993 and again at the Tarragon Theatre from March 9 to April 9, 1995. The director was Daniel Brooks, Clare Coulter played the patient and Daniel MacIvor the analyst.

Scott went to Toronto for some performances and was struck at how the audience laughed in places where he would never have even smiled. He realized that he had underestimated the humorous side of his patient. He was happy when he was told that *Sessions* "outbecketted Beckett himself" (private communication). The reaction of the critics was diverse. The drama critic of *The Star* (March 15, 1995) emphasized "the intriguing relationship between the actual and the artificial sessions." *Sessions* was called a "performance" rather than a play; likening it to real life rather than a representation of real life. The public came out "more enriched than cheated." In the review *Eye* (March 23, 1995), Laura Kosterski described the effect of the set as follows, "The action takes place in a rectangular box, which almost suggests a movie house. Scott's office appears to float as a mirage." In *Now Magazine* (March 23, 1995), J.L. wrote, "The artifice distances the audience from the subjects, and yet the work's greatest success is intimacy, an ability to capture the charged, heightened state—the near hypnotic intensity—of the sessions." Less enamored of the production, John Coulbourn wrote in *The Toronto Sun* (March 16, 1995), "For the rest of us—those who see theatre as more than a bland imitation of life—it's merely interesting. Devoid of meaningful theatrical device, any conflict that exists is largely internal, any resolution, infinitesimal."

In February 1997, *Sessions* was performed in London, England at the Freud Museum (February 24, 1997), then at the Highgate Scientific and Literary Institution (February 27, 1997) and, finally, at the Tavistock (March 4, 1997) with a broader audience. Those performances were addressed to a small audience of psychoanalysts. Marian Milner, a former analysand of Scott, was in attendance. Recently, she wrote a text to be read at the memorial for Dr. Scott on May 25, 1997. While it arrived too late to be read, her memories of *Sessions* and her appreciation of Scott reflect something of the atmosphere in which *Sessions* was received at its 1997 London performances:

> Last February [1997], I was reminded how much we, in England, had lost through Clifford Scott having to return to his country in the early 1950's. It was in February of this year that the Freud Museum organized an evening for a small audience of analysts with a dramatized version of a recording Scott had made, in 1952 at the Maudsley Hospital, of some sessions with a woman patient. It was beautifully performed, the room was small and dark, and at

moments it almost seemed to me as if it was Scott himself in the analyst's chair.

What was so impressive for me was his so early use of the creative aspect of the countertransference. What is painful for me is that, although intending to, ، I never got around to writing to tell him what a splendid occasion it was.

I, myself, was in analysis with him for several years in the late 40's and the early 50's and found that his interpretation had a refreshing simplicity, especially in the area of actual body experiences. For instance, in connection with a child patient of mine (aged 11) who kept threatening to throw a brick through the playroom window, I had interpreted in fairly classical terms her anger with me, but with no effects. But Scott said "I wonder, is it that she perhaps wants to know if her first intercourse will hurt her?" She, at once, stopped threatening to smash my windows (Letter for the Memorial, addressed to E. Scott, May 5, 1977).

Before the performance of *Sessions*, the public was provided with a program for the night in which Scott (1993) had written a summary of the case history of Mrs. J.R. in the following terms:

A woman of 38 who was complaining of fears of being alone outside her house was referred by her physician to a psychoanalyst with whom she began treatment. After several interviews she became so generally fearful, tense, and restless that she was referred to a psychiatrist who cared for her at home, under sedation, for a few weeks until she was admitted to the hospital. There she was treated by insulin comas. Her depressed feelings of guilt and her ideas of having special insight into human affairs gradually lessened.

Her social behaviour gradually improved and after five and a half months she was discharged from hospital to continue treatment as an outpatient. Her chief complaints remaining were fear of being alone and fear of vomiting or seeing anyone vomit.

Treatment by three junior psychiatrists in sequence continued weekly under supervision. During the next two years her complaints had not changed. I decided to take over her treatment by psychoanalysis.

Her symptoms had increased in severity since childhood. She continued schooling until 17, the final few years in boarding school, and became an illustrator and later an author of children's books, both general and religious. At 24 she married and later divorced, and remarried her present reliable and helpful husband. At 33 her first child, a daughter, was delivered by caesarian section due to bleeding. She was ill with much vomiting for several days but recovered well. Accidental pregnancy at 35 ended in unwanted miscarriage after many efforts to preserve the pregnancy.

Her upbringing was in an atmosphere of parental quarreling. A brother, two years older, became eccentric and was successful in business. A brother, two years younger, still lived with their mother and had never succeeded in any type of work. A sister, four years younger, married but was neurotically emotional all her life. The father, the most stable person in the family, died when she was fifteen. The mother, a lawyer who had never practiced, was an excitable, powerful, dominating, and unpredictable woman.

When I decided to treat her, treatment continued face to face for 2 ½ years and was followed by her lying down but still looking at me most of the time. Lying down meant only that she relaxed if she wished. During the 3 ½ years I treated her, we were mostly concerned with the conflicts between depression and enthusiasm and the many conflicting feelings she had about her bodily habits and functions.

When treatment terminated she had greatly improved and, in one late interview, she left the interview to walk alone around the park and return to my office.

Scott went on to add: "In her letter of 1977 authorizing the use of the transcripts of the tapes, she went on to write about how well her life had developed and how well and active she, her husband, and two children were. She recently died and her husband has given me permission for this use of our recorded sessions."

In conclusion, as I was reflecting on *Sessions*, two plays came to mind, one by Samuel Beckett and the other by Luigi Pirandello. In *Krapp's Last Tape* by Beckett (1958), Krapp, the hero, sits alone in front of a table with a tape recorder, the stage in darkness. He listens to the tapes that he recorded at different moments of his life. Krapp wonders about many things: the words he used to express this or that emotion, the relationships that were meaningful to him, the significance of life and death, of time passing. *Sessions* is like Scott's last tape. It is the performance of a lifelong reflection on the nature of analysis, the analytic relationship, and how best to talk about each.

I am struck by the difference and the similarity between Beckett and Scott. In *Sessions*, Scott's protagonist unlike Beckett's is not alone but in a relationship with another, struggling to construct a meaning for her life, to link what was broken and release herself from infantile terrors. Seeking freedom and knowledge, the analytic couple labor together against ambivalence and ignorance. Like Krapp, Scott uses the tapes to recapture and ponder the knowledge he and his patient shared some forty years ago. Contained in the metaphor of the tapes is the analytic process of wheeling backward, replaying scenarios over and over, tolerating knowing and not knowing at the same time, struggling with the impossibility of living the past anew, recontextualizing it, fostering the desire to use what one thinks one knows to face the unknown of creation and destruction. The ultimate desire through drama to outlive ourselves and share the irremediability of time as much as the repeated staging of the struggle to be heard and understood was also part of Scott's project. Some of Krapp's words come to mind as expressing Scott's search:

> Spiritually a year of profound gloom and indigence until that memorable night in March, at the end of the jetty, in the howling wind, never to be forgotten, when suddenly I saw the whole thing. The vision at last. This I fancy is what I have chiefly to record this evening, against the day when my work will be done and perhaps no place left in my memory, warm or cold, for the miracle that. . . (hesitates) for the fire that set it alight. What I suddenly saw then was this, that the belief I had been going on all my life, namely—(Krapp switches off impatient, winds the tape forward, switches on again)—great granite rocks the foam flying up in the lighthouse and the wind-gauge spinning like a propeller, clear to me at last that the dark I have always struggled to keep under is in reality my most—(Krapp curses, switches off, winds tape forward, switches on again)—unshatterable association until my dissolution of storm and night with the light of understanding and the fire (Krapp curses louder, switches off, winds tape forward, switches on again)—my face in her breast and my hand on her. We lay there without moving. But under us all moved, and moved us, gently up and down, and from side to side (Beckett, 1984, p. 60).

In French, Beckett (1959) has translated himself: "L'obscurité que je m'étais toujours acharné à refouler est en réalité mon meilleur. . . indestructible association jusqu'au dernier soupir de la tempête et de la nuit avec la lumière de l'entendement et le feu" (p. 23). Those words in French as much as in English describe the immense capacity of Scott to tolerate ignorance and the lifelong challenge of oscillating between "understanding and fire." *Sessions* is testimony to this creative tension that could only have taken place through the suspension of "desire and memory" (Bion, 1967) and the capacity to tolerate the unknown.

The second play that came to mind was Pirandello's (1995) *Six Characters in Search of an Author*. In the drama, a father brings his family to a director and asks if he could produce a play. When the director asks him if he has a script, the father answers that he wants to put on a play of his life. The whole play then unfolds with each character, a member of the family, offering his or her version of "what really happened." The complexity of the family's history is gradually constructed through the addition of each person's point of view. Scott and I discussed the difficulty of establishing the authorship of *Sessions*. Was it Scott or Mrs. J.R.? Is the psychoanalyst, like the director in Pirandello, not the one who provides a patient with a space, a theater where his entire internal family of characters can gradually develop a script? This multi voiced construction, based on a chorus of memories, will help the patient hear his complete story and, perhaps, understand his difficulties facing love, life, and death. Authorship resides in the shared process of actors with their audience, the analytic couple with their scientific audience.

Notes

1. Scott has accepted also in that spirit to be interviewed by Laurie Raymond in the book *The Inward Eye*, edited by Laurie W. Raymond and Susan Rosbrow-Reich, The Analytic Press Inc., Hillsdale, 1997, pp. 279-309.

2. Elisabeth Rudinesco is the author of the *Dictionnaire de la psychanalyse*, PUF, 1997; *Jacques Lacan. Esquisse d'une vie, histoire d'un système de pensée*, Fayard, 1993, 723 pp. [Translated as *Jaques Lacan* by Barbara Bray and published by Columbia Univ. Press, New York, 1997, 574 pp.]; and *Histoire de la psychanalyse en France. La bataille de cent ans.* Volume 1, 1st edition: Ramsay, 1982, 2nd edition: Seuil, 1986. [Translated as *Jacques Lacan and Co.* by Jeffrey Melman, and published by Chicago Univ. Press, Chicago, IL, 1990.]

References

Beckett, S. (1958). *Krapp's Last Tape*. Written in English in early 1958. First published in *Evergreen Review*, Summer 1958. First performed at the Royal Court Theatre, London, on October 1958.

—— (1959). *La dernière bande*. French translation by the author of *Krapp's Last Tape*. Paris: Édition de Minuit.

—— (1984). Krapp's last tape. In: *The Collected Shorter Plays of Samuel Beckett*. New York: Grove Weidenfeld, 316 pp.

Bion, W. R. (1967). Notes on memory and desire. *Psycho-Anal. Forum*, 2:272-280.

Coulter, C. (August 15, 1977). Letter to M.G.

—— (1997). Memorial Gathering for Dr. W.C.M. Scott, this volume.

Milner, M. (May 5, 1997). Letter to Evelyn Scott.

Pirandello, L. (1995). Six characters in search of an author. In: *Six characters in Search of an Author and Other Plays*. Penguin Books, pp. 5-65.

Scott, W.C.M. (1977). Two recorded interviews. *Psychia. J. Univ. Ottawa*, 2:20-28.

—— (1993). Introductory notes to the play *Sessions*.

Sessions: A One Act Play in 9 Scenes

W. Clifford M. Scott

Scene 1 – Frightened

D Well now here you see, you're frightened as to what you might say but you can say anything and we can try to understand whether it's yours or mine.

P I wish I could oblige by thinking of something to say that was really startling but if – I don't feel I'm frightened. . . and yet I feel frightened – is that what I'm frightened of?

D Well here at least we can make a connection between this "I feel frightened" and "I'm not frightened of what I say." I've asked you to put what you're conscious of into some sort of sound.

Scene 2 – Stuck

P I um I feel as if I am quite stuck and I'm not getting any better you see – I get better in every other way except the ways I um come to get better in. [Silence.] I don't know what else to say – I don't know what you want me to say.

D Just whatever you are aware of here.

P Oh

D You bring your troubles here.

P Yes obviously –

Scene 3 – Water

P Oh – gosh – I don't know what you are talking about. I – um – I want a drink of water – I always do when I'm scared –

D Do you want to go and get one or would you like me to go and get you one?

P No I'll go and get it.

D Which would you like to do better?

P I'll get it.

D Which would you like to do better?

Fig. 25. Clare Coulter and David MacIvor.
Credit: Tarragon Theatre

P I don't know – I don't know – I just feel I want go get out of here.

D Or you want to get water into you.

P Yeah.

D Well – do you want me to give you, – give you water, or do you want to get it yourself?

P You to give it me.

D I'll get you a glass of water.

Scene 4 – Gods and Giants

P Um I have had a a an odd feeling that um something is happening or something's different you see and it's just a feeling and there are no words for a feeling [laughs] are there or very few? Uh [sigh] I have a lot of extraordinary dreams which seemed important when I dreamed them – dreamt them – I haven't had a lot of time to think but I've been thinking, even when I haven't had the time – um I've been trying to catch myself out – I don't feel like telling you this at all – um [laughs] I've been trying to – y-you said about two weeks ago – um – what did you say – that I should talk to you about what I felt or something instead of feeling it and not even knowing it – you didn't put it like this – I forget how you said it – so you see I have been trying to catch myself out in those sort of split seconds when I suddenly think about you – um I've been trying to stop time and find out what I think or feel at that minute you see and if at that minute I put it into words [silence] then I remember what I thought – afterwards I can't believe it – um [sigh] and all of this is is not leading anywhere – I'm only trying to show my good intention of talking to you – one of the interesting things is I find that if I suddenly think of you without knowing I'm going to you see especially just lately you're always so much bigger than life – it's not as if I was young it is as if you had grown enormous which of course is the same thing isn't it – and um it's this extraordinary feeling of it not being anything new at all it feels new to me but I know it's really very old so of course I must really be remembering it or something although it doesn't feel like remembering and um ah it's awfully difficult I can't say anything at all uh therefore in one way that doesn't affect my ordinary life at all although it's all very surprising the things I find myself thinking – um well uh I just ramble on in this sort of aimless uh once I suddenly got a picture of you it was jolly funny because I had twelve people in the house – I was just getting tea for, so I mean I was really busy and I suddenly thought of you for a second or two and I – even at that minute I stopped and thought well what did I think at that second you see and I was surprised in a way because um it felt like – oh god what's the word – desire in a way – very acute – as though it made life seem infinitely rich you know full of possibilities and also very sad of course because of this perpetual grief for something one lost at the same minute or something you know and uh and yet of course it is not real at all I mean there is nothing I would like less than what I think I would like – when I think of you like this but when I think of you like this you see you're three times life size – it's most interesting I only come about up to your knees if that and of course it is awfully easy to see where people get gods and giants from isn't it [laughs] we carry them around with us. I'm not telling you anything yet am I it's awfully difficult to put these things into words.

D You mean you're not telling the original Gods and Giants you're telling me. You're telling me the one that isn't very much bigger than you.

P Oh yes that's right you are only life sized today, yes.

Scene 5 – Seven Minutes

P I feel we've finished haven't we?

D What would you like to do in the next seven minutes?

P Seven minutes is it? Oh I well – I don't know – I haven't any ideas I um I would like in the next seven minutes for you to tell me something that would alter the uh alter my whole view of everything – something that I can continue to um think on and work on afterwards.

Scene 6 – Babbling

D Well this sounds very much like you're feeling that your childish babbling on the – w – was not accepted and, as you put it, everything dissolved, disappeared, whereas out of the babbling – about an idea, comes the better idea – out of the babbling you learned speech for instance.

P Uh yeah, yes.

D For instance you just gave an example you say "yeah" and then "yes."

P That's just lazy, that's me when I'm thinking about something.

D But this laziness goes right back to your babbling when it – when you babbled. energetically, but other people called you lazy.

P Mm. . . .

D Because you hadn't learned to speak English

P Yes

Scene 7 – Screech

P I'm just talking rubbish for the sake of that wretched machine because I feel it's expecting something.

D It's easier to say that it's wretched than that I'm wretched.

P Yeah, I don't think you're wretched at all.

D That I expect some, that I expect something that I expect you to try your best to talk to me – to make a noise – some sort –

P I don't think you're wretched at all, it's the machine.

D Not to pull down the shutters.

P Yeah I don't, no I – think you're gorgeous.

D The machine isn't going to answer you. I can only give you back exactly what you've given it. Whereas what you give me undergoes some change before you get it back.

P [Laughs.] Hm. Yes – sometimes that's true [sighs] Hm – Hm –

D But I think you're feeling it's wretched partly to save me, because you want to keep me unwretched – other than wretched.

P Yes – I think you're quite gorgeous, and I shall keep you gorgeous and abuse the machine. Yes, that's true [clock strikes one] I do like a cuckoo clock have one at home and people always say, how can you bear it? Um – I'm frightfully pleased to find you've got a cuckoo clock – um – can't think of anything else.

D Pardon – I didn't catch –

P I'm sorry, I can't think of anything else to say. I was very pleased to find you had a cuckoo clock, I laughed to myself because I've always had one – um

D Now you see you feel that you can only say a thing once, but if you wanted to keep on talking when you were young you didn't stop at saying it once, if you liked something you kept on saying it and saying it and saying it and saying it, if you wanted to make a noise, but we know there's this conflict between sleepiness and silence and resting – and the fact that if you want to work with me, the outside me, the me that could be gorgeous, you have to perhaps keep on saying the same thing just as you would inside to yourself – over and over and over and over again.

P Instead of going to sleep? Yeah –

D But at time likely, you it wasn't just instead of going to sleep – you likely did it and fell asleep while doing it – and when you woke up couldn't remember just where you had stopped – and how mu- how many of the thing you had said had – could have been heard by anybody else – and how many of them just became a bit of your dream.

P Yes [sighs] it awfully difficult, isn't it, because I've got used to words that make sense. That's another thing I like about this kid of ours, you see, she's quite incoherent – um – she [laughs] hardly says any words that are ordinarily understandable at all.

D For instance?

P Oh, nothing – I mean I already know some of them – I know that carboar is an apple or a carrot but – er – most of the time it's just a sort of husky wa wa wa wa [laughs]. No it's a little bit more expressive than that. She just talks rubbish. Sometimes there's quite a lot of expression. She can't be bothered with ordinary words and she really doesn't seem to need them particularly. Well I feel rather inferior trying to deal with ordinary words, you see, which aren't half so expressive, are they.

D And if you had put expression into the wa wa wa, what would it have been?

P [Laughs.]

D Well. [Imitates P's laugh.]

D [Laughs.] What? At this minute? Mm. [Sighs.] I just don't know. Um – I'm, I'm feeling pretty good at the minute actually. I feel fairly comfortable I quite like you I'm a bit concerned because I don't feel quite as polite and cautious as I usually do.

D Well here – this may have something to do with the fear of asthma? There is this conflict between using sensible words, even words like gorgeous.

P Mm

D and using a wa wa wa wa words

P Mm

D in a different tone to mean something. Here's the fear of talking baby talk to me, talk that I won't understand until you translate it, except I'll just hear it as a song.

P Mm

D But you can try to make a noise – it doesn't need to be sense – it doesn't need to be sensible words –

P It's so awkward – [very softly] I never have anybody to talk rubbish to – I can answer somebody that speaks in rubbish to me.

D You almost said some rubbish, but it was so low I didn't catch it.

P Oh, did I? When?

D Just before you said I can answer somebody if they speak in rubbish.

P Um [sighs]. Well there are so many rubbish languages – I mean –

D For instance?

P [blathers] and wa wa wa wa wa wa wa wa [laughs] and – ah – I don't like the others – they're rather sharp and hard – my favorite is wizza wizza wa wa wa [laughs] all of them are.

D And is that the tone, or is that quieter than you usually like to say it

P Um – wa wa – wawawa – no not much louder than that – not much louder – it's all a matter of inflection you see [laughs] what you said – um – not much louder, no, it carries such weight if it's said quietly.

D It carries such weight if it's said quietly.

P Mm.

D This is as if you're talking to somebody near, but often you talk to people at a distance. This is the difference between talking to the gorgeous me and the gorgeous me at a distance isn't it.

P Mm. [Pause.] Um.

D That is after you learned that your voice could carry – or that you learned that it couldn't carry unless you made it louder. A baby will make a noise no matter whether it's high or low, it feels that it goes every place – there's no distinction is there?

P Mm – no – I wonder whether it enjoys it – I had a baby that nearly drove me dotty yesterday – it's a niece of mine and it's not yet a year and it screeches.

D Like?

P I couldn't even do it.

D Like? Try.

P D'you know, oddly enough, I can't try.

D What?

P Funnily enough I can't bring myself to try.

D Why?

P Um – the first thing I was going to say was because it might split the room in half, which is rather silly.

D This must be a fear that it would really hurt you. The room's all right, but you're not it's you that has the inhibition – you've kept this screech inside so much that you –

P Mm this is a screech – it's supposed to be of pleasure – but it looks um – it probably is pleasure – it's so young one just wouldn't know – but it's a ferocious noise.

D Like?

P Dammit, I can't screech suddenly! Is I I I I um.

D You can try to tell me what she did. Screech is a – is being sensible about it isn't it? To say screech is to be sensible about it.

P Mm

D Instead of saying she did – or she –

P Yes, well if I was sure I could reproduce it, I would, just to hurt your ears the same way it hurts my ears, but I might not be able to reproduce it exactly the same, might I?

D You mightn't reproduce it exactly the same way, and then it would be you not her, hurting my ears. Well, I – I'm not frightened of my ears. Did it really hurt your ears? Did it pain them? Or was that a reaction against it do you think? In other words, do you think you really hurt yourself?

P Didn't really hurt my ears. I don't know – it had the same effect as when a train rushes through a station – no, it probably doesn't actually hurt.

D Well, do you think she was perhaps imitating a train rushing through a station and likes that? Some children are frightened about that and others are –

P Mm

D Love it.

P Do they? I didn't know any baby ever liked it.

D How old is the baby?

P It's not yet a year.

D Well it depends on how she becomes able to master such a noise, to make a noise like it herself. If it's only another baby doing the same thing that she likes – if it's only a big one doing the same thing that she likes – she may enjoy it.

P She might – but she's always made this noise – it just means, that thing has registered with me [laughs] that's all, and she makes that noise.

D Try to tell me what the noise is.

P What do you mean?

D You see, it'll either be her noise or the noise most similar to hers which is actually your noise.

P A screech?

D That you like.

P Do – do you – are you asking me just to screech?

D I ask you to try to.

P [Laughs.] You screech first and then I will.

D She screeched first. And you screeched before you heard other people screech. But now you want me to screech.

P Do you know it makes me absolutely bloody wild, I don't know why – you're making me absolutely furious because.

D You said you are bloody mad because I asked you to let me understand what this screech is that's in you that you heard. Because in trying to tell me it, especially if you aren't sure that you'll imitate her, what you would be doing would be to let me know something about what your shriek is that's somewhat like hers – That would please you, but you have the memory of feeling that others were hurt. Well now here is the link between feeling that you can want to please, and instead you can hurt.

P Oh

D In other words, you don't want to really please me, because you're frightened that I won't take it. Well you can try to tell me. [9 seconds silence.]

P Yes, well it was her screech, not mine, I haven't got one.

D Everybody has.

P [Sighs.] Have they?

D Some of them better one's than others – perhaps – you might envy hers – this is maybe one of the ways of telling me that you envy her.

P [Sighs.] Um. Well now the more we talk about it the more difficult it gets.

D But you can try.

P [Deep breath.]

D At least you see, you took the big breath to get ready,

P Mm. [Laughs.]

D and then you let it out, quietly, and when I mentioned the big breath that you had taken, you chuckled.

P Ye –

D But you can try to tell me her shriek.

P I can't sort of think of it now – is – I I I – mm – how annoying this is – I could have let it out easier when I first s-s-s- said it – um – trying to think what she does – [silence] No, I couldn't do it, it's m- m- much too high pitched and piercing, it's like a train whistle [sighs] and she's absolutely rigid – um – [coughs] can't see the roof of her mouth, but I can feel that even that's rigid, you see, it's scared –

D Like?

P Screech? [Breath.] No, I can't do it. [Giggles.] Hell – I really can't do it, not by myself.

D I didn't say you could – I said you could try.

P [Laughing.] Well, I tried, and I suddenly found I couldn't – it collapses

D You didn't go rigid – you didn't stay rigid.

P Um – well I'll try and think myself into that horrible little baby um –

D You see the fear as to whether you're going to be angry – a moment ago you were quite angry at me – bloody angry at me – and you're wondering whether you're goin- going to give a shriek of delight or a shriek of rage, and you won't quite know what it is until it comes out, because at the very instant it's coming out you may be angry at yourself for not doing it nicely [pause] but try.

P [Silence. Sighs.] It's something colossal's being built up – I've absolutely nothing. I – I could have done it in the beginning, now I can't. I say to myself I don't know where a shriek comes from. Does it come out of my nose or out of my mouth or out of my throat or my tummy? I I've forgotten where it comes from almost.

D   Yes but now you're forgetting her and really remembering all your own life. Remembering all you've forgotten since you last did shriek.

P   Oh hm well,

D   Try.

P   Um – it's so quiet – um – if I could think back to the dog barking and my little brat saying wa wa wa wa wa wa and this baby screeching and [laughs] a sort of tremendous racket of all the – um – noise making things – it would seem to come naturally – but here it's like doing it in church – it's quite different. I'm sorry. . . .

D   Well you see, that's why you want me to make a big noise.

P   Yeah you make a hell of a noise and then I will.

D   So you can so you can do it – you see if I screech like [screeches] if I screech and – then –

P   [Screeches.] That's a bit like the baby was. That was rather a good one wasn't it? Or was it? [Laughs.] No the baby's was better than that. I don't know. I'll try again in a minute now I've broken the ice. [Sighs. Screeches.] No. I can't do it. It's an awful pity. The baby's comes out like a ribbon of steel. Mine's all breathy and coldy.

D   Your's is all breathy and coldy.

P   Mm

D   Well she's practiced a lot and it's a long time ago since you've practiced all sorts of noises. But now you see you immediately gave me a nicer noise, I suggest, than mine. I was more like – mine was more like this whining baby – I didn't know what mine was going to be until it started. But, did you think it was? was it?

P   I didn't think yours was whining. I thought it was quite good.

D   You did.

P   Only it hadn't got much bounce in it, but then, neither had mine – and that baby's had. Now that's a pity.

D   'cause the alternative would be walking a- the the last example of an alternative you gave would be walking well – how long would it take you, three or four minutes, to walk around the square?

P   Three or four minutes?

D   Pardon?

P   Is that really all?

D   Yes.

P   It's so funny because you see it seems to me like an hour or so that it would take.

D Well you can you can look on your watch and see how long it takes you if you want to. Walk around that square and come back in. I'll leave the door open. [Pause.] If you want to.

P Will you tell me what you'd like me to do. What would you like me to do?

D You can tell me what you'd like me to do. What would you like me to do?

P [Laughs.] Hell! I don't know. Let me think how large is it um, ah, three or four minutes is it? It looks like an hour's trip to me. [Pause.] Rather interesting wouldn't it? Because if I had panicked – yes but then what? [Pause.] Yes, I wouldn't mind. I wouldn't mind taking that risk.

D What risk?

P Um [sigh] I wouldn't mind taking that risk. But the annoying thing is that I should feel it was rather a big thing I'd done and you wouldn't think it was anything.

D I'll think it was just as big as you tell me it's big.

P And so that if I tell you I met a dragon on the corner you'll believe me? [Pause.] Will you? Yes.

D I will try to understand, you can tell me more about the dragon and we'll find out what the dragon was.

P Yes and the irritating thing is there might be nothing. Shall I do it just to prove I can do it?

D Well you see here's the other reason that you don't want to go away, that you don't want to – that your you – you're annoyed because you feel that if you do explore the world you won't find the edge. You see this is the child that wants to go and discover, discover the edge.

P Yes, that's true.

D And so it wouldn't go any longer when it ceases to believe that there isn't an edge 'cause it wants to keep up the belief that it's going to find the edge.

P Yes.

D You see you – you can, you can tell me about the dragon without going away. But here, you see, the dragons are really in you. You can tell me what kind of a dragon you want to be.

P Now why am I afraid, I can't still decide how big it is. You see I have to measure up everything and just think in my mind, I know what'll happen, I shall go one side and I shall think oh this is rather [laughs] this is all right! Hooray, it's all right! And then I shall think oh dear I do feel a fool, how silly of me to make all that fuss over this little thing, then I shall get a sudden panic, and then I shall be really frightened and then I shan't be able to walk either way, I shall get paralyzed fright just to. . . .

D Well now you see here's the wondering whether you'll go along with your original intention of walking around the square of whether you'll give it up as it's not worth it, as it's not being worthwhile, and whether you'll come back and then here's the dragon: will you lie, will you say I've been around the square or will you say no it isn't worthwhile it's silly. I can go round if I want to but, I won't go round.

P   But that is also a lie isn't it? [Pause.] That is a lie.

D   It's a statement of your wish, but you hadn't gone round.

P   But I might come back and say I haven't been because I was frightened to.

D   Well do you see the fear is well n- the fear now is whether you'd come back and say well it's silly, I shouldn't have wasted my time or your time I'd get much further by staying here.

P   Oh would I? Yes I would, wouldn't I? I'd forgotten for the minute. I was so intrigued by the idea of um just trying it out. As you might say in god's own front garden, um, that for the minute I h- had forgotten whether I, I, would be wasting time which could be more valuably used.

D   Well you're wondering you see whether you'll waste my time or whether you'll put me out of a job. And if I do anything with anybody else then the fear is that you will be jealous of what I do – you see you don't want me to watch you but there – but that's partly to keep away from saying that you want me to just sit here and think, and dream of you going around the square.

P   [Laughs.] Yes – [coughs] all the time. [Coughs.]

D   Just often – just like people will say "well I'll be thinking of you" whether you, here's the the fear you see as to what you'd feel about asking me, not to think of you until I come back.

P   Yes that's quite true now I don't know what else you've got to do here but,

D   You wonder whether I'd cheat. A moment ago you were thinking whether you'd cheat.

P   You know it really is ridiculous, isn't it?

D   It, or you, or me?

P   It. Me.

D   Well you're wondering whether I'm being ridiculous, I'd

P   [Coughs.]

D   I'd be ridiculous sitting here thinking about you all the time.

P   Um, yes. That's humiliating isn't it but it must be right, since you say it. Is that why I always suppose you never think of me at all?

D   Because you want me to be thinking of you all the time.

P   Yes so that, you know, I'm quite startled even if I um, imagine that you have to think about me even to w- work out wh- when I will have an appointment or something. Yes. I suppose so, 'cause after all you should think of me occasionally, shouldn't you? Um yes, – this is awful, I don't know now whether I ought to say yes I'm going – what is the time – is it really? – Quarter past ten.

D It's about fourteen minutes past ten.

P What time am I finishing with you?

D Half past ten. It'll take you about two to three minutes to walk around.

P Is that really true?

D My, in my best judgement. Because I know it takes ten minutes to walk to the park. [Coughs.] The park's a long way away compared to walking around there.

P Well you tell me whether I, you think it'd be a good idea or not.

D I'm telling you that you may go round. You may stay here. But you've got to decide is it a good thing.

P And you won't even tell me which you would rather I did because you don't even. . . .

D Well if we link this to your, to my wish for you to – be able

P Yeah?

D to get over your trouble.

P Yeah.

D I do- I don't know oth- wha- what we can do other than analyze what it means, is it, wou- would it be worthwhile making such a test and showing yourself how different it is between an hour's and minutes. What is it between having no feelings, just a dream, and having the real feeling of w- of walking around the, well as you said, I've picked up what you said walking around the square.

P So it would be worth it. Yeah well don't lets bloody well argue about it, I mean, um,

[Patient leaves.]

[Patient returns and tape is turned on.]

D Four minutes.

P Four minutes.

D Four minutes.

P Mmmm

D Did you get stuck or did you walk very slowly?

P Oh god it felt like it did feel like about four hours. But I bloody well did it.

D Well how did you get stuck?

P Oh it's horrid though, I should never do it again.

D It's horrid and you should never do it again, what would. . . .

P It's quite a horrible feeling you know, I'd forgotten how nasty it is, um, I just wouldn't have dared do it except that I was here and you were here. Um, shall I describe the whole process? All right. I set off. While I could pretend

I hadn't started because I still hadn't put my coat on, that was all right, and then I got a smoke and then I thought uh "Well I'm still read – getting ready to go out" you see. Then I um realized I was out. I was then on the corner where there's a pillar post box, it's – somewhere about half a mile away [laughs] it seems down that way, um, then I began to get awfully trembly and feel very sick and beastly and thought "Oh heck what am I playing at, I was, uh, just showing off, of course I can't do this, I'll go back," and I began to go very slowly which what usually happens is that I stop dead d'you see, I can't move, I can't move forwards, and I can't move backwards, because the other thing is to run, and I'm very frightened of that too so I don't seem able to just walk. I either have to run like mad and lose my breath, or stop all together. Well then I just went on walking with trembling legs and feeling as if I was going to cry and feeling extremely sick and unpleasant until I got round that corner, then well you – it's just about when I'm nearing halfway anywhere so that it'll be as long to go on as to go back that I get a panic, well then I saw somebody – come out of a house and I thought "Oh well anyway she's a human being in the desert um, I could walk with her if I wanted to" and then I went on, and then when I got round there I found to my horror that I didn't come round this way I had to go out into the great big world of the street, not the square at all, or is it? Anyway it doesn't look like it – it looks like.

D   It's actually still numbered on the square.

P   Yeah it doesn't look like it though it looks like a main thoro – ughfare.

D   You see the fronts of the houses.

P   Oh yeah. Well then when I was out of sight of this house you see it should have felt worse and in some curious way it almost felt better. I nearly felt "Ha! This is me in the great big world" you know [coughs] but the amount it um makes me feel horrid the first half, it's only just worth it. But fancy that was four minutes, you see it's so very odd, isn't it. I, I mean, um, actually, not exaggerating I say four hours, how long does it seem? Well I should have said it was about thirty-five minutes perhaps. S'what it felt like.

D   And it was four minutes because you went so slowly.

P   [Cough.] Yeah that was because it was really rather clever of me to move at all if you did but know it.

P   Oh it's horrid though I shall never do it again.

D   It's horrid and you shall never do it again.

Scene 9 – Dirt

D —how have you been?

P I've been very well thank you, but I haven't been out by myself – um – I've been very well – I was quite pleased with how well I was getting on with all sorts of things and then I got rather depressed because um – I realized I haven't been out anywhere by myself and as soon as I thought "shall I" I couldn't face the idea – and when I thought of walking around your square I thought "Oh dear I wish I hadn't done that – that was a risk" you see [laughs] rather um like the man who hoped he'd had a pork chop because he preferred pork chops to lamb – so he hoped it was a pork chop he'd just eaten I mean – only it was the other way around – I – almost felt I wished I hadn't done it because it was too big a risk to take [pause] otherwise I've done very well you see – I get on so well, with the million things I have to do, and I don't have much time to think, – just sometimes I, note to myself that I've done that such and such a thing rather efficiently and much quicker than I would have.

D Well you see this is the Peter Pan isn't it?

P Yeah.

D This is what you must have done as a child, I mean you exploited the things you could do,

P Yeah

D that you did do so much that you didn't want to be like other people

P Um

D who go about.

P Yes, I am in a bit of a spot because you see I've got to do them now whether I like it or not – I've been so cunning the way I've arranged my life.

D But you don't have to – whether you like it or not – "not go out by yourself" ever.

P No, that is inconvenient – uh, uh, I did this morning before I was properly awake, think "oh what a relief it will be when I can and of course I could now if I really had to" – when I was really awake I knew that wasn't true, but, um – I was thinking about it because, my – John has been having toothache for a month and – nobody knows why you know, and uh – I thought "oh well he'll probably go into hospital for Christmas and that will be very annoying – and that will be Guy's and that's a devil of a long way to get to" – well the little kid we've got has also got to go into Guy's either just before or just after Christmas to have tonsils and adenoids out – we knew this was going to happen – um – my other kid's got a beastly cold and didn't think she felt like going to school anyway – I suddenly thought "good gracious – um – it is a nuisance this – I mean I could – they could all go to hospital and I could still manage perfectly well you see if I could just get there" – um – well it's all right ah – um – I mean it will be all right – but it is a nuisance and I shall be glad when it's all right, but I can't lift a finger to [laughs] make it all right, or shan't I, or don't I want it to be.

D Well this is partly the annoyance that nobody, lifts a finger to, make it all right – in the sense that, as a child you, would have liked to have been like most children, i- in the sense that they were pushed out – and were left –

P But when I was a kid I was – I was, and I did – I went places when I was nine that I wouldn't dare to do now.

D You didn't do them with any feeling though – there was a feeling with which you do them now – that's the other s- inner side of it, isn't it? You had quite a lot of feeling in going around the, the square including the feeling of being a bit interested in discovering a street.

P Mm, mm?

D There is a fear that if you let your feelings go further you'll like something else – and that will be stealing things away as it were, from the people that you are now attached to, or the things you now attach to.

P [Pause.] The one thing I know is different – I suddenly realized this morning – I don't ever now find myself thinking "oh well anyway I'm half way through already, soon I shall be old and then I shan't be expected to go out alone"- [laughs] I mean I do at least look forward to – I have a picture in my mind of being able to, not of – no longer having to excuse myself for not doing so – d'you see – but I still don't understand it because from when I was about five until I was, I don't know, – how old, um,

D How old?

P Well from five until thirteen I went out anywhere without any sort of fear.

D With how much feeling?

P It depends where I was going – oh I didn't – no that's not true to say without any sort of fear – sometimes with an unaccountable dread and a longing to get home again – yes – but, uh, I mean I did have to go to school everyday whether I liked it or not – I very frequently – um – couldn't and wouldn't and felt horrid but – I mean I went to other kid's houses you see – I was much freer then than I am now [silence] and from when I was about, nineteen to about twenty-three – I had about four years when again I could almost go anywhere – and then I enjoyed it – you say with what feeling – well then with a tremendous amount of interest and pleasure and wondering why I hadn't been able to do it before. [Silence.] Well now I've arranged it so cunningly that all the – interest and pleasure is – comes to me most of it – I mean I don't have to, go out to find it. [Silence one minute.]

It's a soporific thing that isn't it? It just ticks a bit and goes round – and I can't help looking at it [22 second silence] – um, I know what happens next – I say what do you want me to talk about and you say anything that's in your head and – um –

D No I don't.

P Don't you? You do usually.

D Anything that's anywhere.

P Anything that you're conscious of – usually you say don't you?

D And you can be conscious of anything anywhere not just in your head.

P Oh, yeah, well – I'm not really conscious of anything except I'm –

D It's as if if you'd like – in other words – to keep things in your head but you're curious about this and it's sleepy, [pause] and then you, touch my chair, with your – foot, and then, you see this is all to keep away from people – because sooner or later you were interested in things, but only because they, were, were substitutes for people that you're interested in.

P But I'm not interested in things – I'm only interested in people.

D Well I'm the only body that you can see.

P At this minute?

D Or touch, without going away.

P I don't touch people – um – [Sigh.]

D And you sigh because you don't – but you used to.

P You're not a person anyway – not the you that is sitting here is not a person.

D Or you make him a thing – you see you're treating me as, well to use the old expression that you used – as just so much dirt. The dirt was a big first word that meant anything that wasn't a body. [10 second silence.]

P Um – yes I don't know – it's not me that makes you not a person – I mean you are not a person on purpose for a reason of your own, and therefore I can't treat you as person, but you're just sufficiently human to make me feel it's all wrong when you're quiet and I'm quiet and I feel I'm not putting anything into the. . . .

D Into this – but here you see if you did put something in this you wonder would you make me more dirty or less dirty – would you make me more of a person or less of a person – more of a body or less of a body – because I've always been what I am, but you f- feel that I make myself not a-person – I've never said so.

P No, but I mean that is so – isn't it – you are like a

D No

P screen aren't you?

D Well you can use me as a mirror – as a screen – if you wish to, but you're keeping me, not a person and just so much dirt, in order to use me that way.

P   Why do you say dirt?

D   In contrast to – persons.

P   Um [pause] but other things are not persons are no- not dirt either.

D   They were to begin with until you – I suggest – they were to begin with until you, began to idealize all these things and found how much you could use them to make something nice out of.

P   Mm. [15 second silence.]

D   I'm suggesting dirt is perhaps the biggest word that means – I mean the shortest word that means most as to what fills in the space between you and people. [12 second silence.]

P   Mm. [Silence.] I don't understand.

D   You said you don't touch people – something that keeps you from touching them – something that you are touching – something that's in between you and people – you can say it's wonderful stuff, or it's not very nice, but I suggest that dirt is the best word to – use to – make you feel about something about – what's in between.

P   Mm – why did I say I don't touch people? Oh that is quite simple – you said you were here to see or touch – well people that touch people are – um – surely everybody's horror – anyway they're mine. People that will come too near, want to paw at you – I mean [laughs] it's not pleasant, um –

D   Well here you feel you don't want to talk about, any wish you might have to touch but I mention this in connection with your touching my chair – for fear then that if you touched me, I might want to touch you and then you'd be horrified – and you feel this fear that I might paw you.

P   Yes that's funny when I said that because of course I didn't mean you – probably I should love you to paw me – I don't know. Um – I was only thinking of people that touch on principal if you know what I mean – and I don't touch on principal. [Sighs.] I don't know what principal is – anyway I don't touch that's all – um –

D   What is principal?

P   I don' think it exists – I don't know what it is [laughs] – I mean it's just a s- s- silly saying isn't it? – principal? On principal? I don't know what it means – people say they don't do something on principal – it's just rubbish isn't it? I mean they don't do it because they don't want to or because something prevents them, or [pause] it's one of those words that just make rubbish all of a sudden I don't know what it means. [Pause.] Dirt – wait a minute – let's get back to this – um – yes it is an idea – that – isn't it? Um [sighs] – as if there is a lot of dirt twixt me and thee – between anybody and me – um [pause] which probably I used to be much more aware of – I mean now I seem to have found a shortcut round it – with most people [pause] but much earlier, when it was difficult to um – just make any kind of relationship with anybody – easily – it might be because there was a lot of dirt – wait a minute though you once said – or did you – that when I expected nothing of anybody I was treating them like dirt didn't you [pause] then there would be nothing but a world of dirt – no people at all – unless there was one person of whom I would – expect something -

D Even if it was expecting them to be alive.

P Mm. [Silence two minutes.] I'm not conscious of anything in particular now – except that you sit there and – I was just wondering whether it was, rather the same sort of feeling as when I am about to have a panic that – I really mustn't move at all – um – otherwise I shall break it – I don't know what it is – um – this – this is quite pleasant though, if I don't move at all – when I, when it's a – a – fear I'm – it's only all right – yes it's the same thing only it's not pleasant. [Pause. Lighter.] I feel this business ought to work – in theory it ought to work anyway, but you see when I get here – it doesn't work like this – I just go stupid and – um – just just stupid [pause] ordinarily, I feel I could tell anybody exactly what I felt – always thinking or something – but I'm half out of myself when I am here you see. . . .

D Well here you feel scared, and feel that it would be stupid to let me know how nice you can be when you're silent, but if you began to tell me what was going on then, it would be like putting a nice you in me, in the same way as you feel you've got a nice me in you, and this will take you back a long time, to the time when you hadn't – a chance to – try to – let your mother really understand how nice you were, how nice you wanted to be. Then the distance between you and peo- you and people – even if it's a fraction of a s- of an inch

P Mm

D can become so horrid – which if you close it by touching them, then you can quite forget – all the difficulties of – telling them – if you're not in touch with them in any other way besides telling them.

P Oh yes.

D [Sneeze.] Pardon me.

P Mm [coughs] yes I suppose words are a poor substitute for touching really [7 second pause] it's funny, I feel, um – I hate the whole subject – I want to be tied up in myself – a very small parcel – um – don't like the whole idea of any of it – I feel quite self contained.

D Well here you feel I'm stealing something, as if I'd – and and the nicer you – the nicer the self that you contain, the more you feel I'll be stealing it if – you really let me know about it – but here, – as you put it – you're so jealous of the thought that I might know – something nice about you – that you feel, you see, and that you feel, not based upon experience with me, but with experience with lots of other people you feel there's something very nice about me – because you feel there's – you've got this nice me – in you.

P Yes.

D [Blows his nose. Silence one minute.]

P I'm stuck again. [Silence thirty seconds.]

D You're stuck on the machine – you like to watch it.

P I'm just fighting the idea of going to sleep – its ex

D Well I'll wake you up if you go to sleep – you can lie down and go to sleep.

P It's an awful waste of time isn't it?

D You don't know what you'd dream on the way to sleep, or while you slept, see this may be a defense against feeling nice when awake – you want to feel the niceness more vividly as you've often done in sleep.

P Mm – yes [pause] well why can't I just enjoy this? It's very pleasant.

D Well lie back and enjoy it – I'll wake you up, by asking you to wake up, after awhile.

P As soon as you tell me I may I – I um – think I mustn't.

D Well this is partly your feeling you mustn't give me the pleasure, in the sense that if you went to sleep and dreamt, dear knows what pleasure you'd feel you'd be giving me – you see if you take me into this pleasure that you're feeling.

P I don't feel it's like this at all – I feel it's all the other way – if I wasted your time by going to sleep I shouldn't dream which would be – a pity, and that would be a disappointment –

D But I think this is a way of talking about what you feel about dreams, that they're waste in the sense that they're not real, here you – you're just telling me that – "you'd really be still out here, even if I go to sleep and dream about you – it'll be a waste because, you wouldn't be feeling the way I'll be feeling it and the way I'll be feeling that you'll be feeling it if I dream about it" – it's seems as if it's your way of telling me "what a waste all this pleasure is if I don't – share it equally with you" – as it has been from the beginning of your life with all sorts of people – if you were happy and they – and you couldn't believe they were as happy as you were.

P Mm.

D Well, you wanted to make them as happy as you were.

P Yes – that's reasonable enough. [13 second silence.] Yes that is so, I suppose – um – this could be very pleasant. It's spoiled because – yes because you don't know how pleasant it is, and because you're sitting here with half an eye on your watch, probably, I don't know but – um – because you're you're here for quite different purpose [laughs] for what I'm here, so that – here in my chair it's as if I'm lying on the beach – and um – it's a long, long afternoon and the water's lapping and it's very pleasant – but if you're just sitting there with that ruddy machine going round, watching me and hoping to God I'll say something that's some, use so that you can – so that we can, quicker um [laughs] I'm so drowsy, I don't know what I'm saying – ah [sigh] – so that the treatment will bear fruit the quicker and, be ended the sooner – I don't mean that you want to, chuck me out but naturally – um – y- y- y- – um – [sigh] – well m- my sitting on a beach isn't leading anywhere is it?

D Are you alone on the beach?

P [Laughs.] Yes, because I'm surrounded – I'm not alone – I mean I am alone – um – no you're there – you are it – you're the sand beneath me, the sky over me and the sea all round you see – it's rather pleasant – you've turned into a [laughs] complete god, but you haven't got

D [Noise.]

P a person. So you don't need to blow your nose or anything like that. You see I'm –

D This is very much the picture of the satisfied baby isn't it? It doesn't make any distinction between the world that it's lying on, that's above it and beside it.

P Mm

D And the mother that it was feeding on and was once upon a time inside of.

P MM

D But sooner or later it finds that all this is – dirt – in contrast to the living body. [13 second silence.]

D but it's as if you're saying you'd like to be independent of any other body – you'd like to be able to roam the world and realize that the world was – that any bit of the world could be like anybody but you see this is only the beginning of the – of the dream and the fantasy – I wonder how it ended – when would you want to leave the beach? [Pause.] And who do you want to find?

P Mm – yes you're quite right there's no end in that – [sighs] uh [silence] yes it's the beginning isn't it? I like people, but I don't want to need people all that much – I don't – I I'm appalled at the idea of people that go and live in a cottage miles away from anybody [pause] um – not wanting people at all – I dislike that but [sighs] uh it's a pity to have to need people too much isn't it [pause] and I don't – except, um, I think I do, to go places – but otherwise I don't need people all that much [pause] oh I wouldn't know, I'm just talking rubbish. [11 second silence.]

D And could I see you at a quarter to ten next week?

P Yes – thank you. Isn't it nearly Christmas or something?

D I won't see you the week after that which is the week after – Christmas.

FIN

Fig. 26. Clifford Scott in his office at home (1984).
Credit: The Estate of W.C.M. Scott.

Fig. 27. Clifford Scott and his second wife, Evelyn Scott (1996).
Credit: The Estate of W.C.M. Scott.

Bibliography of Published, Unpublished, and Other Works of W. Clifford M. Scott

I. Published Works (1924-1995)

Legend:
A – Article/Paper   B – Book Chapter   C – Translation
D – Discussion   I – Interview   R – Broadcast

1924

1A   A pathological anomalous thyroid in the Barn-Door Skate (*Raia Laevis*). *Contributions to Canadian Biology being Studies from the Biological Stations of Canada*, Nova Scotia, 2:131-134.

1925

2B   A comparative analysis of the size of certain public institutions in Canada, with special reference to mental hospitals. *Univ. Toronto Med. J.*, 3: 27.

1926

3A   The relation of the iodine content and the histological structure to the growth curve of the thyroid gland of the Barn-door Skate (*Raia Laevis*). *Trans. Royal Soc. Can.*, 20: 229-237.

1929

4A   A note on the effect of temperature and salinity on the hatching of the eggs of the Winter Flounder (*Pseudopleuronectes Americanus Walbaum*). *Contributions to Canadian Biology being Studies from the Biological Stations of Canada*, Nova Scotia, 4:137-141.

1931

5A   Functional achlorhydria and the histamine test (with S. Katzenelbogen). *Amer. J. Psychia.* 10:829-837.

1936

6A   Cardiovascular effect of benzedrine (with E.W. Anderson). *The Lancet*, 2: 1461.

1937

7D   Discussion of E. Guttman and W.S. MacLay's "Clinical observations on schizophrenic drawings." *Br. J. Med. Psychol.*, 16: 184-205.
Discussion by: W.C.M. Scott, E.A. Bennet, Paterson Brown, "The unwill-

ing patient." (A contribution to a Symposium given at a Joint Mtg. of the Med. Soc. of the Br. Psycho-Anal. and Inst. for the Scientific Treatment of Delinquency, December 16, 1936.) *Br. J. Med. Psychol.*, 17: 76-77.

1939

9A   The chronic uncertified. (Read at the Sec. Psychia., Royal Soc. Med., June 13.) Reported in *Br. Med. J.*, June 24, pp. 1299-1300; *The Lancet*, June 24, pp. 1437-1439.

1941

10D   Discussion of Aubrey Lewis, "Psychiatric aspects of Effort Syndrome." *Proc. Roy. Soc. Med.*, 34: 539-554.

11A   The soldier's defence and the public attitude. (Read at a Mtg. of the Med. Sec. of the Br. Psychol. Soc., Nottingham, April 19.) *The Lancet*, 2: 271-274.

1946

12A   Recent advances in psychiatry. *J. Ment. Sci.*, 90: 509; *Int. J. Psycho-Anal.*, 27: 166.

13A   A note on the psychopathology of convulsive phenomena in manic depressive states. (Read at the Int. League against Epilepsy, London, Oct. 21, 1938.) *Int. J. Psycho-Anal.*, 27:152-155.

1947

14A   On the intense affects encountered in treating a severe manic-depressive disorder. (Read at the 15th Int. Psycho-Anal. Congress, Paris, Aug. 2, 1938.) *Int. J. Psycho-Anal.*, 28: 139-145.

15A   Problems of ego structure. (Mtg. of European Psychoanalysts, Amsterdam, May 24-27.) Summary published in *Int. J. Psycho-Anal.*, 28: 215.

1948

16A   [See 15A.] A problem of ego structure. *Psychoanal. Q.*, 17: 71-83.

17A   A psychoanalytic concept of the origin of depression. (Read at the Sec. Psychia., Int. Congress Physicians, London, Sept. 1947.) *Br. Med. J.*, 1: 538-540.

18D   Discussion of M. Mead's "Guilt and the dynamics of psychological disorder in the individual." (Second Plenary Session, Int. Congress Mental Health Conf. Med. Psychother., London.) *Proc. Int. Conf. Med. Psychother.*, London: Lewis, 3: 49-50.

19D   Discussion of J. Rickman's "Collective guilt." (Second Plenary Session, Int. Congress Mental Health Conf. Med. Psychother.) *Proc. Int. Conf. Med. Psychother.*, London: Lewis, 3: 88-89.

20A   Some psycho-dynamic aspects of disturbed perception of time. (Read at the Med. Sec., Br. Psychol. Soc., 1935.) *Br. J. Med. Psychol.*, 21: 111-120.

21A   Psychiatric problems amongst evacuated children. (Read at the Symposium on Lessons for Children Psychiatry, Med. Sec., Brit. Psychol. Soc., 1946.) *Br. J. Med. Psychol.*, 21: 171-174.

22A   Some embryological, neurological, psychiatric and psychoanalytic implications of the "Body Scheme." (Elaborated from a paper read at a meeting of the Br. Psycho-Anal. Soc., March 19, 1947.) *Int. J. Psycho-Anal.*, 29: 141-155.

23A   Application of psychoanalytic principles to the treatment of in-patients in mental hospitals. (Read at the Symposium on Application of Psychoanalytic Principles to the Hospital In-patient, Royal Soc., Med. Psychol. Section, March 9, 1940.) *J. Ment. Sci.*, 94: 767-772.

24A   Psychopathology of anorexia nervosa. (Slightly altered from a paper read at the Symposium on Anorexia Nervosa at the Med. Sec., Br. Psycho-Anal. Soc., May 22, 1940.) *Br. J. Med. Psychol.*, 21: 241-247.

1949

25C   [See 17A.] Eine Psychoanalytische Betrachtung über den Ursprung der Depression. *Psyche*, 3: 312-319.

26A   The progress of psychoanalysis in Great Britain. *Br. Med. Bull.*, 6: 31-35.

27A   The psychoanalytic view of mandala symbols. (Discussion on archetypes and introjected objects, Med. Section, Br. Psychol. Soc., June 23, 1948.) *Br. J. Med. Psychol.*, 22: 23-25.

28A   The "Body Scheme" in psychotherapy. (Read at Med. Sec., Br. Psychol. Soc., Jan. 26, 1949.) *Br. J. Med. Psychol.*, 22(3-4): 139-150.

1951

29R   Psychotherapeutic treatment of endogenous depression. B.B.C. Latin-America Talks.

30A   Indications for and limitations of psychoanalytic treatment. *Br. Med. J.*, 2: 597-600.

31D   Discussion of W. Mayer Gross' "The treatment of depression." (Sec. Psychia., Royal Soc. Med., March 13, 1951.) *Proc. Roy. Soc. Med.*, 44: 961-966.

1952

32A   Patients who sleep or look at the analyst during psychoanalytic treatment – Technical considerations. (17th Int. Psycho-Anal. Congress, Amsterdam, Aug. 1951.) *Int. J. Psycho-Anal.*, 33: 465-469.

33D   Discussion of Beryl Sandford's "Psychotherapeutic work in maternity and child welfare clinics." *Br. J. Med. Psychol.*, 25: 9.

34D   Discussants: Melanie Klein, S. Nacht, W.C.M. Scott (pp. 60-65), H.G. Van der Waals, "The mutual influences in the development of ego and id." (17th Int. Psycho-Anal. Congress, Amsterdam, Aug. 1951.) *Psychoanal. Study Child*, 7: 51-68.

35C   [See 26A.] The progress of psychoanalysis in Great Britain. Translated in *Medcina y Chirurgia*.

36A   Psychotherapy of schizophrenia. (Proc., Premier Congrès Mondial de Psychiatrie, Paris, Sept. 1950). *Psychothérapie-psychanalyse, médecine psycho-somatique comptes rendus de séances*, Abstract. Paris: Herrman & Cie, 5: 427.

37A   Evolution and present trends of psychoanalysis. (*Proc. V.*) *Ibid*, 5: 140-142.)

38A   Problems of inpatient psychotherapy. The possibilities of psychotherapy and psychoanalysis in a hospital set-up. (Sept. 25.) *Ibid*, 5: 440.

39A   Psychopathology of depressive states. (Contribution to a Symposium on Psychopathology of Depressive States, Sept. 26.) *Ibid*, 1: 394.

40A   Psychopathology of depersonalization. (*Proc. 1*, Psychopathologie générale.) *Ibid*, 1: 260-262.

1954

41A   A new hypothesis concerning the relationship of libidinal and aggressive instincts (18th Int. Psycho-Anal. Congress, London, July 29, 1953; Br. Psycho-Anal. Soc., Jan. 1954). *Int. J. Psycho-Anal.*, 35: 234-237.

1955

42A   A note on blathering. (Read at Br. Psycho-Anal. Soc., June 4, 1952.) *Int. J. Psycho-Anal.*, 36: 348-349.

43A/R Sigmund Freud. (CBC Broadcast Series, 1954.) Published as a chapter in *Architects of Modern Thought*, Toronto: C.B.C. Publication, pp. 25-32.

44A   [See 17A.] A psychoanalytic concept of the origin of depression. Published as a chapter in *New Directions in Psycho-Analysis*, ed. by Melanie Klein, London: Tavistock Publications, 1955. [Paperback, 1971.]

1956

45A   Sleep in psychoanalysis. (Read at Br. Psycho-Anal. Soc., 1950.) *Bull. Phila. Assn. Psychoanal.*, 6: 72-83.

46A   Obituary: Sigmund Freud, 1856-1939. *Can. Med. Assn. J.*, 74: 744-745; *Can. Psychia. Assn. J.*, 1: 57-58.

1957

47D   Symposium/Rumination: J. Richmond, E. Eddy, W.C.M. Scott. Discussion of E. Reichsman, G. Engel, V. Harway and S. Escalona's "Disorders of affects during childhood. Monica, an infant with gastric fistula and depression." (Am. Psychia. Assn. Reg. Res. Conf., Syracuse, N.Y.) *Psychia. Res. Rep.*, 8: 33-34.

48D   Discussion of H. Fox et. al. "Some methods of observing humans under stress." (Am. Psychia. Assn. Reg. Res. Conf., 1957.) *Psychia. Res. Rep.*, (7).

49D   Discussion of Leo Kanner's "Early infantile autisms, 1943-1955" (Am. Psychia. Assn. Reg. Res. Conf., Montreal, 1955.) *Psychia. Res. Rep.*, 7.

1958

50A   Therapeutic results in psychoanalytic treatment without fee. (Am. Psycho-anal. Assoc., Chicago, May 1956.). *Int. J. Psycho-Anal.*, 39: 64-68

51A   Noise, speech and technique. (Int. Psycho-Anal. Congress, Paris, 1957.) *Int. J. Psycho-Anal.*, 39: 108-111.

52A   Obituary: Ernest Jones. *Br. Med. J.*, Febr. 22, p. 463; *The Lancet*, Feb. 22, p. 438; *Can. Med. Assn. J.*, 78: 641-642.

53A   The impact of Meyerian psychobiology and psychoanalytic theory and practice in the development of child psychiatry in Great Britain. (Can. Psychia. Assn., Edmonton, June 1957.). *Can. Psychia. Assn. J.*, 3: 20-31.

54A   Introductory Remarks as Chairman of Committee/Discussion of H. Denber's "Transference and countertransference problems in relationship to drugs." (Conference on Psychodynamic Psychoanalytic and Sociological Aspects of the Neuroleptic or Tranquillizing Drugs in Psychiatry, Montreal, April.) *The Dynamics of Psychiatric Drug Therapy*, ed. G.J. Sarwer-Foner, Springfield, IL: C. C. Thomas, 1959, pp. 319-320.

55A   The psychological effects on the deprivation of liberty on the offender. Discussion of Bruno M. Cormier's "Types of regression determined by the deprivation of liberty and implications in rehabilitation." (Congress of Corrections, Montreal, May 28, 1957.) *Proc. Can. Congress of Corrections*, pp. 147-149.

1959

56A   The impact of Meyerian psychobiology and psychoanalytic theory and practice in the development of child psychiatry in Great Britain. *Can. Psychia. Assn. J.*, 3: 120-131.

57D   Discussion of H. Liddell's "A biological basis for psychopathology." (Am. Psychia. Assn. Reg. Res. Conf., Montreal, Nov. 1957.). *Psychia. Res. Rep.*, 11: 133-136.

58D   Discussion of Howard Liddell's "Stress and maternal protection in animals and men." (Am. Psychia. Assn. Reg. Conf., Montreal, 1959.). *Psychia. Res. Rep.*, 11: 134-135.

1960

59A   Symposium on Depressive Illness: Depression, confusion and multivalence. (Read at the 21st Int. Psycho-Anal. Congress, Copenhagen, July 1959.) *Int. J. Psycho-Anal.*, 41: 497-503.

60A   Panel on Brief Psychotherapy. Introductory remarks and discussion: J. Guild, D.J. Watterson, K. Stern, R.R. Lemieux. (Can. Psychia. Assn. Mtg., Ottawa, June 5, 1959.) *Can. J. Psychia.*, 5: 161-184.

1961

61D   Discussion of Dr. Ostow's "Theory of psychic energetics." *Proc. Int. Symposium Extrapyramidal System and Neuroleptics, Montreal*, 1960, ed. Jean-Marc Bordeleau. Montreal:Thérien Frères, pp. 519-522.

62A   Differences between the playroom used in child psychiatric treatment and in child analysis. (Can. Psychia. Assn., Banff, June 1960.) *Can. Psychia. Assn. J.*, 6: 281-285.

63C   [See 59A.] Depression, Verwirrung und Multivalenz. *Psyche*, 11: 678-689.

64C   [See 59A.] Dépression, confusion et polyvalence. *Rev. fr. psychanal.*, 25: 913-925.

65A   The demonstration of object relations and affect in a set situation in infants of 6-12 months. (20-minute film dealing with an elaboration of Winnicott's observations.) In *Proc. Third World Congress Psychia.*, Montréal, June 1960, pp. 56-59.

1962

66A   The concept of the id. (Panel on Folklore and Linguistics, Indiana Univ. Res. Ctr. Anthropol., May 17-19, 1962.) In *Trans. Indiana Univ. Conf. on Paralinguistics and Kinesics*, Bloomington: Univ. of Indiana Press, pp. 411-445.

67A   Symposium: A Reclassification of Psychopathological States. (22nd Int. Psycho-Anal. Assn. Congress, Edinburgh, Aug. 1961.) *Int. J. Psycho-Anal.*, 43: 344-359.

68D   Discussion of D. Szabo's "Psychodynamics of father-daughter incest." (Symposium on Incest, 2nd Annual Res. Conf. on Criminology and Delinquency.) *Can. Psychia. Assn. J.*, 5: 250-252.

1963

69A   The psychoanalytic treatment of mania. (Am. Psychia. Assn. Reg. Res. Conf., Montreal, April 1962.) *Psychia. Res. Rep.*, 17: 84-90.

70A   A finger-licking, finger-flicking habit. (Am. Psychoanal. Assn., N.Y. City, Dec. 1962.) *J. Am. Psychoanal. Assn.*, 11: 832-834.

71A   Symposium: Psychotherapy in Mental Retardation. The psychotherapy of the mental defective. (Annual Mtg., Can. Psychoanal. Assn., Toronto, June 15.) *Can. Psychia. Assn. J.*, 8: 293-315.

1964

72A   Mania and mourning. (Read at the Can. Psychoanal. Soc., Nov. 1962.) *Int. J. Psycho-Anal.*, 45: 373-377.

73C   [See 67A.] Une reclassification des états psychopathologiques. *Rev. fr. psychanal.*, 28: 169-184.

74A   The limitations of science. (Read at the St. James Literary Soc., Montreal, Oct. 1963.) *Can. Psychia. Assn. J.*, 91: 700-703.

1965

75C   [See 74A.] Deuil et manie. *Rev. fr. psychanal.*, 29: 205-218.

76D   Discussion of Fr. Salman, "The psychology of religious experience." (R.M. Bucke Memorial Soc. Conf. on Personality Change and the Religious Experience, Montreal, Jan. 1965.) *Proc.*, pp. 30-35.

1966

77A   The mutually defensive roles of depression and mania. (Panel on Psychoanalytic Concepts of Depressive Illnesses. Res. Conf. on the Depressive Group of Illnesses. McGill Univ., Montreal, Feb.1965.) *Can. Psychia. Assn. J. Spec. Suppl.*, 2: S267-S274.

1968

78C   [See 77A.] Les rôles défensifs réciproques de la dépression et la manie. *Interprétation*, 2: 95-107.

1971

79A   Problems of psychosis (p. 317; p. 319; p. 344; p. 373; p. 421) (Int. Colloquium on Psychosis, Montreal, Nov. 5-8, 1969. Part 1 – Plenary Sessions, 1969, Excerpta Medica Foundation, pp. 1-264; Part 2 – Discussion, 1971, Excerpta Medica Foundation, pp. 265-451), eds. Pierre Doucet and Camille Laurin.

1975

80A   Remembering sleep and dreams. *Int. Rev. Psycho-Anal.*, 2(3): 252-354.

1976

81C   L'auto envie. *Narcisses, Nouvelle rev. psychanal.*, 2: 253-257.

82C   L'enveloppe sonore du soi, Didier Anzieu. *Nouvelle rev. psychanal.*, Printemps, Paris, 13: 161-180. (Translated by Monique Meloche and edited with the help of Judith Rotstein and Clifford Scott.)

1977

83C   Au sujet de la convulsion: D.W. Winnicott. *L'Arc*, Paris: Gallimard, 69: 84-93.

84I   Two recorded interviews. *Psychia. J. Univ. Ottawa*, May, 2: 20-28.

1978

85A   Common problems concerning the views of Freud and Jung. (Toronto Analytical Psychol. Soc., Oct. 27, 1972.) *J. Analytical Psychol.*, 23: 303-312.

1981

86A   On positive affects. (Read at Panel on Positive Affects, 35th Annual Mtg. Am. Acad. Psychoanal., N.Y. City, Dec. 1979). *Psychia. J. Univ. Ottawa*, 6: 79-81.

87B   The development of the analysands' and the analysts' enthusiasm for the process of psychoanalysis. (Read at the Am. Psychol. Assn., Montreal, Sept. 1, 1980.) In: James S. Grotstein (Ed.). *Do I Dare Disturb the Universe? A Memorial to Wilfred R. Bion.* Beverley Hills: Caesura Press, pp. 571-577.

88C   [See 77A.] Los aspectos mutuamente defensivos de la depresion y la mania. *Psicoanalisis* (Buenos Aires), 3: 419-430.

1982

89C   Melanie Klein (1882-1960). *Psychia. J. Univ. Ottawa*, 7: 149-157.

1983

90R   Part of B.B.C. Broadcast on Melanie Klein by Richard Wollheim, London.

91A   Interview conducted by Phyllis Grosskurth, Oct. 8, 1981. *J. Melanie Klein Soc.*, 1(2): 13-26.

1984

92A   Primary mental states in clinical psychoanalysis. (Panel on Primary Mental States in Clinical Psychoanalysis. William Alanson White Inst. Psychia., Psychoanal. Psychol., 40th Anniv. Conf., N.Y. City, Nov. 6, 1983.) *Contemp. Psychoanal.*, 20: 458-464.

93A   Psychoanalysis of a boy of 26 months with a 20-year follow-up. (First World Congress Infant Psychia., Cascais, Portugal, April 3, 1980.) *J. Melanie Klein Soc.*, 2(1): 3-8.

1985

94A   Narcissism, the body, phantasy, fantasy, internal and external objects and the "Body Scheme" (Advanced Inst. for Analytic Psychother., N.Y. City, May 16, 1980). *J. Melanie Klein Soc.*, 3(1): 23-49.

1986

95A   Mourning, the analyst, and the analysand. (Loss and Mourning: Current Psychoanal. Perspectives, Div. 39, Am. Psychia. Assn., Toronto, Aug. 28, 1984.) *Free Assns.*, 7: 7-10.

1987

96A   Making the best of a sad job. (Br. Psycho-Anal. Soc. London, Oct. 7, 1987.) *Bull. Br. Psycho-Anal. Soc.*

97A   Discussion of M.A. Silverman's "Clinical material, Object relationship." *Psychoanal. Inq.*, 7: 189-197.

98A   Discussion of A. Mason's "A Kleinian perspective." *Psychoanal. Inq.*, 7: 147-166.

1988

99A   Repairing broken links between the unconscious, sleep and instinct; and the conscious, waking and instinct. *Free Assns.*, 12: 84-91.

1989

100A A note about adopted children. *J. Melanie Klein Object Rel.*, 7(1): 22-23.

101C Some personal reflections of Melanie Klein, James Gammill. (First published as "Quelques souvenirs personnels sur Melanie Klein," in *Melanie Klein Aujourd'hui*, Cesura Lyon Edition, 1989. The translation from French is based in part on an earlier more complete English version. This translation was done by Monique Meloche with help from the author and Clifford Scott.) *J. Melanie Klein Object Rel.*, 7(2): 1-15.

1990

102A Transference and counter-transference and wild analysis in the clinical interview. Discussant: Erik L.H.M. van de Loo. *Proc. Fourth Annual Symposium*

Int. Soc. Psychoanal. Study Organization, May 24-26, pp. 378-380.

1991

103A   Entretien avec Clifford Scott, le doyen des psychanalystes. *L'Ane*, Paris, Avril-Juin, 46: 8-9.

104I   Entrevue avec le Docteur Clifford Scott. *Psychiatrie Recherche et l'Intervention en Santé Mentale de l'Enfant*, printemps, 1: 81-85.

105A   Obituary: Bruno Cormier: 1919-1991. *Bull. Soc. psychanal. Montréal*, automne, 4: 4-5.

106A   Le sommeil et le rêve de l'enfant. *Psychiatrie Recherche et l'Intervention en Santé Mentale de l'Enfant*, printemps, 1(3): 81-85.

1992

107A   Making the best of a sad job. *J. Melanie Klein Object Rel.*, 10(1): 1.

1993

108I   Détour autour du transfert: Rencontre avec Clifford W. Scott, par Marie Hazan. *Filigrane*, (2): 190-199.

109D   Discussant: Psy. as a Profession: Canada–China Connections. (Anthropology Soc., May 10, 19th Annual Conference, Montreal, May 9-12.) *Santé Culture/Culture Health*, 1(2): 1992-1993.

1995

110A   An interview with Clifford Scott by Virgina Hunter, *Psychoanal. Rev.*, 82(2): 189-206.

1997

111B   W. Clifford M. Scott. In: Laurie W. Raymond and Susan Rosbrow-Reich (Eds.), *The Inward Eye*. Hillsdale, NJ: The Analytic Press, pp. 279-309.

II. Unpublished and Other Works

Legend:

D – Discussion	E – Essay	F – Unpublished article	
FF – Film	I – Interview	L – Lecture	N – Notes
P – Panel	S – Symposium	SS – Seminar	T – Teaching
V – Video	W – Workshop	G – Book	

1919

1E The effect of motion pictures on the public. English Expression, 2 pp.

2E Atoms and their structure. English Expression, 8 pp.

1920

3E An account of the history of science and civilization during the 18th Century. English Expression, 5 pp.

4E Some causes of labour unrest. English Expression, 3pp.

5F Concerning Einstein – His theories of relativity, space, time and gravitation. 17 Club, 22 pp.

6E Evolution theory. English Expression, 4 pp.

1921

7E Attention. Psychology, 6 pp

8F The claims of science as a human activity to be encouraged, accompanied by a discourse in the meaning of scientific fact. 17 Club, 22 pp.

9E Alcohol question. 17 Club, 3 pp.

1923

10F Diabetes and the pancreas. 17 Club, 14 pp.

11F Islets of Langerhans. Report of work to research club, 4 pp.

12E Cellular fatigue. 17 Club, 2 pp.

1924

13F Review of work on Islets of Langerhans. Physiology Journal Club, 8 pp.

1925

14F Thesis: The paradox observed in the analysis of memory function and a suggested solution. A plea for the assumption of the existence of Pure Time Sensibility. Dept. Psychol., Univ. Toronto, Nov. 18.

1927

15F Thesis: Leucorrhoea. Dept. Obstetrics and Gynaecology. Univ. Toronto.

16F A statistical note on the outcome of illnesses diagnosed involutional melancholia. Manhanttan State Hosp., N.Y. City.

17F Pathology of diabetes. 17 Club, 6 pp.

1930

18N   Biological symptoms. Boston Psychopathic Hosp.
19N   Survey of statistics. Boston Psychopathic Hosp.
20N   Depression. Boston Psychopathic Hosp.
21N   Schizophrenia. Boston Psychopathic Hosp.
22F   The unconscious. Boston Psychopathic Hosp.

1931

23N   Doig and Ashworth. Neurology, National Hosp., London.
24N   Institute of Psycho-Analysis Seminars – 1931-1933.

1934

25F   Constitutional psychopathy. Maudsley Hosp., London, March 13.
26F   A delusion of identity. Br. Psycho-Anal. Soc., Nov. 21.
27F   Projection. Maudsley Hosp., London.

1935

28N   Crying. Maudsley Hosp., London.
29F   Some apparent disturbance of reality due to ideas of omnipotence – With special reference to disturbed ideas about time. (Read at a meeting of the Med. Sec., Br. Psycho-Anal. Soc.)

1936

30E   Mescal Experiment. Maudsley Hosp., London.
31D   Discussion of N. Tibouts' "Child guidance treatment in Holland." New Education Fellowship Conference, Cheltenham, England.

1937

32D   Discussion of Ian Suttie's "Ego development." Med. Sec., Br. Psychol. Soc.
33F   Treatment of psychosis. Maudsley Hosp., London.
34F   Problems of the psychotherapy of schizophrenia. Tavistock Clinic, Dec. 13.

1938

35f   On the intense affects encountered in treating a severe manic-depressive disorder. (Read at 15th Int. Psycho-Anal. Congress, Paris, Aug. 2.)
36F   A contribution to the psychopathology of convulsive phenomena in manic-depressive states. Int. League against Epilepsy, London, Oct. 21.
37F   Psychoanalysis of a manic-depressive patient in an institution. (Read at 15th Int. Psycho-Anal. Congress, Paris.)

1939

38A   The chronic uncertified. Sec. Psychia., Royal Soc. Med., June 13.
39N   Notes on internalised objects. London, April 27 and May 30.

1940

40N   Notes on hallucinations. London.

41F   Discussion: Psychopathology of anorexia nervosa. Symposium, Med. Sec., Br. Psychol. Soc., May 22.

42D   Discussion: Dennis Leigh. Anorexia nervosa.

1941

43**   The soldier's defence and the public attitude. Med. Sec., Brit. Psychol. Soc., Nottingham, April 19.

1943

44F   Emergency Med. Service – Neurosis survey. Reports of Belmont and Mill Hill Hosps.

1944

45S   Contribution to a Symposium on Shock Treatment. Br. Psycho-Anal. Soc., March 15.

46N   Notes on French's book. Psychiatric Social Work, London.

1946

47S   Psychiatric problems amongst evacuated children. Symposium on Lessons for Child Psychiatry. Med. Sec., Br. Psychol. Soc., Feb. 27.

48L   Lecture: Narcissism.

1947

49F   Aggression. Psychia. Sec., Royal Soc. London, Dec. 9.

50F   A psychoanalytic concept of the origin of depression. Sec. Psychia., Int. Congress of Physicians, London, Sept.

51F   The use of patient's drawings in the details of anxiety situations. Conf. European Psychoanalysts. Amsterdam, May 25-27.

52L   Some embryological, neurological, psychiatric and psychoanalytic implications of the body scheme. Br. Psycho-Anal. Soc., March 19.

1948

53F   The use of patients' drawings in the details of anxiety situations. Dutch Psychoanal. Soc., Amsterdam, May 28.

54F   Applications of psychoanalytical principles to the hospital in-patient. Royal Soc. Med., March 9.

55L   Lecture: On sleeping and waking. Psychoanalytic Students, London.

56N   Notes on technique and the concept of a body scheme. Br. Psycho-Anal. Soc., Jan.

57D   Further discussion on archetypes and introjected objects. Med. Sec., Brit. Psychol. Soc., June 23.

1949

58F   The "Body Scheme" in psychotherapy. Med. Sect., Br. Psychol. Soc., Jan. 26.

1950

59F Conditions of happiness: Instincts. Personalist Group and Progressive League Conf. Dorking, Surrey, Oct. 28.

60S Psychotherapy of schizophrenia. 1st World Congress Psychia., Paris.

61S Evolution and present trends of psychoanalysis. [As above.]

62S Problems of in-patient psychotherapy. [As above.]

63S Psychopathology of depressive states. [As above.]

64S Psychopathology of depersonalization. [As above.]

65F Sleep in psychoanalysis. Br. Psycho-Anal. Soc., Jan.; The Psychoanal. Study Group, Seattle, WA, June 1957.

1951

66R Psychotherapeutic treatment of endogenous depression. B.B.C. Latin-America Talks.

67F Patients who sleep or look at the analyst during psychoanalytic treatment. 17th Int. Psycho-Anal. Congress, Amsterdam.

68S The mutual influences in the development of ego and id. 17th Int. Psycho-Anal. Congress, Amsterdam, Aug. 8.

69D The treatment of depression. Royal Soc. Med., Sec. Psychia., March 13.

1952

70S Seminar on sleep: Disorders in children. Maudsley Hosp., London.

71L Lecture: The development of the body ego, the body image, the body feeling and body sensations. Soc. Med. Officers of Health, London, Nov. 14.

72F A note on blathering. Br. Psycho-Anal. Soc., June 4.

1953

73F A new hypothesis concerning the relationship of libidinal and aggressive instincts based on clinical evidence obtained chiefly during the treatment of patients with manic-depressive illnesses. 18th Int. Psycho-Anal. Congress, London, July 29.

74F A new hypothesis concerning the relationship of libidinal and aggressive instincts. Br. Psycho-Anal. Soc., Jan. 1954.

75T Group teaching. London.

76D Discussion on: Anorexia nervosa. Royal Soc. Med., March 10.

1954

77E Retiring Chairman's Address to the Psychotherapy and Social Psychiatry Sec. of the Royal Medico-Psychol. Assn., London, July.

78F Survey paper. Br. Psycho-Anal. Soc., Sept.

79F Patients' drawings depicting the detail of affect situations, Can. Maritimes Psychia. Soc., Dec.

80F Sleep in psychoanalysis. Can. Maritimes Psychia. Soc., Dec.

81Fa Notes: British Psychiatry. Halifax Mental Hosp.

82Fb Notes: British Psychiatry. Moncton Mental Hosp.
83Fc Notes: British Psychiatry. Halifax Univ., Psychia. Dept.
84Fd Notes: British Psychiatry. Moncton Univ., Psychia. Dept.
85Fe Notes: British Psychiatry. Canadian Maritimes Psychia. Society.
86Fa Notes: Psychopaths. [As above.]
87Fb Notes: Psychopaths. [As above.]
88Fc Notes: Psychopaths. [As above.]
89Fd Notes: Psychopaths. [As above.]
90Fe Notes: Psychopaths. [As above.]
91Fa Notes: University Psychoanalysis. [As above.]
92Fb Notes: University Psychoanalysis. [As above.]
93Fc Notes: University Psychoanalysis. [As above.]
94Fd Notes: University Psychoanalysis. [As above.]
95Fe Notes: University Psychoanalysis. [As above.]
96Fa Notes: Depression. [As above.]
97Fb Notes: Depression. [As above.]
98Fc Notes: Depression. [As above.]
99Fd Notes: Depression. [As above.]
100Fe Notes: Depression. [As above.]
101Fa Notes: Interviewing. [As above.]
102Fb Notes: Interviewing. [As above.]
103Fc Notes: Interviewing. [As above.]
104Fd Notes: Interviewing. [As above.]
105Fe Notes: Interviewing. [As above.]

1955

106F Survey paper. Psychiatric Hosp., Toronto.
107F Basic sciences in psychiatry: Psychobiology. Psychia. Sect. Joint Mtg. – Br. Med. Assn., Psychia. Sect., and Can. Med. Assn., Toronto.
108D Narcissism, the body image and the body scheme. Boston Neurol. Psychia. Soc. Discussion by William F. Murphy.
109D Discussant: John R. Reid and Jacob E. Finesigner's "Defences: Their nature and function." Am. Psychia. Assn., Atlantic City, NJ, May 13.
110Fa Noise, speech and technique. Philadelphia Psychoanal. Soc., Nov.
111Fb Noise, speech and technique. Can. Psychoanal. Soc., Dec.
112Fc Noise, speech and technique. Am. Psychoanal. Soc., Dec.

1956

113D Narcissism, the body, the body image and the "Body Scheme." Discussion by Searles and E. Weigert. Washington Psychoanal. Soc.
114D Discussion of S. Lorand's "Therapeutic results in psychoanalytic treatment without fee." Am. Psychoanal. Assn., Chicago, May.
115D Discussion of A. Lussier's "Analysis of a child with deformed limbs." Joint

Mtg. Psychia. Neurological sections of the Med-Chi Soc., March 7.

116F   Panel on Transference. Can. Psychol. Assn., Ottawa, June 9.

117F   Noise, speech and psychotherapy. Second Divisional Mtg. of the Am. Psychiatric Assn., North Eastern United States and Canadian District Branches and Affiliated Societies and a Joint Mtg. with the Psychoanalytic Association of Canada and North Eastern United States. Sheraton Mount Royal Hotel, Montreal, Nov. 8, 11.

1957

118D   Noise, speech and technique. Discussion by M. Getelson. Int. Psycho-Anal. Congress, Paris.

119D   Discussant: Bruno M. Cormier's "Types of regression determined by the deprivation of liberty and their implications in rehabilitations." Congress of Corrections. Montreal, May 28.

121D   Discussion – Symposium: Disorders of Affects During Childhood. Am. Psychia. Assn. Reg. Res. Conf., Syracuse, N.Y.

122F   Psychotherapy under observation. Services Conf., Allan Memorial Inst., Montreal.

123F   Sadness, with or without hope. Dept. Psychia., Univ. Toronto, Feb.

124S   Seminar on the Technical aspects of handling sleepiness and sleep during treatment. State Univ. of New York, March.

125F   The impact of Meyerian psychobiology and psychoanalytic theory and practice on the development of child psychiatry in Great Britain. C.P.A., Edmonton, June 1957.

126F   Problems of training in psychoanalysis and teaching about psychoanalysis. Vancouver Med. Assn., Sec. Neurol. Psychia., June.

127F   Institutional facilities for the treatment of maladjusted children, Vancouver Children's Foundation, June.

128F   Sleep in psychoanalysis. Psychoanal. Study Group, Seattle, WA, June.

129D   Discussion of I.P. Glauber's "Freud's contribution on stuttering." Am. Psychoanal. Assn., Chicago.

130F   Anxieties about pregnancy and childbirth. Services Conf., Allan Memorial Inst., Montreal, Nov.

131D   Discussion of Howard Liddell's "A biological basis for psychopathology." Reg. Res. Conf., Am. Psychia. Assn., Montreal, Nov.

132D   Discussion of H. Fox et al., "Some methods of observing humans under stress." Am. Psychia. Assn. Reg. Res. Conf.

133D   Discussion of Leo Kanner's "Early infantile autism 1943-1955." Am. Psychia. Assn. Reg. Research Conf., Montreal, 1955.

134D   Discussion: Rumination by J. Richmond and E. Eddy, F. Reichsman, G. Engel, V. Harway, S. Escalona on "Disorder of affects during childhood: Monica, an infant with gastric fistula and depression."

1958

135F   Further notes regarding sleep during psychoanalytic treatment. Can. Psychoanal. Soc., Jan. (Re-write of 1957 Seattle paper.)

136F   The psychiatric tragedy of Rudolf Hess. Psychia. Sec., Med.-Chi Soc., April.

137F   Man – A wonder machine. Unitarian Youth Conf., Montreal, April 12.

138E   Introductory Remarks as Chairman of Committee on: Transference and countertransference problems in relationship to drugs. Conf. on Psychodynamic, Psychoanalytic and Sociological Aspects of the Neuroleptic or Tranquillizing Drugs in Psychiatry, Montreal, April.

139F   On identification. Can. Psychoanal. Soc., Montreal, Dec.

140F   The Wolfenden Report. Services Conf., Allan Memorial Inst., Nov.

141F   Presentation of a Vermont State Hospital case of schizophrenia. Held at Vermont State Hosp., Nov. 13.

1959

142D   Discussion of Howard Liddell's "Stress and maternal protection in animals and men." Am. Psychia. Assn. Reg. Res. Conf., Montreal.

143D   Discussion of "Infantile affect situations depicted in 3 Norman McLaren films." Can. Psychoanal. Soc., Jan.

144P   Panel on Pregnancy and Parturition. Can. Psychoanal. Soc. and Soc. Can. Psychoanal., Univ. Montreal, Feb. 26.

145F   The breadth of the problem of crime using arson as an example. Montreal Council of Women, April.

146F   Psychoanalytic treatment of a peptic ulcer. Services Conf., Allan Memorial Inst., May.

147D   Introductory remarks and discussion: J. Guild, D.J. Watterson, K. Stern and R.R. Lemieux, Panel on Brief Psychotherapy. Can. Psychia. Assn. Mtg., Ottawa, June.

148P   Panel: Formation of a Section of Child Psychiatry of the C.P.A. Can. Psychia. Assn. Annual Mtg., Ottawa, June.

149P   Panel: Psychoanalysis in Paediatrics. 19th Int. Congress Paedia., Montreal, July.

150S   Depression, confusion and multivalence, 21st Int. Psycho-Anal. Congress, Copenhagen, July.

151D   Discussion: Depression, confusion and multivalence, with Hoffer's "Psychoanalytic comments on the psychology and psychotherapy of depression." Can. Psychoanal. Soc., Montreal, Nov.

152S   Chairman – Symposium: Psychoanalysis and the Disturbances of the Digestive Tract. 21st Int. Psycho-Anal. Congress, Copenhagen, July.

153P   Panel: Forward from Nationalism Towards Universal Man. Schweitzer Group of the Unitarian Churches of Montreal, Nov.

1960

154D   Discussion of G.L. Engel's "Is grief a disease?" Am. Psychosom. Soc. Annual Mtg., Montreal, March.

155Fa An adult finger-sucking habit. Psychia. Sec., Montreal Med.-Chi Soc., April.

156Fb An adult finger-sucking habit. Pre-Congress Mtg., Br. Psycho-Anal. Soc., London, July.

157Fc A finger-licking, finger-flicking habit. Am. Psychoanal. Assn., N.Y. City, Dec. 1962.

158D   Discussion: Symposium on Incest. 2nd Annual Res. Conf. on Criminology and Delinquency, Montreal, May.

159F   Differences between the playroom used in child psychiatric treatment and in child analysis; read prior to Statten's "Early stages in the analysis of a 4-½-year-old girl." Can. Psychia. Assn., Banff, June.

160D   Discussion of Ostow's "Theory of psychic energetics." Symposium on Extra-pyramidal System and Neuroleptics, Montreal, Nov.

161D   Discussion of H. Azima and G. Sarwer-Foner's "Psychotherapeutic actions"; and Disayima and Sarwer-Foner's "Psychoanalytic formulations of psycho-therapeutic actions." Symposium on Extrapyramidal System and Neuro-leptics, Montreal, Nov.

162F   Conflicts in psychiatry. Int. Club, Montreal, Nov.

163D   Discussion: Family problems in modern society. Montreal Jewish Gen. Hosp., Nov. 2.

164F   Defenses against the affect of depression. The Menninger Foundation, Topeka, Dec.

165F   Theory and treatment of depression and grief. Topeka Psychoanal. Soc., Dec.

1961

166F   Kleinian Teaching. N.Y. State Psychia. Inst., N.Y., March.

167S   The demonstration of object relations and affect in a set situation in infants of 6-12 months. 3rd World Congress of Psychiatry, Montreal, June.

168Fb Film: The demonstration of object relations and affect in a set situation in infants of 6 to 12 months. (20-minute film dealing with an elaboration of Winnicott's observations.) Pre-Congress Mtg., London, July.

169Fc Film: The demonstration of object relations and affect in a set situation in infants of 6 to 12 months. (20-minute film dealing with an elaboration of Winnicott's observations.) Edinburgh Congress, Aug.

170Vd Discussion – Video: Observing an infant in a set situation. Can. Psychia. Assn., Winnipeg, June 17-20, 1970.

171Ve Discussion – Video: Observing an infant in a set situation. 7th Congress Int. Assn. Child Psychia. Allied Professions, Jerusalem, Aug. 5, 1970.

172Vf Discussion – Video: Observing an infant in a set situation. Grand Rounds, Montreal Gen. Hosp., Dec. 3, 1970.

173Vg Discussion – Video: Observing an infant in a set situation. Joint Mtg. Can. Psychia. Assn., Quebec Psychia. Assn, Royal College of Psychiatrists, Queen Elizabeth Hotel, Montreal, June 8, 1972.

174Fh Film: The demonstration of object relation and affect in a set situation in infants of 6 to 12 months. (20-minute film dealing with an elaboration of Winnicott's observations.) 1st World Congress on Infant Psychiatry, Cascais, Portugal, March 31, 1980.

175F [See 1960.] A finger-sucking habit. Pre-Congress Mtg., London, July.

176Sa Symposium: A Re-classification of Psychopathological States. Int. Psycho-Anal. Assn. Congress, Edinburgh, Aug.

177Fb A re-classification of psychopathological states. Can. Psychoanal. Soc., Montreal, Sept.

178Fc Talk on problems of classification (using Congress paper): A re-classification of psychopathological states. Psychotic Interns' Club. Montreal Gen. Hosp., Nov.

179Fd Resume of psychoanalytic nosology. (Used – A reclassification of psychopathological states.) Ottawa Psychoanal. Inst., June 1987.

180D Discussion: P. Greenacre and D. Winnicott's "The theory of the infant-parent relationship." Int. Psycho-Anal. Congress, Edinburgh, Aug.

181F Attitudes to mandalas. Montreal Assn. Jungian Studies, Sept.

182D Discussion of E. Wittkower's "Arachnephobia." Can. Psychoanal. Soc., Nov.

183Fa Psychoanalysis in Canada. (Condensation of brief submitted to Royal Commission on Health Services.)

184Fb Psychoanalysis in Canada. Can. Psychia. Assn., Toronto, June 1963.

1962

185F Brief submitted to The Royal Commission on Health Services.

186F The psychoanalytic treatment of mania. Am. Psychia. Assn. Reg. Res. Conf., Montreal, April.

187D Discussion of J.G. Howett's "Child-parent separation as a therapeutic technique." Am. Psychia. Assn., Toronto, May.

188F Short-lived disappointment, depression and mourning in contrast to anger, in babies of 6-12 months. Am. Psychia. Assn., Toronto, May.

189D Discussion – Panel: The Concept of the Id. Am. Psychoanal. Assn., Toronto, May.

190D Discussant: Folklore and linguistics. Indiana Univ. Res. Ctr. Anthropol., Bloomington, IN, May 17-19.

200Fa Mania and mourning. Can. Psychoanal. Soc., Nov.

201Fb Mania and mourning. Stockholm, July 1963.

203Fc [See 1960.] A finger-licking, finger-flicking habit. Am. Psychoanal. Assn., N.Y., Dec.

1963

204D Discussion of Mrs. Cardozo's "Problems of tongue thrusting from speech point of view." 5th Reg. Conf. Speech and Hearing Soc., Montreal, May.

205D Discussion of A.C. Mendel's "Tongue thrusting from an orthodontic viewpoint." 5th Reg. Conf. Speech and Hearing Soc., Montreal, May.

206F [See 1961.] Psychoanalysis in Canada. Can. Psychia. Assn., Toronto, June.

207D Discussion of The psychotherapy of the mental defective. Can. Psychia. Assn., Toronto, June.

208Fb [See 1962.] Mania and mourning. Int. Psycho-Anal. Assn., Stockholm, July.

209F The limitations of science. St. James Literary Soc., Montreal, Oct.

1964

210F Development of linguistic and paralinguistic utterances: Their role for the psychiatrist and the speech therapist (with Mrs. Cardozo), Montreal Med. Child. Psychia. Sec., March.

211F Freud and the doctors. German Can. Business and Professional Assn., Montreal, Nov.

212D Discussion of J. Aufreiter's "Schizophrenic breakdowns." Can. Psychoanal. Soc., Montreal, Dec.

1965

213D Panel discussion: Psychoanalytic Contribution to Psychiatric Teaching. Can. Psychoanal. Soc., Montreal, Jan.

214D Discussion of Fr. Salman's "The psychology of religious experience." Conf. on Personality Change and the Religious Experience, R.M. Bucke Memorial Soc., Montreal, Jan.

215P Panel: Psychoanalytic Concepts of the Depressive Illnesses. The mutually defensive roles of depression and mania. Research Conference on the Depressive Group of Illnesses, McGill Univ., Montreal, Feb.

216F Review of Isherwood's "Ramakrishna and his disciples." R.M. Bucke Memorial Soc., Montreal, Oct.

1966

217F Talking and communication. Dept. Psychia., Queen's Univ., Kingston, Jan.

218F Discussion of Marcoux-Painchaud's "Un relevé de 65 cas d'encoprésie." Québec Psychia. Assn. Soc., May 20.

1967

219F Defences against the affect of depression. Can. Psychoanal. Soc., Toronto, Feb. 14.

220D Discussion of case presented at seminar on: A methodology for General Hospitals. Montreal Gen. Hosp., May 17.

221Fa Do psychedelic drugs help personality or religious development? Int. Club, Montreal, Dec. 6.

222Fb Do psychedelic drugs help personality or religious development? Humanist

Soc., Montreal, Jan. 26, 1968.

223Fc Do psychedelic drugs help personality or religious development? Chateauguay High School, Feb. 15, 1968.

1968

224Fd [See 1967.] Do psychedelic drugs help personality or religious development? Humanist Soc., Montreal, Jan. 26.

225Fe [See 1967.] Do psychedelic drugs help personality or religious development? Chateauguay High School, Feb. 15.

226D Discussion: Children's ideas of death. Staff of Children's Psychia. Clinic, Royal Victoria Hosp., Montreal, April 22.

227Fa Notes on dreams and sleep. Can. Psychoanal. Soc., Montreal, Oct. 17.

228Fb Notes on dreams and sleep. Can. Psychoanal. Soc., Toronto, Dec. 6.

229Fc Dreams and Sleep (revised). Grand Rounds, Dept. Psychia., Queen's Univ., Kingston, March 5.

230F Dreams in childhood and adolescence. Département de l'enfance et de l'adolescence, Inst. Albert Prévost, Montreal, Nov. 21.

1969

231F The polyglot analysis and the difficulties of analysis in other than the mother tongue. Chairman's Remarks, 2nd Mex-Can. Psychoanal. Colloq., Montreal, Feb. 21.

232D Discussion of C. Brenner's "Dreams in contemporary clinical psychoanalysis." 3rd Pan-American Congress Psycho-Anal., N.Y. City, Feb. 25.

233Fc Notes on dreams and sleep (revised). Grand Rounds, Dept. Psychia., Queen's Univ., Kingston, March 5.

234F The neglect of dreams. Joint Mtg. – Can. Psychia. Assn. and Can. Psychoanal. Soc., Toronto, June 13.

235D Discussant at the 50th Anniversary Albert Prévost Inst., Chateau Champlain, Montreal, Nov. 5-8.

236D Discussant: H. Guntrip's "Schizoid phenomena, object relations and self." Can. Psychoanal. Soc., Montreal, Nov. 20, 1969.

1970

237Fa History of psychiatric outpatient departments in General Hospitals. Reddy Memorial Hosp., Montreal, Feb. 11.

238Fb History of psychiatric outpatients departments in General Hospitals. 3rd Nat. Conf. General Systems Education. Center for Interdisciplinary Creativity, Southern Conn. State College, New Haven, Conn., April 7.

239Fa [See 1961.] Discussion – Video: Observing an infant in a set situation. Can. Psychia. Assn., Winnipeg, June 17-20.

240Db [See 1961.] Presentation and Discussion of Video: Observing an infant in a set situation. 7th Congress Int. Assn. Child Psychia. Allied Professions, Jerusalem, August 1970.

241Dc [See 1961.] Discussion – Video: Observing an infant in a set situation. Grand Rounds, Montreal Gen. Hosp., Dec. 3.

242F Chairman: Colloquium on Neurosis and Acute and Chronic Disease: Treatment. Int. Assn. Child Psychia. Allied Professions, Jerusalem, Aug.

243V Presented Video of: Summary of the contribution to the main themes of the Rome Congress, Robert L. Bak, 1969. Can. Psychoanal. Soc., Montreal, Oct. 22.

244F A review of the psychoanalytic situation (The psychoanalytic rule). Can. Psychoanal. Soc. (Q.E.), Nov. 19.

245F The Jerusalem Congress 1970 Child Psychiatry Allied Professions Grand Rounds. Montreal Gen. Hosp., Dec. 3. [See above.]

246D Discussant: Peter Hartocollis' "Time as a dimension of affects." Am. Psychoanal. Assn., N.Y. City, Dec. 19.

1971

247D Discussion: Problems of psychosis. Int. Colloquium on Psychosis, Part 2 Plenary Sessions.

248D Discussant: D.C. Levin and Dr. J.J. Sigal's "The self in psychoneurosis – A supplement to psychoanalytic technique." Can. Psychoanal. Soc. (Q.E.), Jan. 21.

249D Discussant: Dr. P.G. Thomson's "Wordworth." Can. Psychoanal. Soc. (Scientific), Feb. 18.

250V Video presentation of psychiatric consultation. Allan Memorial Inst., Montreal, March 29 and May 17.

251SS Seminar: Sleep and dreams. Washington Psychoanal. Soc., Washington, D.C., June 12, 1971.

252P Sleep and dreams. Can. Psychoanal. Soc. (Q.E.), Sept. 23, 1971.

253D Chairman: Discussion of Marie Langer's "Psychoanalysis/or social revolution." 27th Int. Psycho-Anal. Congress, Vienna, July 27.

254D Discussant: E.D. Wittkower and J. Naiman's "Psychoanalysis in international perspective." Can. Psychoanal. Soc., Montreal, Nov. 18.

1972

255F [See 1961.] Video of: Observing an infant in a set situation. Joint Mtg. Can. Psychia. Assn., Quebec Psychia. Assn., Royal College of Psychiatrists, Queen Elizabeth Hotel, Montreal, June 8.

256Fa Self reproach, self admiration and self envy as inhibitors of development. Dept. Psychia., Univ. Ottawa, Ottawa Civic Hosp., June 21.

257Fb Self reproach, self admiration and self envy. Queen Elizabeth Hosp., Montreal, Dec. 5.

258Fa Present day common problems of the development of Freud's and Jung's views. Toronto Analytical Psychol. Soc., Oct. 27.

259Fb Common Problems Concerning Freud's and Jung's views. C.G. Jung Soc. of

Montreal, Feb. 3, 1977.

260D   Discussant: Eugene E. Trunnell and W.E. Holt's "The concept of denial or disavowal." Am. Psychoanal. Assn., N.Y. City, Dec. 1, 1972.

1973/1974

261SS Place of psychoanalytic education in the health team. Montreal Gen. Hosp., Feb. 7.

262F   Looking at the patient. Cairo Psychia. Soc., Cairo, Egypt, April 9.

263F   Social implications of psychoanalysis. Dar-el Mokattam Hosp., Cairo, April 11.

264Fa Envy of self and of dreaming. Can. Psychoanal. Soc. (Q.E.), May 23.

265Fb Self envy and envy of dreaming. 24th Annual Mtg., Can. Psychia. Assn., Chateau Laurier Hotel, Ottawa, Oct. 3.

266Fc Self envy and envy of dreams and dreaming. 17th Annual Mtg., Group-Without-a-Name, Chateau Laurier Hotel, Ottawa, Oct. 26.

267Fd Self envy and envy of dreams and dreaming. Am. Psychoanal. Assn., N.Y. City, Dec. 12.

268F   Non-verbal communication in psychoanalysis. 1st Int. Symposium on Non-Verbal Aspects and Techniques of Psychotherapy, Univ. Br. Columbia, Vancouver, July 30.

269F   Report on 1st Int. Symposium on Non-verbal Aspects and Techniques of Psychotherapy. Vancouver, July; Scientific Mtg., Queen Elizabeth Hosp., Montreal, Dec. 3.

1975

270Fa Comments on Freud's views about sleep. Can. Psychoanal. Soc. (Q.E.), Jan. 23.

271Fb Comments on Freud's views about sleep. Can. Psychoanal. Soc., Ottawa, May 26.

272F   Psychoanalysis in education. Queen of Angels Acad., Dorval, Nov. 10.

273Ia Two recorded interviews. Can. Psychoanal. Soc. (Q.E.), Oct. 23.

274Ib Two recorded interviews. Can. Psychoanal. Soc., Ottawa, Oct. 27.

1976

275F   [See 1975.] Remembering sleep, dreams and waking. Grand Rounds, Montreal Children's Hosp., Jan. 26, 1976.

276D   Discussion of A. Lee's "Countertransference." Can. Psychoanal. Soc., Extra Scientific Mtg. (Q.E.), Feb. 5.

277I   [See 1975.] Two recorded interviews. Can. Psychoanal. Soc., Toronto, March 10.

278F   Dissociated personalities without amnesia. Can. Psychoanal. Soc. (Q.E.), March 18.

279F   The relation between teaching, history taking and teaching sex education. VIIth Pahlavi Med. Congress, Pahlavi Univ., Shiraz, Iran, April 27.

280SS Supervisory Seminar. Shiraz Med. Ctr., Nemazee Hosp., Shiraz, Iran, April
       28.

281L   Sleep and dreams. Dept. Psychia., Shiraz Med. Ctr., Nemazee Hosp.,
       Shiraz, April 29.

282D   Discussion of P. Mahony's "The boundaries of free association." Can.
       Psychoanal. Soc., Scientific Mtg. (Q.E.), June 10.

283D   Discussant: D. Levin's "Physics and psychoanalysis: An epistemological
       study." Can. Psychoanal. Soc. Scientific Mtg. (Q.E.), Montreal, Sept. 23.

284F   The early days of the Toronto Psychiatric Hospital. Mtg. Psychia. Historical
       Soc., Clarke Inst. Psychia., Toronto, Oct. 8.

285D   Discussant: Avner Falks' "Freud and Herzl." Can. Psychoanal. Soc., Extra
       Scientific Mtg. (Q.E.), Oct. 28.

1977

286F   [See 1972.] Common problems concerning Freud's and Jung's views. C.G.
       Jung Soc. of Montreal, Feb. 3.

287D   Discussion of Eva Lester's "Imagery during free association." Can. Psycho-
       anal. Soc. (Q.E.), Feb. 17.

288D   Discussion of Milton Viederman's "A special type of transference cure." Am.
       Psychoanal. Assn. Mtg., Quebec City, April 29.

289D   Discussion of Brandt F. Steele's "Psychoanalytic observations on attachment
       and development of abused children." Panel on Child Abuse, Am. Psycho-
       anal. Assn. Mtg., Quebec City, April 30.

290F   Notes on conscious and unconscious religious conflicts in the transference.
       Can. Psychoanal. Soc. (Q.E.), June 16.

291D   Discussant of the Plenary Session on: Affects and the Psychoanalytic Situa-
       tion. Presented at the 30th Int. Psycho-Anal. Congress in Jerusalem, Can.
       Psychoanal. Soc. (Q.E.), Oct. 20.

292SS Seminar: Melanie Klein and child psychoanalysis. Advanced Inst. Analytic
       Psychother., N.Y. City, Dec. 1, 8.

1978

293D   Discussant: G. Maguire's "Iatrogenicity, the transference neurosis, and the
       subordinated position of the self." (A re-examination of the dynamic point of
       view.) Can. Psychoanal. Soc. (Q.E.), Feb. 16.

294F   Adolf Meyer. Allan Memorial Hosp., May 18.

295F   Talking to patients and talking to colleagues: Telling it as it is, gobbledygook
       and scientific discourse. Can. Psychoanal. Soc. (Q.E.), May 18.

296SS Seminar: Psychiatry in China. Canada/Chinese Soc., Sept. 30.

297SS Seminar: Differences and similarities between psychotherapy and psychoanal-
       ysis of children. Montreal Children's Hosp., Oct. 23.

298SS Seminar: Differences and similarities between psychotherapy and psychoanal-
       ysis of children. Child Psychia. Dept., Royal Victoria Hosp., Jan. 31, 1979.

299SS   Seminar: History of child psychiatry. Montreal Children's Hosp., Oct. 30.

300D   Discussant: A. Fayek's "The body image: An introduction to a psychology of the unconscious." Can. Psychoanal. Soc. (Q.E.), Nov. 23, 1978.

1979

301SS   [See 1978.] Seminar: Differences and similarities between psychotherapy and psychoanalysis of children. Child Psychia. Dept., Royal Victoria Hosp., Jan. 31.

302F   Children of psychotic mothers (with S. Dongier). Montreal Children's Hosp., May 7.

303D   Discussant: D. Levin's "Complementarity." Can. Psychoanal. Soc. (Q.E.), June 22.

304F   Learning from experience with analysis of schizophrenics. Can. Psychoanal. Soc. (Q.E.), Sept. 20.

305D   Discussion of J. Wisdom's "Endopsychic objects." Can. Psychoanal. Soc., Ottawa, Nov. 26.

306P   Panel on Positive Affects. Am. Acad. Psychoanal., Waldorf Astoria Hotel, N.Y. City.

1980

307D   Discussant: Harry Anderson's "Theory of technique: The metapsychology of the analyst's working mind - Its place in psychoanalytic science, and potential contribution to theory of technique." Can. Psychoanal. Soc. (Q.E.), Jan. 31.

308D   Discussant: D. Noble's "The creativity of Virgina Woolf." Washington Psychoanal. Soc., Washington, Feb. 8.

309D   Discussant: D. Levin's "Discussion Scott and Kohut - A study in contrasts." Can. Psychoanal. Soc. (Q.E.), Feb. 21.

310Fa   Melanie Klein's work. Chicago Psychoanal. Soc., Feb. 26.

311Fc   Melanie Klein. Montreal Children's Hosp., Oct. 1, 1981.

312F   Sleeping, dreaming and waking. Inst. for Psychoanal., Chicago, IL, Feb. 27.

313D   Discussion: John – Infant analysis. Child Analysts Group, Chicago, IL., Feb. 27.

314D   Discussion of E. Debbane and H. Lee's "Countertransference and the rescue phantasy." Can. Psychoanal. Soc. (Q.E.), March 20.

315F   [See 1961.] The demonstration of object relations and affect in a set situation in infants of 6 to 12 months. Cascais, Portugal, March 31.

316Fa   Psychoanalysis of a boy of 26 months with a 20-year follow-up. 1st World Congress Infant Psychia., Cascais, Portugal, April 3.

317Fb   Psychoanalysis of a boy of 26 months with a 20-year follow-up. Can. Psychoanal. Soc. (Q.E.), Oct. 18, 1984.

318W   Chairman – Workshop: The connection between why we keep secrets and our theories. Can. Psychoanal. Soc. (Q.E.), April 26.

319F   Narcissism, the body, phantasy, fantasy, internal and external objects and the

"Body Scheme." Advanced Inst. Analytic Psychother., N.Y. City, May 16.

320C   Le narcissisme, le corps, le phantasme, le fantasme, les objets intérieurs et extérieurs, le "schéma corporel." Soc. Psychoanal. Montréal, Dec. 16, 1982.

321D   Discussion of G. Maguire's "Transference and genetic continuity." Can. Psychoanal. Soc. (Q.E.), May 22.

322F   Development of the analysands' and analysts' enthusiasm for psychoanalysis. Am. Psychol. Assn., Montreal, Quebec, Division 39B, Sept. 1.

323D   Discussion of P. Harris' "Resolution of childhood mourning – A psychoanalytic study." Can. Psychoanal. Soc. (Q.E.), Sept. 18.

1981

324F   [See 1980.] Melanie Klein's work. M.A. Students in Psychotherapy at Naropa Inst., Boulder, CO, July 24.

325Fb   [See 1980.] Enthusiasm in life and work. Allan Memorial Inst., April 30.

326D   Discussant: Robert Lakoff's "Rumpelstiltskin: The significance of a fairy tale in a beginning analysis." Can. Psychoanal. Soc. (Q.E.), Feb. 19.

327W   Workshop: Working through regressions from and progressions to depression and mourning. 2nd Midwest Reg. Psychoanal. Mtg., Sheraton Ctr., Toronto, Feb. 28.

328F   [See 1980.] Melanie Klein. Given to M.A. Students in Psychotherapy, Naropa Inst., Boulder, CO, July 24.

329F   The treatment of manic-depressive illness. Institute Psychology Symposium: The Psychotic Experience: Nature and Therapy, July 26.

330F   Melanie Klein. Montreal Children's Hosp., Oct. 1.

331F   Buddhism and psychotherapy. Alan Memorial Inst., Oct. 8.

1982

332D   Discussion of Remembering sleep and dreams. Can. Psychoanal. Students (Q.E.), May 10, 1982.

333L   Lecture: Sleeping, dreaming, waking and remembering. Clarke Inst. Psychia., Toronto, Nov. 1982.

334F   The transitions from grief, to denial, to mourning, to zest. Homewood Sanitarium, Guelph, Feb. 10.

335Fa   Melanie Klein (1882-1960). Can. Psychoanal. Soc. (Q.E.), Feb. 18.

336Fb   Melanie Klein (1882-1960). Can. Psychoanal. Soc., Ottawa, May 31.

337Fc   Melanie Klein (1882-1960). Toronto Psychoanal. Soc., Oct. 13.

338F   Melanie Klein's object relationships as related to business management. L'École des Hautes Études Commerciales, Univ. Montréal.

339D   [See 1975.] Discussion: Remembering sleep and dreams. Can. Inst. Psychoanal. Students (Q.E.), May 10.

340D   Discussion of Hanna Segal's *Introduction to the Work of Melanie Klein*. Can. Inst. Psychoanal. Students.

341D   Discussion of Henri Rey's "Interview with a schizophrenic patient." Allan

Memorial Inst., May 14.

342F Contribution of Melanie Klein to technique: Born 1882 – Qualified as an
      Analyst 1919 – Died 1960. A.G.M., Can. Psychoanal. Soc., Montreal,
      June 4.

343D Discussion of Hanna Segal's *Introduction to Melanie Klein*. Argyle Inst.
      Human Rel., Montreal, Nov. 5.

344D Discussion of Hanna Segal's "Transition and loss – An approach to develop-
      mental tasks." Argyle Inst. Human Rel., Montreal, Nov. 5.

345F Introduction to Hanna Segal's "Some clinical implications of Melanie Klein
      – Narcissism and object relations." Can. Psychoanal. Soc., Montreal, Nov.
      6.

346L [See 1975.] Lecture: Sleeping, dreaming, waking and remembering. Clarke
      Inst. Psychia., Toronto, Nov. 10.

347F Denial of mankind's destruction: Fact or fancy? The R.M. Bucke Memorial
      Soc. for the Study of Religious Experience, Montreal, Nov. 24.

348C [See 1980.] Le narcissisme, le corps, le phantasme, le fantasme, les objets
      intérieurs et extérieurs, le "schéma corporel", Soc. Psychoanal. de Montréal
      (Q.F.), Dec. 16.

1983

349D Discussant: A. Fayek's "The psychoanalytic scene and the primal scene in a
      borderline case." Can. Psychoanal. Soc. (Q.E.), Feb. 17.

350S Symposium: Distortions of Grief and Mourning with Inhibition of Mourning.
      Distortions in personality development and their management in psychoanaly-
      sis and psychoanalytically oriented psychotherapy. Clarke Inst. Psychia.,
      Toronto, Feb. 19.

351D Discussant: D. Eyre's "Sixteen-year-old autistic girl." Can. Psychoanal. Soc.
      (Q.E.), Oct. 10.

352Pa Panel: Primary Mental States in Clinical Psychoanalysis. William Alanson
      White Inst. Psychia., Psychoanal. Psychol., 40th Anniversary, N.Y. City,
      Nov. 6.

353Fb Primary mental states in clinical psychoanalysis. Can. Psychoanal. Soc.
      (Q.E.), Oct. 18, 1984.

354D Discussant: J.B. Boulanger's "Early object relationships in the light of con-
      temporary scientific research." Can. Psychoanal. Soc. (Q.E.), Dec. 8.

355D Discussion of J.B. Boulanger's "The primacy of affect in Kleinian methodol-
      ogy and metapsychology." Can. Psychoanal. Soc. (Q.E.), Dec. 8.

356F Participant at Workshop on Oral History. Early history of Kleinian child
      psychology in England and the United States. Am. Psychoanal. Assn.,
      N.Y.City, Dec. 15.

357R Broadcast part of B.B.C.: Melanie Klein. Richard Wollheim, London.

1984

358D Discussant: James Naiman and Paola Valeri-Tomaszuk's "Sophocles' King

Oedipus and Self Analysis." Can. Psychoanal. Soc. (Q.E.), March 22.

359D [See 1947.] Discussion: A psychoanalytic concept of the origin of depression. Montreal Children's Hosp., March 23.

360D Discussant: Louis Couture's "Similarity and dissimilarity between child and adult analysis as seen through a case of pathological mourning in a 6-½ years old child." Can. Psychoanal. Soc. (Q.E.), April 25.

361F Mourning, the analyst, and the analysand. Am. Psychol. Assn. Toronto, Aug. 28.

362F [See 1980.] Psychoanalysis of a boy of 26 months with a 20-year follow-up. Can. Psychoanal. Soc. (Q.E.), Oct. 18.

363F Primitive mental states in clinical psychoanalysis. Can. Psychoanal. Soc. (Q.E.), Oct. 18.

364F Mourning, the analyst, and the analysand. Can. Psychoanal. Soc. (Q.E.), Oct. 18.

365D Discussion of Chapter on Envy – Remembering sleep and dreams. Montreal Children's Hosp., Dec. 7.

366D Discussion of A psychoanalytic concept of the origin of depression. Montreal Children's Hosp., March 23.

1985

367D Discussant: D. Eyre's "The use of the analyst as a dream symbol." Can. Psychoanal. Soc. (Q.E.), Jan. 24.

368F Fact and fancies concerning the nuclear problem. Can. Psychoanal. Soc. (Q.E.), May 23.

369D Discussion: Child Therapy. McGill Univ., Faculty Med., Dept. Psychia., June 5.

370Fa Who is afraid of Wilfred Bion? Bion: His contribution to psychoanalysis. Sponsored by the L.A. Psychoanal. Soc. Inst., Oct. 12-13.

371Fb Who is afraid of Wilfred Bion? Can. Psychoanal. Soc. (Western Branch), Edmonton, June 29, 1986.

1986

372D Discussion of B. Erock's "On the role of projective identification in the psychoanalysis of a homosexual." Can. Psychoanal. Soc. (Q.E.), March 20.

373F Freud's views on transference. Candidates of the Can. Inst. Psychoanal., Ottawa, April 25.

374F Freud's views on transference. Can. Psychoanal. Soc., Ottawa, April 26.

375D Discussant: Sudhir Karar's "Gandhi and the erotic fantasy." Int. Symposium Leadership Practices in Management. École des Hautes Études Commerciales de Montréal, Université de Montréal, May 6.

376F Who is afraid of Wilfred Bion? and The broken links between sleep and the unconscious and waking and the conscious. Can. Psychoanal. Soc. (Q.E.), May 22.

377D Discussion – Leader: The psychoanalyst as isolated practitioner. Can.

Psychoanal. Soc. (Western Branch), Edmonton, June 29.

378D   [See 1985.] Who is afraid of Wilfred Bion? Can. Psychoanal. Soc. (West-
        ern Branch), Edmonton, June 29.

379Da   Discussion: The broken links between sleep and the unconscious and waking
        and the conscious. Can. Psychoanal. Soc. (Western Branch), Edmonton,
        June 29.

380Fb   The broken links between sleep and the unconscious and waking and the
        conscious. '52 Club, London, England, Oct. 1, 1987.

381Fc   Repairing broken links between the unconscious, sleep and instinct and the
        conscious, waking and instinct. Queen Elizabeth Hosp., Montreal, Nov. 3,
        1987.

382D   Discussant: John Memiah's "Child abuse: Remembered fact or fancy? A
        reconsideration." Toronto Psychoanal. Soc., Nov. 19.

1987

383N   Notes for discussion on termination. Can. Psychoanal. Soc. (Q.E.), May 21.

384D   Informal discussion on psychoanalysis. All residents, Montreal Children's
        Hosp., May 28.

385   [See 1962.] Resumé of psychoanalytic nosology. (Used A reclassification of
        psychopathological states.) Ottawa Psychoanal. Inst., June 27.

386F   Discussed: Phyllis Grosskurth's *Melanie Klein – Her World and Her Work*.
        '52 Club, London, England, Oct. 1.

387F   [See 1986.] The broken links between sleep and the unconscious and waking
        and the conscious. '52 Club, London, England, Oct. 1.

388V   Video interview by Riccardo Steiner for Living Archives, Archives Commit-
        tee Br. Psycho-Anal. Soc., London, England, Oct. 3.

389F   Concerning my analysis with Melanie Klein. William Gillespie's house,
        London, England, Oct. 4.

390Fa   Making the best of a sad job. Br. Psycho-Anal. Soc., London, England, Oct.
        7.

391Fb   Making the best of a sad job. Soc. Psychanal. Montréal and Can. Psycho-
        anal. Soc. (Q.E.), June 9, 1988.

392Fc   [See 1986.] Repairing broken links between the unconscious, sleep and
        instinct, and the conscious, waking and instinct. Queen Elizabeth Hosp.,
        Montreal, Nov. 3.

393D   Discussant: Martin A. Silverman's "Clinical material." Montreal Gen.
        Hosp., Montreal, Nov. 4.

394D   Discussant: Albert Mason's "A Kleinian perspective." Montreal Gen.
        Hosp., Nov. 4.

1988

395SS   Seminar: Mental defectives. Senior residents, Montreal Children's Hosp.,
        April 22.

396W   Workshop: The history of the Canadian Psychoanalytic Society: The first two decades. Am. Psychoanal. Assn., Annual Mtg., Montreal, May 5.

397SS   Seminar: Mental defectives. Senior residents, Montreal Children's Hosp., May 20.

398F   [See 1987.] Making the best of a sad job. Soc. Psychoanal. Montréal and Can. Psychoanal. Soc. (Q.E.), June 9.

399D   Discussant: Steven Rosenbloom's "The development of the work ego in the fledgling psychoanalyst." Can. Psychoanal. Soc. (Q.E.), Nov. 17.

1989

400F   Dream theory and Melanie Klein. Southwestern Ontario Psychoanal. Soc., Jan. 16.

401D   Discussant: Ely Garfinkle's "The double and confusion between dreams and remembrances in multiple personality." Can. Psychoanal. Soc. (Q.E.), Jan. 19.

402F   Learning to talk simply about babies and corpses. Queen Elizabeth Hosp., Montreal, Jan. 24.

403F   Change from non-verbal to verbal communication. Queen Elizabeth Hosp., Montreal, April 18.

404F   Introduction: Donald Meltzer, Annual Clinical Day, Can. Psychoanal. Soc. (Q.E.), May 6.

405Na   Notes on an example of dissociated personalities without amnesia with "Further notes." Can. Psychoanal. Soc. (Q.E.), May 18.

406F   Notes on an example of dissociated personalities without amnesia with "Further notes." Can. Psychoanal. Soc. (Q.E.), May 18.

407F   [See 1986.] The broken links between sleep and waking and the unconscious and conscious. St. Mary's Hosp., Psychia. Unit, Montreal, Sept. 21.

408F   The relationship of drawing to script, to music, as illustrated by the art of Maurice Sendak. 2nd Symposium on Creativity, Psychopathology and Adaptation. Montreal Gen. Hosp., Psychia. Unit, Nov. 11.

1990

409F   Debate: "Hypnosis, sleep and wake, conscious and unconscious," W.C.M. Scott; and "Sleep, hypnosis, conscious and the unconscious," Maurice Dongier. Can. Psychoanal. Soc. (Q.E.), Jan. 18.

410F   Object relation theory – Personal reflections. Montreal Gen. Hosp., Psychia. Unit, Jan. 24.

411F   How to talk to children and adolescents about pregnancy. Queen Elizabeth Hosp., Psychia. Unit, Jan. 30.

412D   Discussant leader with Isabel Menzies. "Transference and countertransference in organizational consultation" (Members Session). Int. Soc. Psychoanal. Study Organizations. École des Hautes Études Commerciales, Montreal, May 23.

413D   Discussant: Erik L.H.M. van de Loo's "Transference and countertransference and wild analysis in the clinical interview." Int. Soc. Psychoanal. Study Organizations. Clinical Approach to the Study of Managerial and Organizational Dynamics. École des Hautes Études Commerciales.

1991

414F   Pictures, music, dreams and creativity – Maurice Sendak. Queen Elizabeth Hosp., Psychia. Dept., Jan. 8.

415F   Object relationship theories. Montreal Gen. Hosp., Lecture to junior staff and students, Psychia. Dept., Feb. 20.

416D   Discussant: Ostrich in Eden when anality is denied: A clinical case study by Sidney Perzow. Can. Psychoanal. Soc., March 21.

417F   Three themes in the development of an analytic career. Toronto Branch of the Int. Soc. History Psychoanal., April 6.

418F   More on drawing when the drawer cannot speak. (The use of cartoons in psychotherapy.) Queen Elizabeth Hosp., April 16.

419D   Narcissism and instinct theory. Klein Study Group, Can. Psychoanal. Soc. (Q.E.), April 26.

1992

420F   Understanding early childhood, Montreal Gen. Hosp., Dept. Psychol., April 1.

421F   A student intern at the new Toronto Psychiatric Hospital – 1925. History of Canadian Psychiatry Research in Progress, Seminar 1992. Queen Street Mental Health Centre Archives, Toronto, May 1.

422F   Psychiatry as a profession: Canada – China connections. Can. Anthropol. Soc., May 10, 19th Annual Conf., Montreal, May 9-12.

423F   History of child analysis in Canada and its relationship to other psychotherapy of children. Can. Psychoanal. Soc. A. G. M., Montreal, June 5.

424G   Morning and Zest – Melancholy and Mania. Book finished in 1992.

1993

424F   Understanding early childhood. Montreal Gen. Hosp., Dept. Psychol., April 25.

425T   Little Hans, First Year Candidates. Can. Inst. Psychoanal. (Q.E.), May 4.

1994

426F   Importance of psychoanalysis in understanding infant development. Montreal Gen. Hosp., Residents' Seminar, March 30.

1995

427F   Importance of psychoanalysis in understanding infant development. Montreal Gen. Hosp., April 5.

1996

428T   Teaching – Patrick Mahony and W. Clifford M. Scott, "Object relation point of view." Can. Inst. Psychoanal., Nov. 11.

Fig. 28. Photograph of Clifford Scott in his son Robert's garden in Boston (June 28, 1992). Credit: The Estate of W.C.M. Scott.

Conclusion

Michel Grignon

This book started and finished with the writings of W.C.M. Scott. He was often there to initiate projects and would never miss a chance to raise questions after their creation. We are sad that he is not with us anymore. We regret all the missed opportunities for collaboration and inspiration. We hope to be able together to continue his work propelled by his energy and animated by his intensity while always remembering his long search for a zest for living through psychoanalysis without any compromise.

Index